Drip-dry shirts:
the evolution of the graphic designer
Lucienne Roberts

LEARNING
RESOURCES
CENTRE

ava |Academia
the environment of learning

An AVA book

published by

AVA Publishing SA
Rue des Fontenailles 16
Case Postale
1000 Lausanne 6
Switzerland
t: +41 786 005 109
e: enquiries@avabooks.ch

distributed by

ex-North America
Thames & Hudson
181a High Holborn
London WC1V 7QX
United Kingdom
t: +44 20 7845 5000
f: +44 20 7845 5055
e: sales@thameshudson.co.uk
www.thamesandhudson.com

**English Language
Support Office**
AVA Publishing (UK) Ltd
t: +44 1903 204 455
e: enquiries@avabooks.co.uk

design by
Lucienne Roberts
sans+baum

production and separations by
AVA Book Production Pte Ltd
Singapore
t: +65 6334 8173
f: +65 6334 0752
e: production@avabooks.com.sg

ISBN 2 940373 08 6

10 9 8 7 6 5 4 3 2 1

01 **Drip-dry shirts:**
02 **the evolution of the graphic designer**
03 Lucienne Roberts

01
The term drip-dry first
appeared in the 1950s along
with high-rise and hi-fi,
hovercraft and sliced bread,
and graphic design.

02
Evolution:
gradual development
OED

03
with contributions
from Ray Roberts,
Kelvyn Laurence Smith
and Rebecca Wright

**Margaret Calvert's studio
1979 to the present**

When Margaret Calvert set
up her own practice she
moved some of the objects
from her previous studio
to her home. The objects,
gathered over 40 years
of working life, continue
to be added to still.

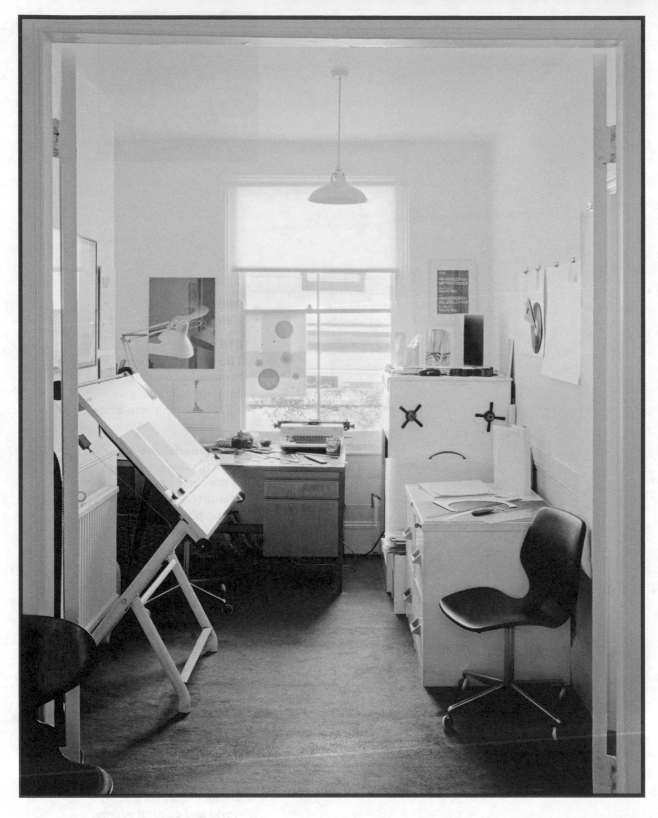

Contents

006 : 007
drip-dry shirts

The **dimension pieces** are preceded by the introduction and contents list.

An example of a spread from a **dimension piece**. All title blocks fall in the top right-hand corner.

Using this book

The structure is simple.

There are **six dimension pieces**. These are brief scene-setters for the **discussion pieces**. Some show the work of the interviewees to illustrate more general points about the time, approaches to work or methods of production. The **dimensions** are intended to be overviews only.

There are **nine discussion pieces**; a series of illustrated interviews with Wim Crouwel, Milton Glaser, Ken Garland, Rosmarie Tissi, Colin Forbes, Geoff White, Karl Gerstner, Margaret Calvert and Ivan Chermayeff.

Each has been invited to reflect on their formative years and long careers from historical and personal perspectives. They have each contributed a self-portrait and suggested a soundtrack to evoke their own chosen mood – listen as you read.

Each principal contributor has named a colleague or student over whom they feel they have had some influence. With the contributions of these secondary interviewees the pieces are mini design family trees and the symbiotic nature of work and teaching becomes apparent.

The book closes with the **reference section**. This includes an extensive **timeline** covering 1945–69, which identifies some cultural and world events that were the backdrop to this formative period of graphic design. Entries are not necessarily of equal significance but are chosen to give a sense of any given year.

The **reference section** includes the **timeline**, the first spread is shown here. On the left-hand page are listed all the different categories that are covered. Each year forms a column.

The discussions

The **discussion pieces**
are preceded by this colour-
coded contents list. Each
contributor has been given
a colour, used throughout
their text.

008 : 009
drip-dry shirts
using this book

Each **discussion piece**
starts with a spread like this.
The left-hand page shows
the principal contributor's
self-portrait. Their soundtrack
is listed on the right.

The right-hand page also
introduces the colour-coding
and the division of pages
that is used throughout.
The secondary contributor's
comments and images are
always at the top of the page.

The second spread of each
discussion piece looks like
this. The biography of the
secondary contributor runs
across the top. The principal
contributor's biography takes
up the rest of the spread.

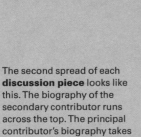
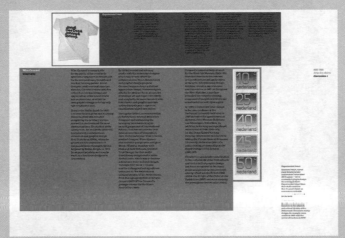

The interview pages of
each **discussion piece** look
like this, with the secondary
contributor's comments
and images always running
across the top.

The far left-hand column
is a navigation zone. In it are
the names of the contributors,
repeated on every spread,
cross-referenced subject lists,
to show what each spread is
about, and all captions.

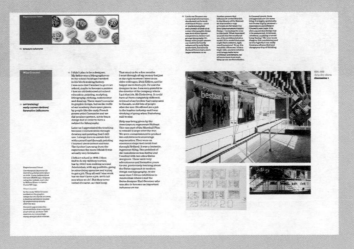

Introduction

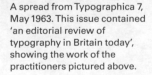

A spread from Typographica 7, May 1963. This issue contained 'an editorial review of typography in Britain today', showing the work of the practitioners pictured above.

Its editorial is full of expectation describing contemporary design graduates as not content 'to scratch around for new tricks, gimmicks and ways of manipulating the alphabet for the purposes of amusement and profit... [instead] exploiting with imagination, intelligence and a sense of responsibility the vast opportunities for visual communication'.

The portraits reveal diverse personalities. A mix of pop stars, gangsters and boffins. Perhaps not much has changed today.

In keeping with all issues of Typographica, print techniques are used inventively on this spread. Images are black-and-white halftones printed on a silver coated stock. Each designer's name is printed in red on a translucent overlay.

'When we talk with Wim Crouwel and he tells us about himself as a young man visiting Piet Zwart, we are bridging three, almost four generations of designers, in one conversation. But it doesn't feel like history at all. It feels extremely close by.' Experimental Jetset have summed up the essence of this book. History is really the telling of stories, hundreds of thousands of individual stories.

I hoped that, free of many of the insecurities of youth, the principal contributors to this book would speak honestly about what it was like to make design history. They did, but not necessarily as I had expected. With each interview a different approach and assessment was revealed. Each time I was surprised and enriched by the personality I had just encountered. One myth was dispelled in an instant; that people of the same age share the same perspective.

Introduction

01
Oh no. More stuff to look at. More stuff to read and it must be better than the last lot because it's new and new obviously means best. It says so, so it must be.

02
How can I keep up? It's changing all the time. I'll be irrelevant soon. What am I going to do? I'm so depressed. Help me. It just goes on and on. She's doing better than me. Everyone's doing better than me. Was Emil Ruder jealous of Müller-Brockmann? Don't be stupid. I'm a disaster.

03
Don't panic. There's got to be more to design than this. What does it all mean? Does life mean anything? Stop it. It'll be fine. There have been lots of designers before and they all seem ok. Don't they?

The choice of contributor was not in any way intended to be conclusive. From a purely historical point of view there are omissions. However, there is breadth of vision and experience: designers from different cultures and countries, workaholics and globe-trotters, those who have been successful in business and those whose influence is more quietly disseminated through teaching.

There are defenders of the 'profession' and those who are sceptical of any designer club; committed modernists, early post-modernists; artists and visionaries; intellectuals and freethinkers. They are all here.

This was always going to be a personal book. Not just because it is about the sharing of memories, observations and anecdotes, wisdom and insight, but because the generation on which it focuses has been the most influential on me. I wanted to hear it directly from them, to check that my admiration was not misplaced. It's not, and this has been confirmed by all the secondary interviewees too.

Brookie Maxwell for example, said that Milton Glaser spoilt her for lunch with anyone else. I feel the same about his interview. Each of his answers was a gem, rich with resonance. Big issues explored through small observations that will serve to stimulate me in years to come.

01 Every season, with alarming predictability, yet another graphic design book sets out to capture definitively the zeitgeist.

02 The blurb always makes the same claim: that the book shows the work of the newest, youngest, most innovative designers. This restless search is self-perpetuating, can never be sated and ultimately intensifies nagging fears and insecurities among designers.

03 An understanding of design history has the reverse effect. It explains who we are and sets contemporary work in an expansive and broad landscape, one that is more objective and less introspective. Without knowledge and experience we are lost, floating in a sea of unanswered questions. **Drip-dry shirts** seeks to answer some of the questions.

Ken Garland, a strong influence since my student days, is probably the closest to being a kindred spirit of all the interviewees. Not because of his resistance to design ideology – something I have keenly embraced – but because he is slightly removed from the profession and because of his political and cultural concerns. In talking to him I felt a useful sense of vindication that will bolster me in the future.

I have long been an admirer of the work of Wim Crouwel and Karl Gerstner. Crouwel's rigour allied to political commitment will I think inspire me for the rest of my life. Gerstner's paintings are simply beautiful, uplifting, aesthetically challenging, near perfection. Sitting in his kitchen, snow falling outside, I could almost touch what it was he aspires to: a quality of physical, intellectual and spiritual life, the possibility of which is for many simply unrecognised.

So much in life is chance; the right person, the right connection, meeting someone who helps unlock potential that would have otherwise stayed dormant. This arbitrariness is simultaneously reassuring and terrifying, but in all the stories Glaser, Forbes and Chermayeff told, I felt there was an optimistic belief that it can 'all be all right' and that it is this that has helped in their success.

Introduction

Graphic design was the successor to commercial art and is now the precursor of visual communication – the current, one-size-fits-all term, which perhaps attests to a personality crisis within the industry today. This book however looks at a time of great confidence in graphic design, on the part of both its practitioners and those who employed them.

Before the Second World War graphic design wasn't quite as we know it today. There was type and there were images of course, but the term 'graphic design' didn't exist. **Drip-dry shirts** looks at the inception of graphic design as we still recognise it: a job that includes the day-to-day running of a studio, the dealings with clients, the notion of the problem to be solved and the production of inventive, visually arresting, sometimes beautiful and usually useful solutions.

At the end of the Second World War western society was fragmented, the old order had been all but destroyed. Sociological, political and economic changes were absolutely inevitable. The stratified deference of previous generations was rejected. Both class and gender expectations were shifting. No more women 'who did' either as paid or unpaid labour. The 'stuffed shirt' was out; drip-dry was in.

The term drip-dry first appeared in the 1950s along with high-rise and hi-fi, hovercraft and sliced bread, and graphic design. The drip-dry nylon shirt quickly became an icon of the bachelor lifestyle, the 'wash and go' of the '60s, combining as it did speed and technology with colours as bright and artificial as the fabric itself. It became a metaphor for all things modern.

When I was a child in the '60s, our bathroom was full of them. My father was not a groovy bachelor, nor was he an unquestioning exponent of all things modern, but he was a graphic designer – a recently defined profession whose members felt charged to build a new post-war world. For this generation it was a time of unprecedented possibilities; of expansion and inventiveness; of optimism, freedom and above all wondrous excitement. They embraced their role with an enthusiasm and conviction which, from a post-modern, cynical, ironic perspective, seems naive, but engendered enormous personal satisfaction.

'Her advice to us has always been to be yourself,' said Margaret Calvert's ex-students Frith Kerr and Amelia Noble. This too is an overarching message I took from the interviews. It is a prerequisite to success to follow one's heart, the opposite results in diminished motivation and disappointment, regrets for what you haven't done and so on...

Ambition and drive can be sated in different ways and I found Rosmarie Tissi's quiet confidence in the benefits of freedom inspiring. For her, being able to leave work behind and travel has been an essential ingredient in her success. Quiet conviction also characterises Geoff White and his work. Over the years so many fellow designers have referred to his influence upon them as their teacher. His belief in modernism is unwavering and his teaching methods continue to resonate with his students to this day.

Margaret Calvert was right. When I went to interview her she astutely observed that I was doing this book because I was trying 'to work something out'. I'll confess I have been in a quandary of late. I wanted to know what to do next. Now I have some answers.

Of course, with hindsight we laugh about the sparks that flew off nylon and its roughness to the touch. Now only natural is good and even my underwear is made of organic cotton. We are rightly cautious about the invasiveness of the human-made world and many had similar concerns then, but the drip-dry shirt was embraced as a demonstration of inventiveness and the ability to make things better – which is what I think graphic design practitioners also set about trying to do.

Initially I called these first graphic designers 'pioneers', but they all resisted such a notion, seeing themselves as part of a continuum. The use of a new term however demonstrates that there was a change in the perception of their role.

Printing – the multiplication of text and image, initially in book form – had been around for 500 years when the industrial revolution gave rise to advertising. At the turn of the nineteenth and twentieth centuries a gradual recognition of the design decision, as distinct from the print decision, emerged and this required the existence of the typographer and the designer. In the '20s and '30s there was a dramatic shift away from the previously revered ideals of 'craft' production. The intrinsic characteristics of the machine and the democratising potential of mass production acted as a stimulus for artists and designers alike.

To be truly modern, typography had to be asymmetrically arranged on the page and the type predominantly sans serif. Typographers looked to abstract painting as a source of theoretical and aesthetic inspiration and this led to a different approach to the integration of type with images. Images, particularly photography, started to be used more abstractly and simply, like type, whilst type was exploited visually in the manner of an image. This marks the start of graphic design thinking that is still relevant today.

By the end of the last war the scene was set for the arrival of the modern graphic designer. A politically engaged, but not uncommercial sort of chap – at that time they generally were chaps – enterprising, thoughtful, broadly educated. By the early 1950s art schools started to teach 'graphic design' instead of typography separated from illustration. The advent of government loans and then grants also changed the socio-economic breakdown of the student intake. The war resulted in a new social order, democratisation, the growth of capitalism, mass consumption and an economic boom in the West. So, what better time to set up a new business selling a newly defined trade?

The following **dimension pieces** are designed as brief scene-setters, giving context to the **discussion pieces** that follow them. Here we look at the arrival of 'commercial art' and the emergence of modernism [the history], the impact of right and left in the design of a new post-war world [the politics] and, of course, typography, from Grot 215 to Univers 55 with some nineteenth-century slab serif for good measure [the type].

A love of abstract form gave rise to less mechanical representations of words [the lettering], skills that were then applied in the design of logotypes and symbols; the iconic focus of the 'house-style' [the trademark]. Technology played its part, affordable full-colour was about to arrive on the scene, but designers still had to be inventive with limitations of colour and process producing images that are now so evocative of their time [the imagery].

The nineteenth century

The term 'graphic design' is relatively recent in the history of visual art, although the activity it denotes is as old as the earliest scratchings on cave walls. The greater part of that history is concerned with the transmission of information and ideas – religious, cultural, social, political and practical – with aesthetics generally conditioned by the purposes that images and texts are there to serve. Since the beginning of modern industrial production, in the late eighteenth century, 'making' gradually became divorced from distribution and retail. Promotion and marketing have subsequently grown, supported by an increase in literacy resulting from the widespread elementary education needed to sustain industrial life at all levels.

From the inception of printing with movable type until the early nineteenth century, the bulk of production was devoted to the making of books. Then, in a rapid process of change, posters, handbills, catalogues, packaging, newspapers and magazines, all became part of a new promotional landscape for providers of goods and services.

Most early printed advertising was crude and haphazard, conceived in a loose relationship between client, printer and engraver, who were all facing problems of a new kind. Type designs of greater variety, style and weight were developed to provide impact in the marketplace. Division of labour increased in the preparation of images, with artists passing their drawings to highly skilled engravers in wood or metal, who interpreted these on to printing surfaces from which thousands of copies could be made.

Newly founded advertising agencies were concerned with obtaining and time-planning the use of space in the press, or on hoardings, not with the visual and verbal content. Fine artists meanwhile concentrated more on the projection of their personal reactions to life, rather than visual solutions to these essentially non-artistic problems.

Gradually, this chaotic situation reordered itself, and a more meaningful integration of the creative, technical and economic aspects of promotional printing came about. Agencies began to provide design, illustration and copywriting services, thus becoming responsible for the content of spaces booked on behalf of their clients. General publicity and informational material was less profitable to agencies than direct advertising, and this opened the way for individual designers to work in close association with the client on those aspects of promotion. These developments began in the late nineteenth and early twentieth centuries, but became more clearly defined during the 1920s and '30s.

American poster
c1831
designer unknown
dimensions unknown

Most nineteenth-century advertising was crude and haphazard; type designs of greater variety, style and weight were developed to compete in the marketplace. This poster, advertising the travelling menagerie American National Caravan, is typical of such work, despite its charm to modern eyes.

Gustav Klimt
First Secessionist Exhibition catalogue cover
1898
dimensions unknown

Art nouveau, in its Viennese manifestation, had many contributors, such as Oskar Kokoschka, Josef Hoffmann, Kolo Moser and Bertold Löffler. Among these, Gustav Klimt demonstrates the flowing line, flat colour, rich patterning and organic structure of the style.

Design ideologies

Words and images in earlier work were treated as separate entities, like illustrations with captions. The integration of production processes, however, led to a consolidation of pictorial and verbal content and to more visually arresting results. A reassessment of approaches to architecture and engineering led to greater consideration of function in relation to form. New discoveries about colour and abstraction, exampled in fine art, also affected design at all levels.

In the late nineteenth century, a growing awareness of Japanese art encouraged the use of flattened perspective, heightened colour, and strong simple forms. This was one of the sources from which art nouveau was distilled, a style that used flat colour and sensuous, sinuous line to strongly organic effect with lettering freely drawn as an integral part of a design. This movement was at its height in the early twentieth century and influenced applied art in America and most European countries, especially Belgium, France and Austria. The arts and crafts movement in Britain, with its parallel developments in America and Germany, implanted ideas about fitness to purpose and truth to materials. Both movements set the atmosphere for applied design immediately before the outbreak of the First World War.

Design processes and education

As is always the case, new techniques open the way for experimentation and change. Between 1890 and 1910 the technology of reproduction for printing underwent a minor, but profound revolution. Photographic techniques were used to transfer images to metal and other surfaces from which printing plates could be made. Hand-engraving was replaced by controlled etching to make blocks in line or halftone. By 1900, theories about colour were converted into practical colour halftones, making full-colour reproduction a commercial possibility. All forms of image reproduction were made faster, cheaper, and generally more accurate. It became possible to enlarge or reduce image sizes, to reverse from black to white, and to integrate lettering or typography with ease.

Sadly, these technological changes led to the almost total disappearance of skilled engravers – craftsmen who had learnt within the trade. At the same time the study of graphic work of all kinds was beginning to provide an expanding market for students who wanted to train more academically at art school.

018 : 019
drip-dry shirts
dimension 1

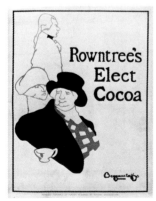

J&W Beggarstaff
Rowntree's Elect Cocoa
lithographic poster
1896
38 x 28 5/8 inches

The British artists James Pryde and William Nicholson worked as the Beggarstaff Brothers when creating applied design. They used cut paper, woodcut and other techniques to make strong shapes printed in flat colours. Freely drawn line work and lettering combined aspects of art nouveau with popular imagery in their designs.

El Lissitzky
Veshch/Gegenstand/
Objet cover
number 1–2, April 1922
dimensions unknown

El Lissitzky worked in Russia and the West. His strongly geometric structures, with lettering integrated as an important design element, became hugely influential in the development of the modern movement in graphic design.

Design ideologies

The power of words and images was fully exploited by government bodies during the First World War. Well-known fine artists made contributions to the cause, but much of the material came from studios that were loosely connected with the printing trade or advertising agencies.

Before the war ended, the Russian revolution had changed the social and economic structure of that country and issued a challenge to the then developed world. Many Russian artists considered themselves to be at the forefront of change and a part of new artistic developments in the West. Among many others, individuals such as Malevitch, Kandinsky and El Lissitzky were major contributors to the modern movement, which had abstraction at its heart.

At this time political propaganda was an important concern, combining new ideas about society with a revolutionary approach to design. Movements such as constructivism, futurism, dada and later, surrealism, all influenced applied design, while typography gradually assumed a more central role as a powerful contributing element. Kurt Schwitters, for example, was influenced by constructivism and worked as a typographer, using collage in both one-off items and publications, such as his own periodical Merz; a mouthpiece for many important modernists including Mondrian, Man Ray, Picabia and Arp.

In Germany, the Bauhaus school, founded in 1919 by Walter Gropius, set out to educate would-be designers in a proper understanding of industrial production methods, allied to an analysis of design function. Most aspects were covered, from architecture, through furniture and textiles, to typography and graphics. Many of the pioneers of the modern movement either taught at the Bauhaus or had some influence upon its work. In many ways, the school welded earlier ideas into a more coherent and appropriate approach to modern design problems at all levels.

Although some of the ideas explored at the school were not successful, a great deal of its teaching led to underlying principles that still have currency today. Unfortunately, the Bauhaus was seen as politically left-wing, which resulted in its closure by Hitler in 1933.

A movement with close sympathetic ties to the Bauhaus, de Stijl, was founded by a group of artists and designers in Holland in 1917. Here various companies and public bodies were prepared to work with advanced design ideas. Strong abstract geometrical forms, photographic imagery, powerful typography and pure colours characterised their work. Vertical-horizontal stresses were contrasted with elements placed obliquely to create dynamic emphasis. The visual approach of de Stijl became influential on the work of sophisticated designers throughout Europe; but their working methods were also important. A close cooperation with the client, from original conception to responsibility for all production aspects of the job, was considered vital to success. This concern with process pointed the way to modern practice.

Kurt Schwitters
Merz inside spread
number 11, 1925
dimensions unknown

Schwitters, influenced by constructivism and the New Typography, experimented fully in his publication Merz. The important principle here was 'do it in a way no one has ever done it before'.

Herbert Bayer
Bauhaus magazine cover
volume 3, number 3,
July to September 1929
dimensions unknown

Herbert Bayer, a former student at the school, was appointed to direct typographic work at the Bauhaus after its move from Weimar to Dessau in 1925. Influenced by Moholy-Nagy, he did much to create Bauhaus typography, promoting the use of sans serif and including experiments with single alphabets that abandoned capital letters.

Another important movement crystallised in 1925 at the International Exhibition of Modern Industrial and Decorative Arts in Paris. Art deco combined influences from cubism, art nouveau, the industrial forms found in streamlined aircraft and cars, with shapes and lines expressing speed and movement. Highly stylised treatments of human and animal forms, in brilliant colours, were translated into a wide range of materials, from textiles to stone, wood and metal. Art deco was a style applied to the surface of products and little concerned with their function. It is often referred to as 'moderne', to distinguish it from 'modern', as in the modern movement. The style spread rapidly during the 1920s and '30s, but its influence was particularly strong in France, where some brilliant designers made convincing use of its possibilities in posters, books, textiles and furniture. Hollywood also exploited art deco, most notably in the musical films of the 1930s starring such luminaries as Astaire and Rogers.

Design processes and education

By the early 1920s the whole business of promotion had become more ordered and sophisticated. In addition to advertising agencies, specialist studios appeared providing images and camera-ready artwork for all forms of publicity. A network of trade typesetters supported the agencies and studios. Individual designers were already working in a freelance capacity, although generally as specialists in fields such as illustration, and were known increasingly as 'commercial artists' producing 'commercial art'.

A growing number of educational institutions formulated courses that started to acknowledge the needs of industry. The printing trade had supported the idea of day-release education for apprentices, and it was seen as sensible to base such facilities within art schools. Unfortunately, both printing proprietors and trade unions were wary of allowing design students to share technical equipment. This meant that typographic education for future graphic designers was largely theoretical, with practical experience gained by stealth in all but a small number of art schools.

020 : 021
drip-dry shirts
dimension 1

Piet Zwart
Film cover
number 9, 1933
dimensions unknown

Close cooperation with the client, and attention to production methods and costs, were seen by members of the Dutch de Stijl movement as part of the design process. Theo van Doesburg, Mondrian and Oud were among the founders, while one of those who projected these ideas most powerfully was Piet Zwart. His combination of dynamic typography with photography is illustrated by this cover for the magazine Film.

AM Cassandre
New Statendam
Holland-America Line
lithographic poster
1928
75 x 105cm

The French poster artist AM Cassandre was outstanding in his decorative use of industrial forms, expressed through surface textures derived from aspects of modern painting. His lettering is part of the total conception.

Design ideologies

This was a period of great disquiet, in which the world economy was only just recovering from the economic depression. Trading conditions were uncertain, there were still millions of unemployed people, and social class divisions were clearly defined by experience, attitude and financial status. Europe was also suffering political division and fear, with rising right-wing dictatorships in the West and the powerful communist presence in the East. By the late 1930s it was clear that war would be the inevitable outcome.

During the Second World War there was again a great need for government publicity and information. The switch of resources from peace-time manufacture to war production changed the nature of advertising. Companies often continued to publicise themselves, but emphasised their contribution to the war effort, while apologising for the lack of their goods or services in the market.

The skills of advertising agencies and individual designers were used by government departments to inform, direct and encourage the public. The pressures of that time increased a general understanding of the nature and place of graphic design. There were many more freelance designers with knowledge of production methods, and some powerfully conceived and executed work was created with images and words fully integrated.

In Britain, the Central Office of Information was a successful coordinating body, organised and operated in ways that would influence future practice in the post-war design profession. It commissioned and guided the creation of all forms of publicity, including films, and maintained a creditable standard of production against a background of material and human shortages.

Although involved in the war, the American economy was so strong that much everyday production continued alongside an enormous war effort. Designers, therefore, served the demands of a relatively normal market, while promoting the cooperation of the whole nation in fighting the war. Among the developed central European nations, Switzerland remained neutral, and was able to maintain its market-based economy.

The rise of oppressive Nazism in Germany led to many individuals leaving to settle in more liberal states. Among these were designers who went to America, Britain and Switzerland. Most had advanced ideas and had been connected with schools, publishing houses or agencies that actively supported such thinking. In this way the host countries received an intellectual boost to their understanding of the aims of the modern movement. For example, Bayer and Gropius went to America; Hoch and Schleger to Britain; Tschichold to Switzerland.

Abram Games
Your Britain,
Fight For It Now poster
1942
dimensions unknown

A very individual contribution to British wartime publicity was made by Abram Games in posters combining awareness of modern art movements with an understanding of the basic need to communicate ideas. This poster expresses the hope for a world that is physically and politically transformed after years of destruction. It is one of a series of three designed for the War Office on the subjects of health, housing and schools.

Herbert Matter
Pontresina Engadin
travel poster
1936
dimensions unknown

The powerful posters by Matter, using dramatic contrasts, photomontage and rectilinear structures at an angle to the vertical, show Swiss awareness of modern design principles in the late 1930s and '40s.

In Switzerland, despite the difficulties of its position surrounded by participants in the war, the study of theoretical and practical aspects of design continued in the design schools, while the high standards of its printing industry were maintained.

The Swiss and American approaches were both very influential in the years following the end of the war, the first in the formal aspects of design, the second in the realm of ideas. The geographic and political position of Switzerland, a small land-locked country with few resources beyond its long history and magnificent scenery, could not be more different from the huge, well-endowed United States. It has been said that the kind of knowledge and human skill required to turn a few pennyworth of brass and steel into a fine precision watch is absolutely necessary for the comfortable survival of a highly populated but tiny country such as Switzerland. The need for strong social order and maximum contributions from its citizens, are reflected in the finely detailed quality of its typography and graphic presentation. At its best, beautiful restraint typifies Swiss design in all areas.

In contrast, the abundant competitive American approach embraces everything from the vibrantly crude to the most elegantly refined, Las Vegas to Lloyd Wright. Their finest typography and graphics bring together careful craft with the full exploitation of wit, humour, drama and contrast in the way words are presented visually, and images reinforce verbal ideas. Paul Rand is prominent in a generation of such designers, which included William Golden, Lester Beall, Alvin Lustig, Bradbury Thompson, Aaron Burns, Herb Lubalin and Gene Federico among others.

With the return of peace, new design magazines, such as Graphis and Domus, began to raise awareness of international developments, while renewed travel made experience of people and their problems more immediate. Art and design schools sought to provide courses more relevant to the needs of industrial society, often under pressure from governments who saw design as an important factor in promoting trade and increasing the appeal of products. Large exhibitions such as Britain Can Make It, the continental Expo presentations and, a little later, the Festival of Britain, had much to do with opening markets for trade in a recovering world.

022 : 023
drip-dry shirts
dimension 1

Paul Rand
Direction cover
volume 4, number 4, 1940
dimensions unknown

Paul Rand is prominent in a generation of American designers who bring together careful craft with the full exploitation of wit, humour, drama and contrast in the way words are presented visually, and images are used to reinforce verbal ideas.

Josef Müller-Brockmann
Beethoven concert poster
1955
dimensions unknown

Müller-Brockmann was among the first post-war Swiss designers to practise across the field from exhibition design to books. He used abstract and figurative imagery and was fastidious in detailing, large or small. A fine teacher, his writings had worldwide influence on a whole generation. This illustration is an example of his powerful and appropriate use of abstract forms serving an abstract subject.

Italian ruin
exact date unknown

A ruined street after bombing
during the Second World War,
1939–45.

Festival of Britain
1951

Visitors enjoying the various
outdoor exhibits on a sunny day
at the Festival of Britain.

In the face of immense physical destruction and shortages of materials, the late 1940s and early '50s were a time of huge optimism and great hope for a better future. After the suffering imposed by economic depression in the years between the wars, democracies involved in conflict were determined to change life for the better for the mass of their people. Who were better suited to build this new world than a generation of keen young designers and architects committed to the notion that contemporary design could, in a practical way, make the world a better place? This ethos was made concrete and given substance by various European 'expos' designed to inspire enthusiasm for the changes ahead. These national exhibitions, for example Britain Can Make It, 1946 and All Hands On Deck in Holland, 1952, acted as a testing ground for many young designers.

The seeds of the economic recovery in Europe that made the boom of the 1960s possible were sown partly by the financial aid of the American Marshall Plan announced in 1947. The intention was to encourage regrowth in Europe, but this was partly motivated by a fear that economically dislocated nations would be susceptible to communist influence. Indeed, in 1945 a majority of western people did regard Russia as heroic in its defeat of Nazism. The communist cause was attractive and adopted by western countries in various forms of socialism. In Britain, for example, the Labour victory of 1945 led to the foundation of the National Health Service and architecturally adventurous programmes of social housing.

Legislation opened education to all regardless of social class or wealth, for example in America, through the 'GI Bill', 2.2 million Second World War veterans accepted the government's offer of a free college or graduate education. The effect of these changes was that the first of several generations of young people entered the whole spectrum of higher education that had previously been closed to them through the lack of financial resources. These students were joined by recently discharged members of the armed forces who brought added maturity and determination to their studies.

In matters of art and design much of the most progressive work was found in printed material with left-wing tendencies, especially that which had connections with the modern movement. Relativism held little sway, and distinctions between good and bad were drawn clearly. Against this background educationalists, critics, teachers and students attempted to create courses of study that were coherent and could be seen to contribute to the betterment of life for everyone.

One of the issues that was deemed important was the distinction between style and substance in design solutions. It was believed that the final appearance of a design should arise from the careful working out of the problem, and should not be an applied face, no matter how attractive that might be.

Looking back from the present time, much of the thinking of those days seems idealistic, but flawed by its wilful reduction of complex interrelations between purpose, method of manufacture, nature of materials and economics.

Nevertheless, the perception of an activity that came to be known as graphic design grew apace. It was realised that a practitioner of this craft would require a sound general education in visual art, with skills in drawing, plus a broad understanding of the technologies of printing and graphic reproduction. He or she would also need some knowledge of the economic aspects of such work, and be a resourceful team leader when necessary, directing the work of specialists such as illustrators, photographers and writers. Often, the creative role of the graphic designer would be in shaping the overall concept, rather than executing the many specialised aspects of the work. At most times, these efforts would be directed towards the solution of problems existing beyond purely artistic concerns.

By the early 1960s those who wished to be educated, those who taught and, increasingly, those who used such services, had a much clearer understanding of what could be defined as 'graphic design'.

026 : 027
drip-dry shirts
dimension 2

Hertfordshire Architects Department
Cadmore Lane Junior School, Cheshunt, Britain
1959

Exterior and interior views.

Development Corporation and Sir Frederick Gibberd
Harlow, Britain
c1958

Stairs up to the galleries, between the Painted Lady and the back of the Market House as reproduced in issue 737, Architectural Review, June 1958.

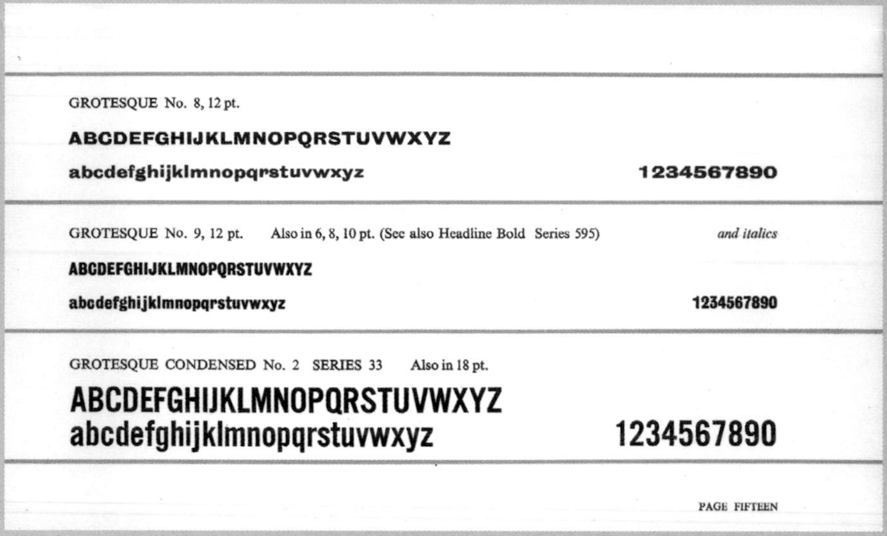

GROTESQUE No. 8, 12 pt.

ABCDEFGHIJKLMNOPQRSTUVWXYZ

abcdefghijklmnopqrstuvwxyz   **1234567890**

GROTESQUE No. 9, 12 pt.   Also in 6, 8, 10 pt. (See also Headline Bold Series 595)   *and italics*

ABCDEFGHIJKLMNOPQRSTUVWXYZ

abcdefghijklmnopqrstuvwxyz   **1234567890**

GROTESQUE CONDENSED No. 2 SERIES 33   Also in 18 pt.

ABCDEFGHIJKLMNOPQRSTUVWXYZ
abcdefghijklmnopqrstuvwxyz   **1234567890**

GROTESQUE No. 2 SERIES 51, 10 pt.   Also in 6 and 8 pt.

ABCDEFGHIJKLMNOPQRSTUVWXYZ

abcdefghijklmnopqrstuvwxyz   1234567890

GROTESQUE BOLD EXTENDED No. 1 SERIES 150   Also in 6, 8, 10, 12, 14, 18, 30, 36 pt.   *and italics*

ABCDEFGHIJKLMNOPQRSTUVWXY
abcdefghijklmnopqrs   1234567890

GROTESQUE No. 1 SERIES 215, 10pt.   Also in 6½ on 7, 8, 13 pt.   *and italics*
ABCDEFGHIJKLMNOPQRSTUVWXYZ

abcdefghijklmnopqrstuvwxyz   1234567890

Norwich School of Art   **Helvetica** Medium

Stempel Type Foundry West Germany

abcdefghijklm
nopqrstuvwxy
z &.,;:-!?'£$/
ABCDEFGHIJ
KLMNOPQRS
TUVWXYZ 12
34567890

72 point

Grotesque specimen pages
circa 1950

The sans serif faces known as grotesques were the forerunners of Helvetica, Univers and many of the sans serif fonts used today. The selection featured here is gathered from a variety of sources dating from 1898 for Grot 8, to 1926 for Grot 215.

Helvetica specimen sheet

When designer Max Miedinger collaborated with the Haas'sche foundry's Edouard Hoffmann in an effort to improve Akzidenz-Grotesk, the result was Neue Haas Grotesk. In 1960 the design was sold to the Stempel foundry and produced as Helvetica. It reinforced the qualities espoused by many advocates of the international style; clarity, consistency and objectivity. The Helvetica family extends to a full range of weights, widths and italics.

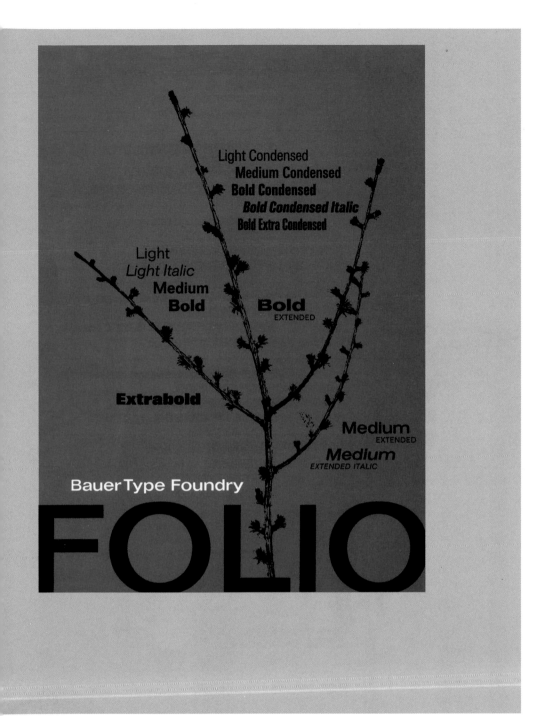

Folio specimen book

Folio was designed by
Konrad Bauer and Walter Baum
at the Bauer foundry in Germany
in 1957 and was one of a series
of key sans serif typefaces
available at the time. It refers to
the nineteenth-century face
Akzidenz-Grotesk and was used
widely in America where Bauer
had particularly strong sales.

Palatino

MICHELANGELO **SISTINA**

Palatino
Italic
Semi Bold
Swash
Characters
Small Caps

Among today's types in the Renaissance roman style, the Palatino family designed by Hermann Zapf has not only stood the test of use throughout Europe, but has in addition won unique acceptance in the United States. The reasons for this success are to be found in the special qualities mutually shared by the companion faces of that group. Their letters are not arbitrarily or timidly drawn, but spring from the edged pen's natural motion, whence the Palatino types derive their fresh individual forms and their vital rhythms of word-spacing and page-texture — merits which together confer upon these faces a high rating in originality. Palatino itself is a dynamic type of ready legibility for extended texts in books, periodicals and catalogues. In advertising, its unmistakably expressive individuality is widely esteemed. Available for title designs and for special compositional tasks are the two titling faces — elegant Michelangelo and full-bodied Sistina. These vigorously supplement Palatino's basic grades and extend the range of the family's joint typographic possibilities.

D. Stempel AG Typefoundry Frankfurt am Main

Palatino specimen literature

Inspired by the letterforms of Roman inscriptions and the Italian Renaissance, Palatino received international acclaim on its release in 1949. Its designer, Hermann Zapf, was a master calligrapher and art director of Frankfurt's Stempel foundry.

Zapf intended Palatino to be a display face. Its repeated use in books caused controversy as some designers believed its calligraphic subtleties made it less legible in continuous text. With the limitations of lithographic and gravure printing in mind, Zapf had compensated for the mediocre paper in Germany after the war by giving Palatino open counters and a stroke weight slightly heavier than most Roman fonts.

**Monotype Newsletter 83
Rockwell cover**
March 1968

The first slab serif type was Vincent Figgins's Egyptian of 1817. Designed for impact rather than legibility, it was described as a true expression of the new industrial age with its 'sledgehammer' even weight. The term Egyptian was used because these types were redolent of the weight and scale of the architecture of ancient Egypt, a cultural obsession at the time. Of twentieth-century versions, Heinrich Jost's Beton, 1931; Monotype's Rockwell, 1934; and Serifa by Adrian Frutiger are good examples.

**Monotype Newsletter 88
Neographic cover**
February 1971

Robert Barbour's Neographic is indicative of the approach to type design in the early 1970s. With the advancement of phototypesetting, manufacturers rushed to offer an impressive variety of fonts and many typographers gave in to the temptation of inventively distorting type and introducing rather 'wild' aesthetics.

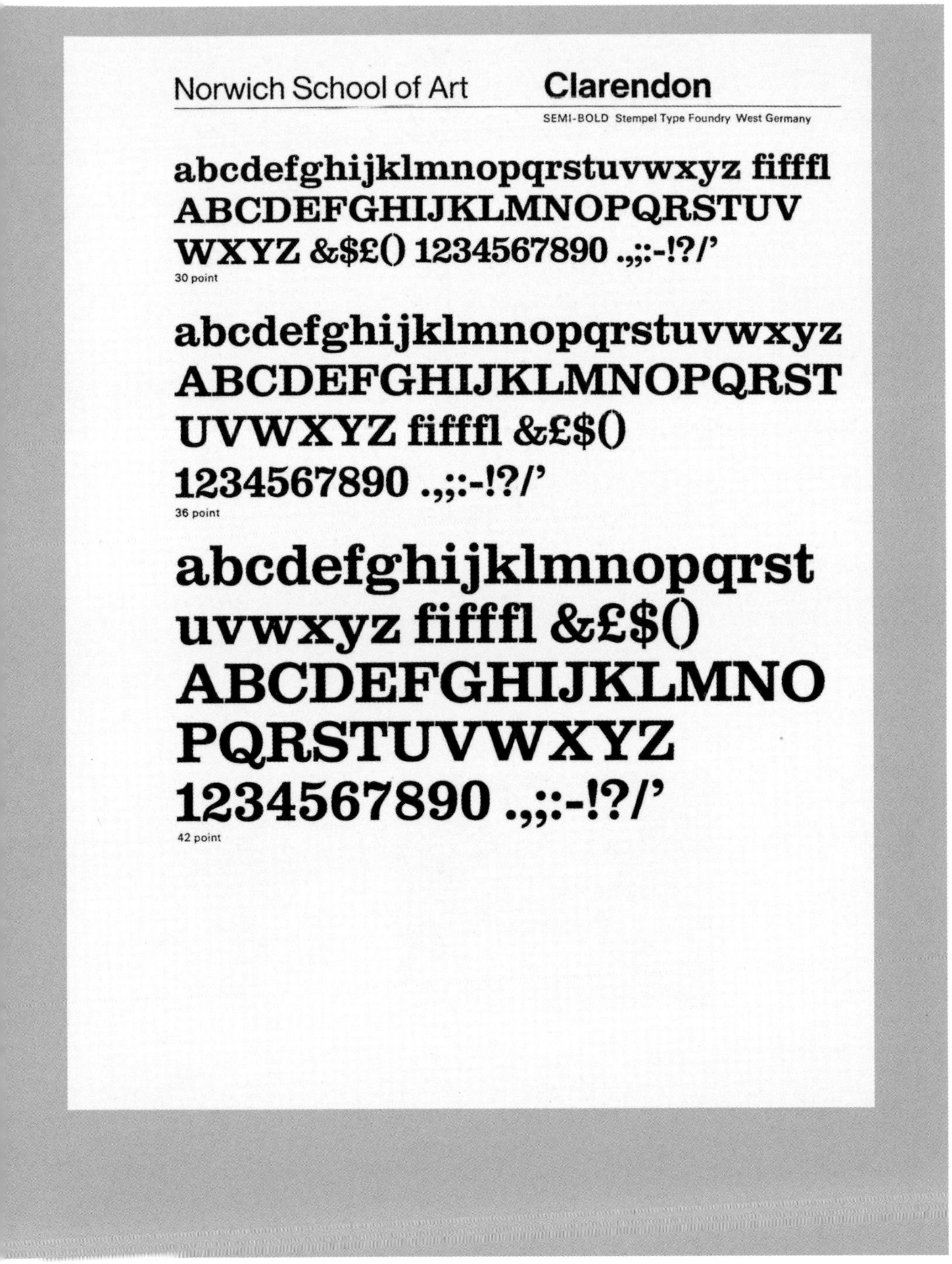

Norwich School of Art   **Clarendon**

SEMI-BOLD Stempel Type Foundry West Germany

abcdefghijklmnopqrstuvwxyz fifffl
ABCDEFGHIJKLMNOPQRSTUV
WXYZ &$£() 1234567890 .,;:-!?/'
30 point

abcdefghijklmnopqrstuvwxyz
ABCDEFGHIJKLMNOPQRST
UVWXYZ fifffl &£$()
1234567890 .,;:-!?/'
36 point

abcdefghijklmnopqrst
uvwxyz fifffl &£$()
ABCDEFGHIJKLMNO
PQRSTUVWXYZ
1234567890 .,;:-!?/'
42 point

Clarendon specimen sheet

Clarendon was designed in 1845
by Robert Beasley as a reaction
to the interest in Fat Faces and
Egyptians. It was intended for use
as a bold face for emphasis in
reference books. The strokes are
moderately heavy, with some
variation in weight, rather than
the consistent thickness of most
Egyptians. The serifs have square
terminals with elegant brackets
joining them to the main strokes.

Clarendon had a revival during
the 1950s. Influential new versions
include Haas Clarendon by
Hermann Eidenbenz, 1953; Fortune
(later Fortuna) designed for the
Bauer foundry in 1955 by Konrad
Bauer and Walter Baum; and Claw
Clarendon for American Type
Founders by Freeman Claw, 1956.

Fiat goes Univers

At the end of 1967 the Fiat organisation in Italy completely revised the graphic image presented in all its communication media. In order to simplify the process of communicating the complexity, vastness and variety of the company's activities and products, a new symbol was adopted, and this was based upon the unit of a rhombus shape. Each unit, containing a capital letter or number, is used like a module in architecture to build up different graphic shapes of the names of the company and of its products: an idea which reflects the mass-production assembly process in a modern car factory. It is instantly recognisable, and it has the advantage of infinite adaptation which is so often lacking in other company symbols.

The redesigned symbol was only one part – the most important part – of the new house style which aimed at simple identity and disciplined order. Rules were formulated about the style of writing, which had to be straightforward, informative and direct: never affected, ambiguous, pompous or authoritarian.

Rules were also laid down regarding illustrations, both photographs and drawings, one of these being the exclusion of people except wherever absolutely essential.

Last, but not least, it was decided to utilise only one typeface – Univers; and, in the case of advertisements, to use it only in the italic version of the four different weights of the normal width. The reproductions on these two pages show just how successfully this scheme was carried out in practice during 1968.

ABCDEFGHIJKLMNOPQRSTUVWXYZ&
abcdefghijklmnopqrstuvwxyz

ABCDEFGHIJKLMNOPQRSTUVWXYZ&
abcdefghijklmnopqrstuvwxyz

ABCDEFGHIJKLMNOPQRSTUVWXYZ&
abcdefghijklmnopqrstuvwxyz

ABCDEFGHIJKLMNOPQRSTUVWXYZ&
abcdefghijklmnopqrstuvwxyz

Univers italic series 696, 693, 689 and 685 – the four weights of the normal width of the Univers range

6

Monotype Newsletter 86
Fiat goes Univers feature
December 1969

Univers was designed by Adrian Frutiger in 1957 for the French type foundry Deberny & Peignot, where he was consultant. He removed many of the idiosyncratic features of grotesque producing a simple and neutral font, highly legible both as a text and display face.

Univers consists of an extensive range of weights and variations and Frutiger, the master of systems, employed a numbering code as a means to identify these variations. The first digit refers to the stroke weight, three being the lightest and eight the heaviest; the second digit makes reference to the width of the letter from condensed to expanded. Romans are allocated odd numbers and italics even numbers. Univers 55 is the weight from which all other variants were generated.

This article promoted the basic Monotype series of Univers. Unlike the original Deberny & Peignot family of 21 fonts, the Monotype series was extremely limited. Monotype chose to ignore Frutiger's revolutionary coding system and continued to use their own nomenclature, Univers 76 for example, became Monotype series 696 Univers extra bold italic.

034 : 035
drip-dry shirts
dimension 3

Following the Second World War, economic prosperity and expansion were seen increasingly as linked to the health of national and international corporations. Companies large and small became conscious of the need to create and project a cohesive image and looked to graphic design as a tool to achieve this. The challenge of expressing identity through graphic form offers exciting opportunities for designers to test their aesthetic ingenuity, and to create durable and enduring solutions for a broad range of clients.

Designers embraced identity design, perhaps with hindsight rather naively, and developed a notion of visual identification beyond the trademark and logotype. This was the period of the 'house-style'; manuals were designed to guide firms in their usage of the mark and ensure consistency across a range of situations, surfaces and scales. The design of these complete visual systems established the concept of corporate identity, recognised today as a powerful branding and marketing tool.

Trademarks are visual marks of identification and fall loosely into three categories: the descriptive, symbolic, and typographic. Descriptive trademarks generally relate to the client's actual product or service; symbolic trademarks, most frequently abstract forms, offer some essence of the company, product or service; typographic trademarks utilise letterforms in a visual organisation relevant to the client or activity and are often combined with descriptive or symbolic elements.

These trademarks were designed by Chermayeff & Geismar, consultants to many leading corporations and institutions. They have designed and developed a vast number of visual identities and comprehensive corporate identification programmes. Famously describing good identity design as having 'some barb to it that will make it stick in your mind', Chermayeff & Geismar have created many memorable and recognisable trademarks including those shown here.

 Mobil

 Pan Am

XEROX

040 : 041
drip-dry shirts
dimension 5

Chermayeff & Geismar
Screen Gems
1966

Loosely descriptive of the
activities and services of the
film-making and distribution
company it represents, this
logo is a simplified image
of film feeding into and
off a roll. It communicates
the process and product
concerned, while cleverly
suggesting the typographic
forms of both the 'S' and 'G'.

Chermayeff & Geismar
Chase Manhattan Bank
1960

The logo for Chase Manhattan
Bank was one of the most
influential and striking of its
time; the interlocking abstract
symbol demonstrates that
a form free from typographic
or pictorial connotations
can function successfully as
a visual identifier.

Chermayeff & Geismar
Mobil
1963

This trademark replaced the
red flying horse with a simple
and elegant solution. Using
a sans serif typeface, the
logotype is constructed with
five vertical lines, the angle
of the M and two circles. The
distinctive red 'o' distinguishes
the logotype from others and
retains a link to the previous
identity. The emphasis on the
circle and cylindrical forms
is a theme running throughout
the identity, and was utilised
in the design of Mobil station
forecourts.

Ivan Chermayeff
Pan Am
1955

Chermayeff & Geismar
Xerox
1965

The breadth of post-war art and design education meant that graphic designers graduated well versed in image-making. Ken Garland, Colin Forbes, Rosmarie Tissi and Milton Glaser, whose images and design work are shown here, were all confident in generating as well as commissioning images. Garland and Glaser in particular are defined as much by their image-making as their design work.

The distinctive visual style of the imagery of this period was determined not only by aesthetic sensibility and fashion, but also evolved as a result of printing technology and economic considerations.

In the 1950s most jobs were printed using letterpress, a relief method, or silk-screen for larger items like posters. Full-colour was expensive and so designers were often limited to using two or three colours. These were inks straight from the pot – pure, bright and stronger than many of the flat colours four-colour process can achieve.

Designers explored the limitations and virtues of the printing process as a creative aid in design and illustration. A combination of line work, tints and halftone, with colours overprinted to ingeniously make secondary colours, characterise the period.

Photographs were initially printed as halftones, in black or one colour, and sometimes overprinted areas of flat colour. Despite the development of lithographic photomechanical printing, colour remained expensive well into the 1960s. However, the commercial availability of full-colour at that time generated an interest in the creative potential of photographic realism. This was particularly true in the markets of fashion, food and travel, where money flowed more easily.

Photography suited both the new photomechanical means of reproduction and the ideology of modernism. The camera was able to depersonalise its subject and produce an objective image. It also met the demands of the modern aesthetic, which favoured the machine-made over the hand-drawn. The advancement, availability and affordability of photography allowed designers to shoot, art-direct or appropriate ready-made and found photographs and by the 1960s it had become an integral part of the graphic designer's visual vocabulary.

Designers combined photography with illustration. Collage, which had been used powerfully but rather crudely in the inter-war period, was now applied to the production of images that were clever, witty and sophisticated.

Illustration was rich and varied in the post-war years. The ability of photography to represent the real reinvigorated illustration as an imaginative, conceptual and expressive medium for ideas. During the war painterly or hand-drawn graphics had been used successfully in information and propaganda. Divisions between disciplines had blurred; both illustrators and fine artists made important contributions to commercial illustration. Many practitioners used autographic processes, forming the printing surface by drawing on to the lithographic plate, engraving in wood, or etching.

In books and magazines it was then still economically possible to combine processes by binding illustrated sections with sections of text matter, using different printing methods and printed on different papers. The scope for imaginative presentation was very wide: colour could be reserved for some sections and contrasted with others in monochrome.

The economic, commercial and technical situation allowed a great deal of experimentation to spill over from fine art into graphics and vice versa. Surrealism, for example, with changes of scale and disturbing juxtapositions of images, allowed illustration to reflect imaginative texts, serious or comic.

Milton Glaser
250 courses poster
The School of Visual Arts
1967

Glaser experimented with a range
of media and materials, from
his recognisable use of thin black
contour line with strong flat colour,
to ink washes and adhesive colour
films. Like many image-makers
he explored the printing process
as a means of creating images and
effects not possible to achieve by
hand. These included the split-duct
technique, which involved the
blending of a variety of inks on the
rollers of the printing press to
achieve a multicolour result, similar
to the accidental blending that
occurs in Glaser's watercolour work.

Milton Glaser
Bach poster
Columbia Records
1967

Graphic designers often drew
inspiration from fine art, particularly
in image-making. Drawing on the
configurations, distortions and
dimensional illusions of surrealism,
Glaser sought to encompass
graphically the work of Bach in this
poster of 1967. Combining delicate
outline and watercolour washes
with geometric forms, perspective
lines and a dramatic use of colour,
he created a dream-like space rich
with musical associations.

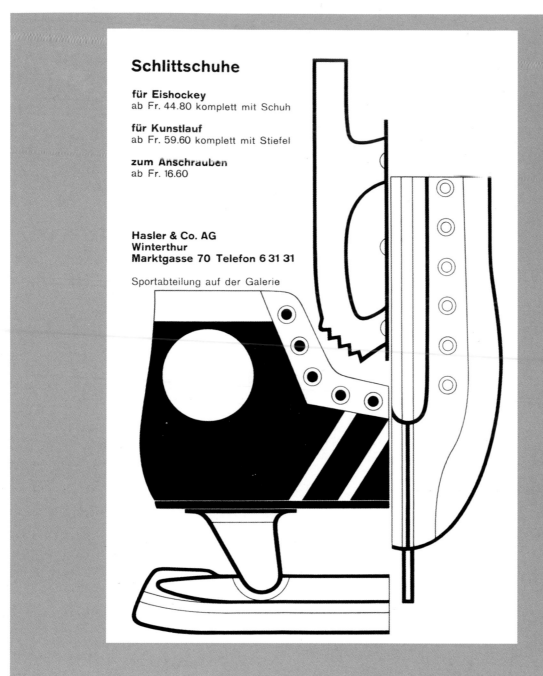

Schlittschuhe

für Eishockey
ab Fr. 44.80 komplett mit Schuh

für Kunstlauf
ab Fr. 59.60 komplett mit Stiefel

zum Anschrauben
ab Fr. 16.60

**Hasler & Co. AG
Winterthur
Marktgasse 70 Telefon 6 31 31**

Sportabteilung auf der Galerie

Rosmarie Tissi
Skates advertisement
1957

In the 1950s and '60s line
drawings were often used for
their immediate impact and
clarity. Free of excrescences, they
were deemed to be the illustration
equivalent of modern typography.
As Tissi demonstrates, subtleties
could be articulated through
changes in line weight and scale,
while object placement maximised
the abstract quality of the forms
without losing definition.

Ken Garland
Design magazine covers
1958, 1960, 1962, 1967

Garland's covers for Design
demonstrate his versatility as
a designer and image-maker.
The images shown here are
a mixture of the commissioned
and self-generated. Using a variety
of techniques – photographs
reproduced in single colour as
cut-outs within fields of bold,
flat colour, or montaged with
axonometric projections and
outline drawings, they reinforce
the idea of image as information.
Juxtapositions of scale and
colour with asymmetric layout
combine to give visual impact.

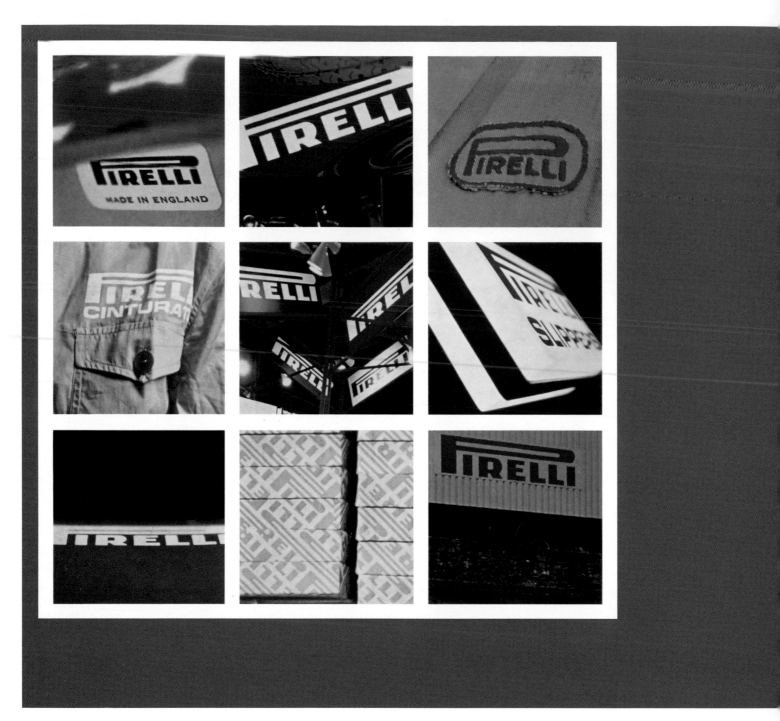

Colin Forbes
Pirelli brochure
late 1960s

Full-colour printing heightened
the visual relationship between
reality and its printed image, and
opened up to the designer new
possibilities for documentary
approaches. Within advertising,
promotion and corporate design,
this provided opportunities
to authenticate and reinforce the
image or identity of a company
or product. Forbes's images for
this Fletcher/Forbes/Gill-designed
Pirelli brochure employ tight
cropping and details to reduce
complex images to the graphic
essentials of shape and form.
Forbes transformed neutral,
straightforward photographs into
dynamic graphic constructions of
colour, pattern and information.

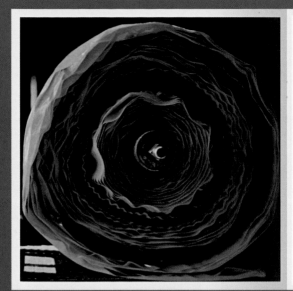 

046 : 047
drip-dry shirts
dimension 6

Wim Crouwel
self-portrait
Crouwel's 1949 MG/TC
'restored nut and bolt,
it took me 10 years'.

Experimental Jetset

Wim Crouwel

**Wim Crouwel
soundtrack**

Arvo Pärt
Fratres from
Tabula Rasa

Philip Glass
Einstein on the Beach

Crouwel's recording
of Einstein on the Beach is
on four LPs from 1979 on
the Tomato Music Company
label, New York. The
accompanying booklet was
designed by Milton Glaser.
The opera was performed at
that time in Amsterdam.
Crouwel saw it and 'it made
a great impression'.

Experimental Jetset
biography

Experimental Jetset is an
Amsterdam-based design
group founded in 1997 by
Erwin Brinkers (born 1973,
Rotterdam), Marieke Stolk
(born 1967, Amsterdam)
and Danny van den Dungen
(born 1971, Rotterdam),
who met while studying at
the Gerrit Rietveld Academy,
Amsterdam.

Wim Crouwel
biography

Wim Crouwel is remarkable for the purity of his resolutely systematic approach to design and for the extraordinary breadth and reach of his long career. Artist, designer, professor and museum director, Crouwel's many mantles reflect his rich knowledge and appreciation of the world of arts and architecture, of which he sees graphic design as being only one component part.

Born in the Netherlands in 1928, Crouwel trained at the Art Academy Minerva (1946–49) and after completing his military service, started his professional life as an abstract painter. He studied at the Amsterdam Art Academy (1952–53) and joined the architectural, exhibition and graphic design firm Enderberg (1952), where he gained his first experience of the possibilities of graphic design. Inspired by Swiss design, in 1954 he stopped painting and sought work as a freelance designer in Amsterdam.

By 1956 Crouwel had set up a studio with the industrial designer Kho Liang Ie with whom he collaborated on three-dimensional and graphic design projects. Crouwel began to forge a distinct approach to design. Harnessing his affinity for abstract form, principles of abstract art and regard for clarity and simplicity, he experimented with letterforms and graphic systems, and embarked upon a rigorous examination of grid structures.

During the 1950s Crouwel travelled to Switzerland meeting with other designers and witnessing the emerging international style; an avid proponent of international debate, Crouwel became the first general secretary of Icograda in 1963. In the same year Wim Crouwel, product designer Friso Kramer and architect and graphic designer Benno Wissing, together with Paul and Dick Schwarz, founded Total Design, the first multi-disciplinary design studio in the Netherlands, which was to become a dominant force in Dutch design. Through their work, Crouwel and his colleagues had significant influence on the national and cultural identity of the Netherlands; from the signage system at Schipol Airport (1965–67) to Crouwel's postage stamps for the Dutch Post Office (1968).

Faithful proponents of Helvetica, they acknowledge their relationship to modernism but are keen to claim that the influence of pop culture, punk rock and conspiracy theories are equally important in shaping their work. They liken their studio model to that of a music band: a small group operating as one unit with a collective responsibility for the work they produce; working at the margins of graphic design yet part of an international design underground.

Experimental Jetset enjoys and exploits the physical qualities of design; its inventive graphic projects span the spheres of culture, fashion and music and include stamps for Royal Dutch Mail (2002), T-shirt design and the new house-style for the contemporary section of the Stedelijk Museum (2004).

Its manifesto Experimental Jetset vs The World was published in Dot Dot Dot magazine (number 3, 2000) and work by the design group was featured in the exhibition of recent European design titled Somewhere Totally Else at the Design Museum, London (2003).

Crouwel's extensive body of work for the Stedelijk Museum (1964–85) demonstrates his achievements in the refinement and application of the grid. His systematic design thinking was also experimental and innovative: in 1967 he designed the New Alphabet, a typeface intended for computer reading, composed of simplified letterforms constructed as units upon a grid.

In 1980, Crouwel left Total Design to become professor at the Technical University Delft and in 1985 accepted the appointment as director of the Museum Boijmans van Beuningen, Rotterdam. In addition to his long and significant association at Delft (1965–85), he also consolidated his long running commitment to education taking the Private Chair at Erasmus University, Rotterdam (1987–93) and a visiting professorship at the Royal College of Art, London (1981–85).

Crouwel's considerable contribution to the cultural life of the Netherlands and to the field of graphic design has been recognised in the many prizes and awards he has received, among which are the British OBE (1989), the Knight of the Order of the Dutch Lion (1993) and most recently the prestigious Oeuvre prize (2004).

Experimental Jetset

Ramones T-shirt, one of many designs for the independent T-shirt label 2K Gingham – 'we're constantly trying to design the archetypal shirt'. Experimental Jetset liken their studio model to that of a music band: an autonomous unit with a collective responsibility for the work.

Wim Crouwel

Total Design had significant influence on the national and cultural identity of the Netherlands. Crouwel's stamp designs, for example, were used from 1968 until the arrival of the Euro in 2002.

Wim Crouwel

01 **art training/
early career choices/
formative influences**

Experimental Jetset

The Stedelijk Museum CS
moved to a temporary space
in 2004. These badges show
the new SMCS logo, slogans
using the initials, and refer
to Milton Glaser's classic
I Love NY logo.

Wim Crouwel

In the early 1950s Crouwel
worked on the graphic
design for All Hands on Deck,
a floating exhibition funded
by regeneration money
after the war.

Crouwel appreciates the
hand-skills he first acquired
at art school, as these 1967
sketches for his postage
stamp designs demonstrate.

01 I didn't plan to be a designer.
My father was a lithographer so
in the school holidays I worked
in his block-making factory.
I was sure that I wanted to go to art
school, maybe to become a painter.
I had an old-fashioned art school
education: painting, sculpting,
lithography, etching, watercolour
and drawing. There wasn't a course
in graphic design, but on the walls
of our academy there were pieces
by people like the early French
poster artist Cassandre and we
did produce posters, not to learn
design but in order to have a
subject for lithography.

Later on I appreciated the teaching
because I learned skills through
drawing and painting that I still
use. I always have to sketch first
with a pencil and through painting
I learned about colour and tone.
The further I am away from the
experience the more I think it was
actually very formative.

I left art school in 1949. I then
had to do my military service,
but by 1952 I was walking around
Amsterdam, with my portfolio, going
to advertising agencies and trying
to get a job. They all said 'nice work
but we don't have a job, we'll call
you when we do'. But they never
called of course, so I felt lousy.

That went on for a few months.
I went through all my money but just
at the right moment I went to an
older colleague, Dick Elffers, and he
helped me to find a job. He saw the
designer in me. I am very grateful to
the director of the company where
I got that job, Mr Enderberg. It could
have all been completely different.
A friend of my brother had emigrated
to Canada, as did lots of people
after the war. He offered me a job
in the lumber industry and I was
thinking of going when Enderberg
said to stay.

Help was being given by the
Americans to regenerate Holland.
This was part of the Marshall Plan
to rebuild Europe after the war.
We were commissioned to produce
two exhibitions to encourage
regeneration. They were on
enormous ships that could float
through Holland. It was a fantastic,
ingenious thing. The architect of
the installations was Italian and
I worked with two other Swiss
designers. These were very
adventurous and formative years
for me, particularly learning about
the Swiss approach to modern
design and typography. At the
same time I did an exhibition in
Amsterdam where I met the
Swiss designer Karl Gerstner who
was also to become an important
influence on me.

01 Linda van Deursen was a very inspirational tutor, she showed us the work of Richard Prince – a sort of 'punk-minimalism' and a breath of fresh air at a time when graphic design was more about layered compositions, techno- and grunge-typography. It's funny, some people assume our work to be heavily influenced by early Swiss modernists, but actually Richard Prince had a much larger influence on us.

Another person that influenced us was Bob Gill. In the library of the Rietveld we discovered a copy of Forget all the Rules You Ever Learned about Graphic Design – including the ones in this book. What impressed us most was his consistent use of the problem/solution model. It's a model that some might find outdated, rigid, one-dimensional. To us, it is beautiful. Of course, it has a tragic side, as every solution only brings forth more problems; and besides, we all know there is no such thing as one perfect solution.

In Crouwel's work, form and approach are the same thing. It is highly systematic, but it's also highly personal – organisation according to Crouwel's own logic. It is often argued that design has to be unexpected, irrational, rebellious; anything to avoid being 'boring'. We very much disagree: it is consistency and an iron logic that can really throw you off your feet and change your way of thinking.

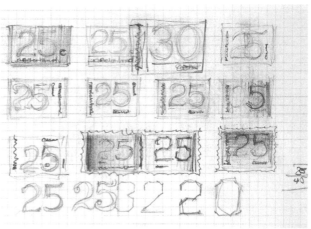

Wim Crouwel

02 **modernism/
finding direction/
Univers/
Anthony Froshaug/
minimalism**

Experimental Jetset

Two of a series of three posters hung in New York bus shelters as exhibits for the 2004/05 group exhibition Terminal Five. Each uses an early modernist quote to advertise a fictitious airline company. Can modernism retain its utopian dimension in such a commodified world?

Wim Crouwel

These calendars from 1965 and 1973 show Crouwel's interest in using more mechanistic sans serif fonts. In 1957 the font Univers was issued. Crouwel and his colleagues at Total Design never looked back using predominantly Univers and Helvetica from then on.

02 A while ago, in an old issue of Emigre, a group of American academics were discussing a trip they made to Europe. They wrote how shocked they were by the indifference of European designers towards history. We don't think it is indifference – we just don't fetishise history as much as some American academics tend to do. History is part of the here and now.

For example, when we talk with Wim Crouwel and he tells us about himself as a young man visiting Piet Zwart, we are bridging three, almost four generations of designers, in one conversation. But it doesn't feel like history at all. It feels extremely close by.

03 We're not really interested in the narrow definition of the word 'function'. To us, a chair isn't simply something to sit on, it also functions as the embodiment of a way of thinking. This broad definition of function is closer to that advocated by early rather than late modernists.

In Theory and Design in the First Machine Age, Reyner Banham, for example, shows that Rietveld's armchair is a highly symbolic structure. It is a statement about the infinity of space. This is something we're quite interested in: the function of design as an embodiment of ideology.

02 I was a child of modernism, influenced by the period around 1930; a high time for modernism in painting, design, architecture – and the Bauhaus period. In art school we were not taught about it, but in the early '50s, as soon as I discovered the beauty and logic of Swiss typography I thought 'this is it'. That was a real breakthrough. These connections made at the beginning of my career completely shaped what happened later. I also met the Dutch designer Piet Zwart. It was crazy that I did not know about him in art school. Modernism was far away from that school, although we were in a building that was the first modernist building in Holland. Maybe I was more influenced by the building than by the teaching. Anyway, by 1957 I had found my own way and was sure. I wasn't looking sideways any more. I was 29.

Looking at my early work you can see that I was searching for the right direction. I even searched for the right type to use. In 1957 we discovered Univers was the right answer. This was the first typeface where the 'x' height was the same in all weights when used at the same size. Bold, extra bold, light, you could use them in one line close to each other if you wanted. This was a real step forward.

In 1963 we started the company Total Design. The only typefaces we used for many, many years were Univers and Helvetica. If a client wanted something else there was initially some kind of fight.

The publisher Abrams, for example, had asked me to design a book about Rembrandt's etchings, but felt that Rembrandt and Univers just 'didn't go together'. Why should we try to get the kind of atmosphere of Rembrandt through the type, I asked? It's never real when you try to simulate such a thing. However, I didn't win the fight so I chose Bembo which the client liked very much. Whenever I have had to use a classic typeface, it is almost always Bembo and occasionally Garamond. Anyway, these are the only exceptions that you can find in all the work in my period at Total Design.

The English typographer Anthony Froshaug was also a hero of mine. I learned of him in 1954 when he was teaching at Ulm. I was absolutely intrigued by him. He was impossible, but a great man and a fantastic typographer and teacher. He was a typical English designer and yet he was a modernist. He visited me when he felt lousy and that was always Christmas time. He would come over to Holland and spoil my Christmas – fantastic! During those years I felt lousy too because I was divorced. Together we had lousy Christmases!

Later on in the '60s my interests were refreshed by minimal art. I found my roots again. Then, at the beginning of the '70s, the work of Robert Wilson in the theatre and the composer Philip Glass influenced my further development. I saw Robert Wilson's first opera. It was Baroque minimalism – absolutely fascinating.

056 : 057
drip-dry shirts
discussion 1

04 We are firm believers in the utopian dimension of design. It's something we're absolutely convinced of. However, we're not sure if this can be found in utilitarianism or obviously social work as we are sceptical about the potential that this work has to change structurally ways of thinking.

We believe we are living in a fragmented society. One way to counter this alienation is through the 'inner logic' of design. However, you can define this in many different ways: Herbert Marcuse speaks of 'the aesthetic dimension' in his essay of the same name, but you can also refer to it as the dialectical dimension, or the critical dimension, or the inner logic, or the internal whole. This is where we locate the utopian dimension of design.

We have ideals but recognise they are unachievable, a concept better expressed by this quote from Jorge Borges: 'Nothing is built on stone. All is built on sand, but we must build as if the sand were stone'. We think this is an excellent definition of design. Building on sand, as if it were stone. It's the ultimate idealism.

Wim Crouwel

**03 post-war optimism/
politics and design/
idealism**

**04 post-modernism/
changing attitudes
towards design/
business competition**

Wim Crouwel

Crouwel's work has spanned more than five decades but is consistently modern and rigorous.

The Hiroshima exhibition poster, designed in 1957 for the Van Abbemuseum, combines strong lettering with minimal typography. The 1961 IBM brochure shows restraint and clarity whilst the letterforms used in the 1976 calendar are powerful and inventive. Contemporary work is no less impactful as demonstrated by the Kieler Woche poster of 1998 and the poster for Vier Generaties designed for the Centraal Museum Utrecht in 2000.

03 When I look back, the 1950s were absolutely marvellous. For us it was absolutely glorious because we were rebuilding the country after the war. We all had this feeling.

The Dutch Federation of Applied Arts was founded in 1945 by museum director and graphic designer Willem Sandberg and others. There were graphic designers, interior designers, textile designers all under the umbrella of this Federation. It had a very idealistic approach. You could hardly become a member if you did not follow left-wing ideology that was demonstrated in your work. If you had been a collaborator in the war, for example, you couldn't join.

We had two associations at the time. The other was the Federation of Publicity Designers and Illustrators. In this society there were several members who had worked for the Germans during the war. Publicity design was regarded as something a little dirty because it is more overtly about making money. The notion of publicity seemed wrong; an attempt to influence people and restrict freedom of choice. So the associations were political enemies.

During the '60s we discussed merging the organisations. I left the board of the Federation of Applied Arts for a while because I didn't want to battle any longer.

Once they merged I rejoined, but about ten members left permanently. They were the older members who were active during the war. People who had been part of the Resistance so they couldn't stand it.

I sometimes wonder what is driving designers today. I can understand why young designers are enthralled by the speed of technological development and that this is their focus, but there's a lack of idealism now. No utopian ideals, no belief that graphic design could be important in making this a better world.

That's what we believed until the end of the '60s when post-modernism came along. Until that moment we thought that a house-style was something to make people aware of the difference between companies, a signage system was so you don't lose your way and typography was something neutral that should not stand between the sender and the receiver.

I miss that point of view today. I talk to younger designers who are active and intelligent and they have something else that makes them tick. I guess it is the fascination for the job in itself.

04 In the mid-1960s I read Complexity and Contradiction in Architecture by Robert Venturi. This marked one of the first steps towards post-modernist thinking. Venturi advocated combining fragments of old architectural devices with the modern, as you see, for example, in his work on the National Gallery extension in London. In the beginning these ideas seemed to be about a kind of romanticism, but the more I considered them the more convinced I was of my own modernist position.

I was teaching in Delft at the time. I have always advised my students to keep their radar going; everything that happens is important. Although I didn't like it I showed my students the work of post-modern designers. They needed to know in order to make an informed choice and when I was director at the Museum Boijmans van Beuningen we bought quite a lot of models from that period for the history department of the museum.

In Holland in the early '70s, combined with post-modernism, there was a wave of anti-design feeling. The feeling was that designers were destroying traditional aspects of life and spoiling the cities.

People turned against our company Total Design because they thought our objective was to unify everything. There were symposia, articles in the papers and magazines. In my opinion this was partly a result of post-modern thinking.

At the same time we saw other design offices springing up. We suddenly had competition. We didn't really have competition in the '60s. We had to cope with this just as society turned against design. The '70s were a kind of down period. I myself felt stronger and stronger though because the opposition helped me to develop.

There was a journalist who wrote weekly articles against design in quite an influential magazine. I was one of her targets. I still remember a symposium evening that the magazine organised when I was confronted by this journalist for the first time. Myself and colleagues explained our position then someone in the audience shouted 'fascist!' at me. They thought design was a form of fascism. It was very upsetting.

Then came the '80s and suddenly everything had to be 'designed', which really meant 'made pretty'. Professionally design flourished at this time. In the '90s new minimalism came in, but I didn't really trust it. Suddenly all designers were shaved bald and dressed in black. I was part of another design forum, on the same stage as previously, with five bald-headed, black-dressed British designers. They were all in the same uniform! It was crazy!

05 We're a three-person studio operating on the margins of graphic design. We feel very much like a band. K Records, a record label from the States, often used the catchphrase 'the international pop underground'. In a way, we feel very much a part of an international design underground. We never participate in 'pitches' or advertising award shows, we don't go to industry receptions etc. It just isn't our world.

As a small group of people operating as one unit we have the advantage of a cooperative, collective way of working whilst the 'smallness' ensures that every member is responsible, and nobody is alienated from the end product. We want to be responsible for the whole design, and that includes the boring part.

06 We have to admit, there are often quite aggressive confrontations during the design process, as we are quite difficult people to work with (and our clients are usually quite stubborn too). But in the end, our clients usually appreciate the blood, sweat and tears we put into a project and are enormously proud of the stuff we do for them

Wim Crouwel

Experimental Jetset

The house-style for SMCS in its temporary new home, an old sorting office. Univers, the font Crouwel also used, is combined with the stripes of airmail letters to make an arresting and contemporary logo. An ingenious, flexible system is applied to print, exhibition and web design.

Wim Crouwel

Crouwel designed extensively for the Stedelijk Museum for over 20 years. The 1968 poster demonstrates his fascination with grid structures, the bulletin announces a show of his own work in 1979, whilst the 1971 poster for inflatables in art shows his inventiveness with letterforms.

05 Most clients became friends. Even if it was very business-like, people trusted us, people knew what we stood for and that's why people came to us. We were the first design office in Holland and so we proved ourselves on some very important jobs. We visited the British designer FHK Henrion before we set up Total Design. He advised us that institutions like to talk to institutions. They like the guarantee that even if someone is ill the work will still go on. We went to Fletcher/Forbes/Gill too. They had just started the year before us and invented the idea of partners who had their own clients. So, we shaped our office to their model.

My client the director of the Stedelijk Museum was with me for 30 years. He was my dearest client and I did my best work for him. The shape of my whole career can be seen in that work. I was lucky that I had this cultural commission steadily going on while I was doing other business-orientated work too. One of the most interesting commissions I had was the design of the Dutch postage stamps. These lasted until the Euro arrived! Also my work on the New Alphabet, as this started an interest in computers and technology.

I never felt unsure. I feel myself just lucky. In Total Design we were able to do nice jobs and were not forced to accept things that we didn't want. However, compromise is something you have to live with. For example, we produced the corporate identity for SHV (Steenkolen Handels Vereniging). We discovered they had sub-brands that were not using our identity. We said this is against our idea of what corporate identity is and we had enormous discussions with our clients about whether we could accept this. We compromised because we understood that the realities of business required something other than a purely applied corporate identity. This experience made us grow up, it taught us a lesson. It's not even compromise, it's learning lessons.

07 We definitely see graphic design and art as functioning within different infrastructures, but they do overlap. Trying to truly separate them can be as dangerous as parting Siamese twins. It is its historical link with art that gives graphic design its utopian dimension in the first place.

It's interesting to see how the relationship between art and design changed in modernism. Striving towards a synthesis of art and design was quite an elementary characteristic of early modernism, quite possibly its most defining one. Late modernists, on the other hand, seemed eager to cut the umbilical cord. It must have something to do with the forging of graphic design as a profession. In graphic design's adolescent phase it is trying to create some distance from its closest relative, art.

Wim Crouwel

Experimental Jetset

A SMCS poster for the exhibition Sandberg Now, a homage to the legendary museum director and graphic designer Willem Sandberg. It is rather melancholy, the name and time gradually slip away.

Wim Crouwel

Crouwel is interested in technology. In 1967 he designed the New Alphabet intended for computer reading and composed of simplified letterforms constructed as units on a grid.

06 I am of the generation who believe there is a large distance between painting and graphic design. The most important thing as a graphic designer is that you are dedicated to your commission, you find a solution. It has to do with responsibility. Design became, more or less, art when David Carson designed the magazine Raygun at the beginning of the '90s. The pages were beautiful in an expressionistic way, but you couldn't read the text. Occasionally I admit to feeling jealous of such a free approach, of not having this burden of the things we learned from modernism.

07 I worked like crazy. Probably my first marriage broke down because I was a workaholic. I think that if you want to achieve something professionally you have to work very hard. Maybe your private life should be number one, but my work was. I always have been ambitious, maybe a little less now. I'm afraid to be overloaded with things now and that has to do with my age.

I think that people like Armin Hofmann and Karl Gerstner were more groundbreaking than I was, but in Holland I had quite an influence. The strictness of using grids, the way we explained our work, everything we did in Holland in corporate identity programmes was very important – and groundbreaking now and then.

Of course I felt a little envy of what some other designers did. For instance I admired Karl Gerstner greatly. He was my age. I have known him since 1952. He was theoretical, he was so strong, so sharp, and the books he published... one book after another and they were all very influential.

The strange thing is that in the '90s British designers were suddenly very interested in my work. The Foundry digitised my font designs, young British designers visited me and produced exhibitions of my work, only in England, very strange. Now the Japanese magazine Idea wants to produce 100 pages on me. That's half the magazine so I must be part of design history! Even if I don't believe it myself, others seem to.

08 It occupies every minute of our lives. It's beyond Total Design, it's a Total Existence.

All three of us are slightly dysfunctional and oversensitive, which means that we don't have the right personalities to deal with the deadlines, the responsibility that comes with working on large projects and the constant pressure to perform. It's resulting in headaches, overeating, dizziness and sleeplessness. But we still think it is worth it.

We're living in a world that seems divided between neo-conservatism and religious fundamentalism. Both are post-modern phenomena. Working in graphic design, an inherently modernist profession, gives us the chance to explore values and themes that offer consolation and reduce our sense of alienation.

08 I started teaching in 1954. Crazily young. I have always enjoyed it. I have taught all the time and loved it.

09 I love technology in general. I'm restoring an old car because I like the technology. I was always intrigued by technical inventions. In our profession I became very aware of it at the moment when letterpress printing disappeared and offset printing came in its place. We had to work in a completely different way. Then came the computer. In the '60s the first generation of phototypesetters arrived and I was immediately intrigued. The results were typographically awful and this inspired me to design fonts specifically for the computer. That's why I made my New Alphabet. The computer has been very influential. We'd struggle with different layers in the '50s, doing a lot of things by hand for offset printing. Now you can do 12 layers easily and produce layouts that we couldn't dream of.

I am a positive thinker, I always have been. There is constant change and every period is fantastic and interesting. I'm not pessimistic at all. I see that there is a lot of rubbish produced but there always has been. Even in the '50s, when we thought we'd found the solution, there was rubbish produced. It multiplies but the good stuff does too. So percentage-wise it's the same amount of good to bad.

I would hardly know how to start now and I'm not jealous of the young people today who have to because it's very difficult. On the other hand once you see the possibilities then it's a fascinating period. I would always advise to find out as soon as possible what your strong points are and develop them. When you are strong you can absolutely reach something. For me 1957 was a very important year because I found out what my strengths were and also what I should not do. All things considered I would do it all again the same way.

062 : 063
drip-dry shirts
discussion 1

Milton Glaser
self-portrait

Brookie Maxwell

Milton Glaser

**Milton Glaser
soundtrack**

Handel
opera Alcina

Bach
selections from
A Well-Tempered Clavier

Muddy Waters
Baby, Please Don't Go
from Muddy Waters
and Otis Spann,
Tomato Records

Brookie Maxwell
biography

Brookie Maxwell (born 1956, New York) is a passionate advocate of art as a means of addressing issues, transcending boundaries, and inspiring and transforming lives. She studied media arts at the School of Visual Arts, New York (1974–77) and her career has encompassed playwriting, illustration, fine art and public art projects. Maxwell is currently the director of Gallery 138 in Chelsea, New York.

Milton Glaser
biography

Milton Glaser is an extraordinarily prolific designer and illustrator whose distinctive work and personal vision occupy a unique place in the collective American experience. A giant of American design, Glaser is a master of reinvention. His career has been propelled by his ability to consistently create innovative solutions and by his restless exploration of media, materials and techniques that make his work hard to categorise.

Born in 1929 in New York City, Glaser was educated at the High School of Music and Art, New York (1944–47) and the Cooper Union art school, New York (1948–51) before gaining a Fulbright Scholarship to the Academy of Fine Arts, Bologna, Italy (1952–53), where he studied etching under Giorgio Morandi.

In 1954 Milton Glaser, Seymour Chwast and Ed Sorel founded Push Pin Studios, an influential consultancy that challenged the convention that design and illustration were separate components. Glaser explored a range of graphic techniques, motifs, perceptual and conceptual iconography and applied them with wit and verve to memorable effect. His Dylan poster of 1967 succeeded in transcending both subject and function to become a popular cultural icon.

Critical to Glaser's enduring success is his vision for seeing and seizing opportunities and challenges. In 1968 he co-founded New York magazine with Clay Felker, in 1983 he formed the editorial design office WBMG with Walter Bernard and redesigned various publications, among them Fortune and the Washington Post. In 1974 Glaser moved from Push Pin to set up Milton Glaser Inc. Here his projects expanded to include large-scale environmental and interior design; a 600ft mural for the New Federal Office, Indianapolis (1974) and the design of the interior and graphics of the restaurant and observation deck of the World Trade Centre, New York (1975). His place in graphic design history was confirmed in 1976 with his creation of the I Love NY logo. Glaser's varied projects include his 15-year relationship with the Grand Union Company supermarket chain and the AIDS symbol and poster for the World Health Organisation (1987).

Maxwell was the founder, executive and artistic director of Creative Arts Workshops for Kids (1986–96), a community arts programme that used visual and performing arts to teach survival and problem-solving skills to inner-city children. In 1995 Maxwell designed and directed Peace Place in East Harlem; a half-acre art park, play area and gardens incorporating a large collaborative mural between artists and CAW children. In 1991 she received the Big Apple Award from the Mayor's office.

Her practice embraces painting, sculpture, writing, dance and theatre. Visual bodies of work include Desire 1–4 (2000–05), Pieta (2005), Fear No Evil (1999–2003), Celebrate Life (1999–2004), Witness (2001), Deep Water (1990–99), Building America (1987–90) and 42nd Street: A Walk Across (1983–87).

She has exhibited widely, often at alternative spaces throughout New York including the Henry Street Settlement (2000) and the John Jay College of Criminal Justice (2004). Her public art has been exhibited at the Port Authority, Bellevue Hospital and in the NYC Subway system.

Maxwell has two plays currently in development, The Hurricane Reports: Jonesing for Shango Macho and Incident on the F Train.

He has exhibited worldwide and his solo exhibitions include the Museum of Modern Art, New York (1975), Centre Georges Pompidou, Paris (1977) and Cooper Union, New York (1984). In 1991 he was commissioned by the Italian Government to create an exhibition in tribute to Piero della Francesca and his illustrations of Dante's Purgatorio were exhibited in Venice in 1999. He is represented in many permanent collections, among them MOMA, New York and the Smithsonian Institution, Washington DC.

Glaser has received numerous awards and is an active member of the design and education communities. He was a co-signatory of the reissued First Things First 2000 manifesto calling for a more considered and responsible approach to graphic design. He won the Prix Savignac for the World's Most Memorable Poster of 1996 and he is the recipient of The Society of Illustrator's Gold Medal from the Cooper Union. He is a member of the Art Director's Club Hall of Fame and the American Institute of Graphic Arts and holds nine honorary doctorates, including one from the School of Visual Arts, New York and the Royal College of Art, London.

Brookie Maxwell

True Value, 2005, from the Desire series, which explored four aspects of desire over a five-year period. True Value considers human rhythms tied to the rhythms of nature; the seasons of life, death and rebirth, 67 x 82 inches.

Milton Glaser

Glaser's I Love NY logo of 1976 continues to resonate with graphic designers of all generations. Experimental Jetset refer to it on page 54 where they show some of their recent work for the Stedelijk Museum CS in Amsterdam.

Maxwell's materials include tar, caran d'ache crayons, acrylic, found objects, blood, stone, ashes, gold and silver leaf, and wood.

Brookie Maxwell

01 **the initial appeal
of commercial art/
lasting impressions
of Milton Glaser**

01 I studied media arts at the School of Visual Arts during the '70s when people in the fine arts department were setting fire to the staircase, chewing up sandwiches and spitting them out, and drawing self-portraits masturbating while they were menstrual. I was concerned about making a living; I chose commercial art for my major.

During my first year I worked for a photographer who sent me to see Milton at New York magazine. The office was blasting Mozart; it was alive with flowers and sunshine. It was not like any workplace I had ever been to before or since. Picture the moment in Rothko's work when he discovers colour field painting and the sun comes up over the whole universe. That's what it was like meeting him.

I went to Milton's post-graduate night class when I was only 17. There were assignments given every Wednesday for the following week. I cried 'till Sunday, then got to work. The following week I did it again. By the time we were halfway through the year, I was 17. I was able to work within any time-frame, a skill that stood me in good stead later as an illustrator.

Milton Glaser

01 **early interest
in the visual arts/
the mysterious
life of the painter/
the initial appeal
of commercial art**

02 **breadth of vision
and learning/
early professional
experience**

Milton Glaser

Glaser had a sense of becoming design history early when his Dylan poster of 1967 became a popular cultural icon. A Marcel Duchamp silhouette had inspired him as had Islamic painting. Six million copies were printed and included with a Dylan album.

Glaser refers to the influence of Japanese calligraphic wash drawings and Picasso's aquatints when he produced this 1960 cover for Push Pin's journal Graphic.

The early 1970s' covers of New York were consistently bold and arresting, fighting as they did in an increasingly competitive market.

I will continue to think about these lessons for the rest of my life. At first I didn't understand, but I knew not to waste the information. Anyone who has ever worked with Milton knows he is a genius. He has intellectual and artistic capacities that other people do not: he is also able to present ideas very simply. Everything seems clearer to him than it does to other people.

01 My impulse always was to be an artist, without ever understanding what the term means. Early in my life I decided that I didn't want to be a painter. Although I had nominal contact with people who painted for a living – at 12 I began learning to draw from life – I couldn't imagine their life. I literally didn't understand the construct – painting pictures, showing at galleries and selling work. It seemed like a very curious idea. I did have an enormous desire to make things and to create form, to make pictures and to tell stories, but what I didn't have was the idea that the appropriate way to express this interest or passion was by becoming a painter.

On the other hand, I was very interested in comic strips and narration. I learned to draw by copying comic strips – that's probably true of many fledgling designers and painters if you dig into their histories. I loved the idea that tens of thousands of people could experience my work. I thought that was fabulous, particularly as compared to the work of a painter that might reside in someone's living-room. The social reward of being visible was greater than the aesthetic reward of high art. I wanted my work to be public and I knew there was a way to enter into the public consciousness through what was then called commercial art.

02 A lot of people in the visual arts don't have a literary interest. The tradition of modernism removes people from those interests to a degree, but I've always been interested in storytelling and narration and I see this as part of the role of picture-making and imagery. I found that this was not at the core of graphic design training or practice. It began to draw more on ideas of abstraction and pure form. However, I went to Cooper Union – a terrific school – and I got a very good, solid education. It was very broad and to some degree reflected Bauhaus principles and the spirit of twentieth-century modernism.

I went to work at the promotion department of Vogue magazine for about six months after I got out of college. It is the only job I've ever had. I ended up having a disagreement with the art director who was very happy to see me go to Europe when I got my Fulbright. I spent some time in Bologna studying etching with Giorgio Morandi. This made me realise how parochial and narrow my understanding was, but I didn't know how I was going to apply my new learning.

Brookie Maxwell

02 We share the belief that art can address life's intractable problems and that artists have responsibilities that come with our gifts. Glaser's vision of design is partly based on the idea that design should be for the good of all people.

In my work I have dealt with the rape and murder of children, the suffering of the perpetrators themselves, and the healing of families who are dying of AIDS. I don't consider my work to be overtly political. I think it is about life; as such, politics and injustice are recurring themos. So are love, war, desire, hope, loss, light, rage, peace, shadow, transgression, transcendence and the little girl on my block whose parents are getting divorced.

Milton Glaser

Brookie Maxwell

In 1995 Maxwell designed and directed Peace Place in East Harlem; a half-acre art park incorporating a large collaborative mural between artists and Creative Arts Workshops children. Glaser wrote to every important New York artist, from Christo and Jeanne-Claude to Alex Katz, and they all contributed work.

Milton Glaser

Glaser's powerful AIDS symbol was designed in 1987 for the World Health Organisation.

03 There was a sense of possibility once the war had ended and a tremendous release of energy and constraint. This was unprecedented. There was a real change of sensibility during that time. It was a very formative moment for the profession, the studio and for myself. Attitudinally, and to some degree stylistically, the period shaped my approach to work, although I think that over the last 20 years my work has departed significantly from those influences.

There was a tremendous sense that power could rest with the people. The success of the civil rights movement led us to believe that we were on the way to overcoming the dark side of the culture. But what we discovered, as everyone discovers late in life, is that it is always with us and occasionally wins. This struggle between light and dark is a constant manifestation of the human condition and so ours was only a temporary success. The durability of evil is something that has obviously concerned humankind since the beginning of our species, but whatever gains you make are obliterated by the passage of time.

I am mindful that as a graphic designer you are responsible for transmitting ideas that occur in your work to others. I don't think you can remove yourself from the idea that your work has consequences. The First Things First manifesto expressed that idea in a strong way and so I thought it was appropriate to sign it.

04 In retrospect we had tremendous advantages. The field was not populated to the same degree as now. It was not entirely a desert, but it was much less competitive. There were designers who cleared the way for us, most notably Paul Rand, Lester Beall and Lou Dorfsman. They basically said 'this is possible'. However, I tend to refer more to art history and to the general visual history of our species than to a particular moment in time that is officially designated as a design moment. I've always been more interested in going outside the field for my influences than staying within it.

03 Milton is in love with design because he is so in love with life. If you look on his bookshelf, you will see books on every conceivable topic, indicating the depth of his curiosity. Hokusai's Woodcuts, Muybridge's Complete Encyclopaedia of Human and Animal Locomotion, Mystic Art of Ancient Tibet and Cuisine of the Sun are a few of the titles. Having a mentor who lives this way proved to me that it was possible. It was the encouragement I needed to fly in the face of convention.

He's been wildly successful in his career. His energy is not blocked by spending his days doing senseless things he hates. He has always divided his week with firm boundaries: a short design week in the studio – four days – followed by a long weekend making art in the country.

Milton has been behind every undertaking I have tackled in my career. He never told me 'no'. Many of the projects we have done together were planned during lunch as we talked about good and evil, creation, chaos and destruction, joy, old master drawings, truffles from Tuscany, paper from New York Central Arts Supply, brushes from Japan, seduction and betrayal, addiction and recovery... and cats. It has ruined me for lunch with other people.

An example of a project worked on together is the Peace Place mural in East Harlem. Milton wrote to every important New York artist, from Christo and Jeanne-Claude to Alex Katz, and they all contributed work. The mural still stands today, loved and protected by the community.

Brookie Maxwell

04 Every limitation provides opportunity. Compromise was essential when I was starting out as an illustrator, because the product always came first. Subject matter was assigned by the client and this greatly expanded my range of interests.

When I had been working as an illustrator for ten years, Milton suggested it was time for me to expand my horizons. Shortly afterwards, I submitted a proposal to the Public Art Fund and it was accepted. I also began as artist in residence at a summer camp for homeless children, which led to developing my own Non Profit organisation. Our relationships with funders were always positive because we always told them the truth.

We were aware of what an essential part they played in the lives of the people we served together. We did not bow to their constraints, together we identified the best possible way to be of service. A similar process exists in the fine art community. Artists must find a balance between personal expression and marketability in order to make work that is accessible.

Milton Glaser

05 Certain clients were absolutely central to my development because ours went beyond a business relationship. They were personal and affectionate relationships. Professionalism, when I was growing up, meant you take a job, you do it and move on to the next. Very few relationships endure beyond a couple of jobs in professional life, but in many cases my relationships have lasted 20 or 30 years. I depend on that and I find that I really cannot work for someone I don't truly like. As a designer your ability to establish relationships with others is part of your talent. You need to find people with whom there is a sense of affinity and commonality. This makes everything possible, without it nothing is possible.

One of the instrumental people in my life has been Silas Rhodes, the co-founder of the School of Visual Arts. He has been enormously supportive in all my work, helping me find a way of expressing my ideas and so on. Another guy was Joe Baum, the great restaurateur, who was a marvellously interesting man, and who I worked for for over 25 years doing a lot of restaurant interiors and graphics. He was a splendid, splendid guy, a wonderful friend and again, someone who was completely open to my ideas. We had a great ride together. I actually had a very good relationship with Sir James Goldsmith; our personal relationship managed to transcend our political differences. We did a lot of good work together in the supermarket business. Another person who's been tremendous for me is Shirley Kenny who is president of Stony Brook University; together we have helped transform the campus.

Brookie Maxwell

Be Aware, 2001, from the Politics of Racism collective. Shortly after a young friend was arrested for 'walking while black', Maxwell watched a red tailed hawk catch and eat a smaller bird – it looked over its shoulder after every bite, 30 x 63 x 2.5 inches.

Milton Glaser

Glaser has enjoyed long and fruitful client relationships and remains a master of reinvention as the Tomato Music Company covers and poster for the School of Visual Arts, 1996, demonstrate.

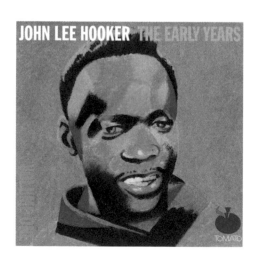

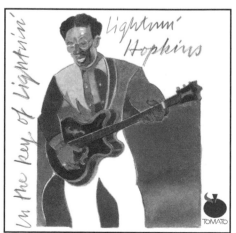

06 Compromise is a loaded word. It implies the designer has been diminished but I don't think it happens that way. I have had many clients, particularly resistant ones, whose input has improved my work. If you look at the work as self-expression, which I do not, of course you feel compromised, because anyone who tells you not to do what you want is an enemy. But that really is more a manifestation of narcissism than of professionalism.

If you don't have resistance, boundaries, constraints, you can't do your work. Constraints and limitations are as much a part of developing a brief and of design as anything else. The worst thing that anyone can ever tell you is 'do whatever you want'. Your mind flattens out into nothing.

07 My principle is that ideology is a short-term truth. Eventually you learn that nothing is true enough to be loyal to and that belief really represents an end to inquiry. I grew up with modernism. Anything that is systemic and can be easily repeated becomes untrue. I knew that modernism was useful for a while and I still like it as one of the options you have in thinking about things, but I would say that I was a premature post-modernist in my thinking. There is as much inspiration to be found in the Viennese Secession as in the Bauhaus.

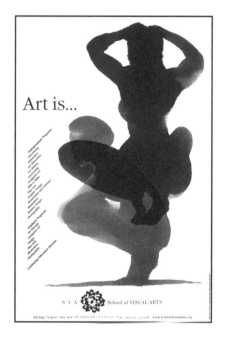

Milton Glaser

Brookie Maxwell

Witness, 2002, created for
a 9/11 memorial exhibition.
Walking by the Hudson
the half-submerged pilings
of the piers reminded Maxwell
of people escaping – in up to
their ankles, stopping to help
others and in over their heads,
7 x 3 x 4ft.

Milton Glaser

The Rubin Museum of Art
identity was completed in
2004 and gave the museum
a striking street façade
(far right). Shown here are
three of the large window
panels (this page), the logo
applied to signage and for
use in print, and the cover
of one of the many items
of publicity produced.

08 I loved the idea that Picasso didn't
have loyalty to any style, that just
because he did something for
ten years he didn't do it forever.
I have tried assiduously to see how
far I could take this idea. Often you
start on a path, you pursue it but it
loses interest for you so you have
to find another. You often see people
who have been in the field for ten
or 20 years and have lost interest,
they've learnt a methodology and
they repeat it forever. But the work
loses energy and meaning. There's
an enormous tendency to repeat,
by virtue of what your clients
ask for, which is usually what you
have already succeeded at.

Push Pin Studios, which I had been
instrumental in starting, had to
end for this reason. I had become
identified with doing a certain thing
very well, but for me it represented
an end to possibilities. After 20 years
it's hard to give up something you've
created, but it was inevitable. The
hardest part was thinking about it
beforehand, the easiest part was
doing it and moving on.

I've always believed, probably
because of my mother's assurances,
that I could accomplish anything
that I set out to do. I didn't feel
worried about the next stage of my
working life. I never spent more
money than I had, which is a
tremendous protection against
anxiety. If you really have to worry
about where your next dollar
is coming from you're in a very
perilous position. I've also received
a very strong basic education and
so have confidence to move towards
what I don't know.

Over the last ten years I've become
more interested in the relationship
between language and visual
things. It's an inquiry I really want
to continue because it's so central
to the profession. Most recently
a project that really changed my
idea of my work was the illustrations
for Dante's Divine Comedy. They
were monoprints – I went back
to doing printmaking – and they
really represented a shift in my
consciousness. Also the work that
we did at the Rubin Museum
inevitably represents a kind of
maturity and understanding that
I didn't have earlier.

05 I have had several overlapping careers: illustrator, public artist, artistic director of a Not for Profit organisation, fine artist, playwright, gallerist. The education provided to me by Milton's mentorship has carried me fairly smoothly from one career into the next. There have been growing pains, but it worked. I am always relentlessly positive when we are together. Nothing is ever impossible. Time and space bow to our will. Money appears when it is necessary. The materials are defined by the solution to the problem.

09 In my last book I said 'don't call it art, call it work'. This detoxifies the situation a little bit. I like what Gombrich says at the beginning of The Story of Art, that there is no art, only artists. Art is simply defined by the 'art community' every ten years or so. Then somebody else comes up with another definition that includes new people and excludes others. It's one of the nonsensical obsessions of human beings, specifying that 'this is art, this is not'. This is like the search for the true cross. Lord knows why, but it is probably related to the priesthood and to the idea of defining what the spiritual is.

All through history art has been purposeful and commissioned. 'We want a mural that scares people, so show them hell and people being eaten up and squashed.' There was no work being produced for purely expressive purposes until relatively recently, say the last 150 years.

People get confused because it's hard enough to create an object that creates transcendence let alone having to sell a product as well. But when you look at Lautrec's paintings and his posters you discover that the posters are every bit as significant, as artful and as moving as the paintings. This means that occasionally it's possible to produce art and integrate it with a specific purpose. One thing we also observe is that most paintings are not necessarily art either. It isn't that the commercial enterprise makes something not art. It adds an extra layer of difficulty to the process.

The important thing to acknowledge is that art is a mechanism for survival. Having art in our lives produces a greater possibility of the species surviving. It gives people commonality. If you like Mozart and I like Mozart, we already have a relationship. So it provides a mechanism for people to increase the likelihood of not killing one another.

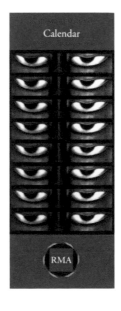

06 I hope to be always learning
and growing. Without that,
a person becomes 'phuerto
muhalo', one who is dead and
doesn't know it.

Milton Glaser

Brookie Maxwell

The Gospel According to
Marcy Avenue 1, from the
Fear No Evil series, 2000.
Maxwell documented her
models walking in their
neighbourhoods. The colour
paper suggests emotional
changes in the landscape,
33 x 26 inches.

Milton Glaser

Two of Glaser's monoprints
for Dante's Divine Comedy,
Purgatorio, 1999; 'they really
represented a shift in my
consciousness'.

This 1967 School of Visual
Arts poster is probably one
of Glaser's most famous.
It announces a show of large
nudes and shows a nude too
large to fit on the poster.

10 I discovered that I didn't want to
run a large office. We once had
45 people working for us when we
were doing a lot of supermarkets.
It gets very hard when there is so
much managerial work to do.
I really think my role in life is to
make forms, not to tell other people
what to do. I don't look at this
simply as a business, it's a way for
me personally to make things and
that's what I've pursued in my life.

Of course it gets complicated when
you're meeting a payroll and you
always worry about where the next
dollar's going to come from, but
I've been very lucky. I've been in
business for 50 years and managed
to do quite well. I've never lived
above my means, I learnt the value
of this as a child in the Depression.
At one point I made some money and
put it away and now I have enough
never to think about it again.

If you have a family to support,
sure you're fearful. There's no one
who doesn't face that issue, it's not
peculiar to designers. Does the
fear sometimes lead you to do work
that you know doesn't suit you, or
that is mediocre? Yes, I think for
a lot of people it does. One has to be
sympathetic, but conversely I think
that there are a lot more choices
in life than people are capable
of seeing.

11 I still teach every Wednesday night,
I enjoy it, I've learned how to teach –
it takes a while. It's not just about
passing on information, what's more
important is that the students get
who you are. Morandi and I only had
two conversations about art in the
entire time I was living in Bologna,
but what I was inspired by was his
commitment to his work. Students
need to see a life that they want
to emulate.

12 I always wanted to be the best there could be. I certainly am competitive, but I've never felt jealous of anybody else's accomplishments. I would use as a standard not my peers in the field, but what had occurred in history. So if I do a drawing, I don't compare it to an illustration that was done recently, I compare it to a Leonardo da Vinci and realise that I've got a way to go.

I had a sense of entering into design history when my Dylan poster became iconic, although the reasons were accidental and had more to do with Dylan's reputation than my artwork. I also had a one-man show at the Museum of Modern Art early in my life. Museum approval is one of the ways you think that you may have entered into the official culture; I have had that kind of reassurance a number of times. These things are self-generating. You also come to recognise how ephemeral all of this is so one cannot be arrogant about it.

13 My work is the centrepiece in my life, it is defining. It is the means by which I have understood the world and understand myself. I don't treat it as a job. It is absolutely core in terms of how I see myself. To a large degree it gives meaning to my life, it is more meaningful than anything else except human relationships.

You have to learn what it is you're doing and if you want to be good at it you have to devote your life to it. This is not a casual thing. Everybody I know who's amounted to anything in his or her field has basically worked night and day and madly with very little room for anything else; it ain't a hobby. It's a privilege coming to work each day and feeling that there's a possibility of learning something new, it's one of the great, great things about the field.

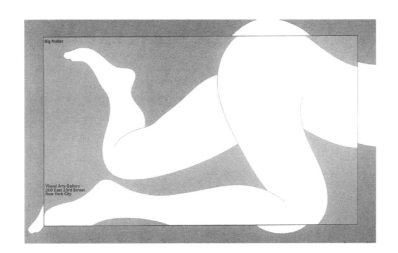

```
     Date: Thursday, September 9, 2004 9:17
       To: lucienne roberts <endash@dircon.co.uk>
   Subject: self portraits(s)
                                           .....

lucie: one self-portrait seemed inadequate, so here are 6

[8-)  [8-(  [8-X  [8-/  [8-?  [8-£

if you wish to label them, they are

kg happy, kg sad, kg abusive, kg sceptical, kg inquisitive,
kg mercenary

kg
```

vienna
Addre...
popm...
Micro...

Ken Garland
self-portrait

Peter Smith

Ken Garland

Ken Garland
soundtrack

Tracy Chapman
Talkin' bout a Revolution
1988

**Peter Smith
biography**

Peter Smith (born 1956, Lancashire) trained at Bolton College of Art and Design (1972–76) and the London College of Printing (1977) where he studied advanced typography. He worked for the Design Research Unit (1977–78) before studying graphic information design at the Royal College of Art (1978–80).

**Ken Garland
biography**

Ken Garland is a maverick of British design: political in a broad sense, independent and outspoken. Never constrained by the boundaries of his subject, Garland's references and inspiration reach beyond the realm of graphic design and reveal his curiosity and breadth of knowledge about the world. A writer and photographer as well as a designer, Garland sees these activities as equally important, reflecting his inclusive view of the world. His wide-ranging work includes educational toys, political posters and museum graphics and demonstrates his pleasure in graphic design as a language of engagement, discussion and discovery.

Born in Southampton in 1929, Garland trained at the Central School of Arts and Crafts, London (1952–54) where he received a broad graphic design education under the tutelage of, among many, the influential course director Jesse Collins. He became art editor of Design magazine (1956–62), before leaving to start his own studio, Ken Garland and Associates in 1962. Although he worked on many commercial projects and his client list was diverse, an agenda emerged: not to work with large multinational corporations and to remain a small company where designer and client could work 'eyeball to eyeball'.

Garland's many long and creative relationships with clients include his consultancies for Galt Toys (1961–81), for whom he designed educational games as well as graphics, Barbour Index (1962–73), Ministry of Technology (1962–67) and projects with photographer Fay Godwin, the Science Museum, London and the Arts Council of Great Britain. Significantly, Garland also produced posters (fee free) for the Campaign for Nuclear Disarmament (1962–68).

In 1964 Garland published the First Things First manifesto with 21 designers and photographers as co-signatories. Interpreted as a rallying call for designers to question the priorities of their profession, the manifesto expressed dismay at the squander of talent and resources on selling unnecessary consumer products. Revised and republished in 2000 with a new set of signatories, First Things First is still regarded as a relevant yet largely unheeded document.

Starting as a freelance design consultant (1980–84) he went on to work as creative director at Raymond Loewy International (1988–90), Lloyd Northover (1990–93), Dialog (1993–96) and Luxon Carrà (1996–2003). In 2003 he co-founded the company Openmind, which specialises in brand strategy and corporate identity.

Smith is fascinated by letterforms, typography and the possibilities of graphic information design systems.

He has led major branding, identity and communications programmes for clients including BAA, Barclays, Courtaulds, Aer Lingus and Toyota and his work has included the design of corporate literature, packaging, exhibitions and interactive media design.

He has recently been involved in the design, strategy and positioning of Enjoy England for England Marketing, responsible for the profiling and promotion of England.

Smith is a fellow and membership assessor for the Chartered Society of Designers and has won awards from the New York Art Directors Club (1995) and the New York Type Directors Club (1994). He is a recipient of the Minerva Award for corporate identity (1995). He has lectured in graphic design at Central Saint Martins and Ravensbourne College of Design and Communication.

Garland's work reflects his First Things First credo in its bias towards informational and educational graphics and in his aspiration to be true to his subject; aesthetically broad, Garland has never settled for one style, preferring to respond to each brief rather than adhere to any restricting design doctrine.

Garland is a respected and influential teacher, lecturing across the breadth of graphic design courses from the University of Reading (1971–99), to the Royal College of Art (1977–87), Central Saint Martins (1986–91) and the National College of Art and Design, Dublin (1982–92). In 1995 and 1997 he toured Great Britain and America talking about his work. He is currently visiting professor at Brighton University and was visiting professor in information design at the Universidad de las Americas, Pueblas, Mexico (1999–2004).

Widely published, Garland has contributed articles to design periodicals worldwide and his own publications include: the Graphics handbook (1966), Mr Beck's Underground Map (1994), A Word in Your Eye (1996) and most recently a book of his writing and photographs, Metaphors: A Portfolio of Text and Image (2001).

Peter Smith

The symbol for Narvesen, a Norwegian newsagent chain, was designed in 1987 by Smith and clearly demonstrates his fascination with both letterforms and identity design.

Ken Garland

'That we designed this game which has proved so satisfying to so many generations is absolutely wonderful.' Connect was designed by Ken Garland and Robert Chapman in 1968 and originally produced by Galt Toys.

Peter Smith

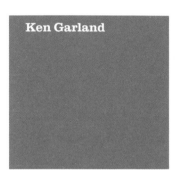

Ken Garland

Peter Smith

The Maze Book, a self-initiated project produced in 1981. Smith explored the abstract potential of letterforms by redrawing each letter of the book title as a maze.

Ken Garland

In 1968 Garland and his team designed the lettering and sign system for the Paramount and Plaza cinemas in Lower Regent Street, London – one of the largest signs they were ever to work on.

As a student Garland had started to experiment playfully with letterforms, as demonstrated by this project of 1953.

01 At school I had a good friend whose uncle worked as a commercial artist. I was good at art at school and so I asked him for advice. He suggested that I went to art college to do a foundation course and whilst there I was introduced to graphic design. Although I didn't really understand the range of the subject, I decided this was the path for me.

When I was studying at Bolton we went to the Icograda seminars in London. Ken was one of the speakers. He gave a very theatrical performance including how to answer the telephone to different types of clients by taking on various personas and wearing different costumes each time! He also demonstrated how to get the best out of your design solutions by adapting and modifying concepts to suit different clients. It was very funny, controversial and thought-provoking. So, my first impression of Ken was that 'this guy is crazy, fascinating, challenging and extraordinary'.

A few years later I started at the Royal College of Art and one Tuesday morning this guy turned up wearing a woolly hat and bicycle clips and said 'hi, I'm Ken Garland, I will be teaching on the course one day a week'. I was delighted. By then I'd read some of his articles, seen the First Things First manifesto and was familiar with his design work for the Campaign for Nuclear Disarmament, Galt Toys and Design magazine.

 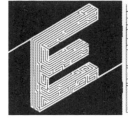 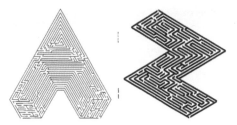 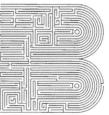

01 It was slightly haphazard. I decided I wanted to be a commercial artist when I was still at grammar school. I left school at 16 and went to the West of England Academy of Art in Bristol. They didn't have a course in graphic design, in fact the term wasn't known. They did offer commercial design, which was a rather low-brow activity. It involved 'trade drawing' among other things – doing representative drawings of industrial equipment and so forth. I felt very quickly that it lacked some of what I was looking for, life drawing for example, and I made a great fuss. As a result I spent two years doing a rather hybrid course and went quite eagerly into the army to do my conscription. When I got out I came to London.

I already had an idea that I wanted to do something to do with industry and business that would use my skills to un-muddle. I started at the John Cass College of Art, but after a short while I realised it wasn't providing me with enough in the way of graphic design.

At the instigation of one of my teachers there, whom I think of very fondly to this day, I went to the Central. They accepted me there without fees all year, until I managed officially to get myself away from John Cass. I spent the next two years at the Central School. Then I really did get a grasp of graphic design.

There was daytime teaching given by Jesse Collins, Herbert Spencer and George Mayhew. Keith Vaughan and Paul Hogarth taught illustration. I took evening classes in experimental typography with Edward Wright and experimental photography with Nigel Henderson. This was enormously important to me.

In the UK before the war, there were four designers who were shining and brilliant and led the way for us. Henrion, Abram Games, Hans Schleger and Tom Eckersley. I don't think we were pioneering, but we were constructing the notion of a graphic design business. People insist on calling it a profession but I never do, I call it a craft or a business, a trade.

02 The atmosphere was enormously enthusiastic at the Central. We had a feeling that we were a generation of some significance. Most of my fellow students had not been in the war, but there was something to be done, there was a world to be made. It was definitely there, a feeling of building a new society.

Graphic design was not something that people thought, 'ahhh we must have some of that'. We had a world to make there too, but that in itself was exciting. We had to make a case for what we were doing. We enjoyed the Festival of Britain but as graphic designers we were critical because it was imbued with a notion of Britishness that we rejected totally. We were drawn to the international and were impatient about this narrow-minded Britishness.

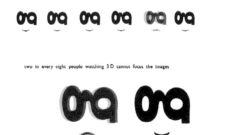

two in every eight people watching 3 D cannot focus the images

Ken Garland

02 I came from a working class background. Living and studying in the north-west of England during the 1970s meant that I witnessed first hand the crisis-prone state of the country.

Luckily at this time grants were available so I was able to go into higher education. Like many art students I thought I would end up as an illustrator doing music album covers. Music has been a passion for me and I've always been interested in the way popular culture reflects or represents a political message. A lot of my political and social ideas came through these influences; as Bob Dylan says 'the answer is blowin' in the wind'.

I moved to London in 1976, which was a shock to my system. I got to see people like Elvis Costello and Billy Bragg. The Sex Pistols were also doing their stuff (God Save the Queen and her Fascist Regime). I always felt very privileged studying in London and tried to make the most of it, a bit like the film Educating Rita, or Peter in my case, which is one of my favourites.

03 Jesse Collins, our head of department, came to me and said, 'Garland, you're going to be an art editor' and I said, 'what is an art editor?' He'd found me a job on Furnishing magazine. I had a feeling it might be my kind of thing, and my God, it was. Initially three months of agony, but I loved it. I spent two years in that job and then I got another job as art editor on Design magazine, which I loved even more. I was there for six years.

I had the pleasure and honour of being one designer among a group of people who had other skills. They were printers, photographers and I was in the middle of them trying to organise the appearance of the magazine. It was amazing. It was a revelation, it was a totally stunning experience. I've enjoyed myself hugely since then but never more. It's part of the agony of finding oneself, grappling with situations that are totally unfamiliar.

I was immersed in the job, but I could sense what was going on elsewhere. I didn't agree with some of the enthusiasms of my fellow designers who were passionately fond of Swiss graphic design. I did find out about it. I spent six weeks in Switzerland, through the summer of 1960, studying Swiss graphic design and I had some respect for it, but this was not some kind of holy grail for me and I went my own way.

Ken Garland

Garland was art editor of Design magazine for six years from 1956. The covers shown on page 45, and the cover and spreads here, demonstrate that his inventiveness and organisational skills were repeatedly put to maximum effect.

I lived in Brixton at the time of the riots. The Clash sang London's Burning and it was. These experiences made me very socially aware and continue to influence my working life. I try to work from a socially responsible point of view. John: 6: 27 do not work for food that goes bad; instead, work for the food that lasts for eternal life.

During my time at the RCA Ken became my most influential tutor. He was a constant source of new challenges and inspiration. He would probe every detail of a project not only from the point of view of content and aesthetics, but also from a social responsibility standpoint. Twenty-five years later, corporate social responsibility has become a major topic in design. I think this demonstrates his visionary outlook.

04 We are more prone to claim absolutes in the visual arts than almost everything else. In poetry, literature, politics, people are forever pointing out that our attitudes and our achievements are mediated by time and experience and they don't have any absolute significance. People in the visual arts are quite often arrogant in this assumption that there are absolutes. I don't think there are in art or design or architecture.

I don't think I have many set principles, although in my own work clarity and a lack of obfuscation and unnecessary ornament is essential. I don't necessarily hold that for other people. Some work is delightfully obfuscated. I can accept it in other people as long as they don't impose it on me.

I'm barely aware of fashion in relation to design. For example, in the panels I produced for the exhibition Children of Bangladesh, I used handwriting and was told, 'that's terribly fashionable – doing it by hand'. It wasn't meant to be, it was just the way I responded to the subject. This is disingenuous in the sense that we are all aware of some kind of fashion and we do respond to it. But less than most people I know, I'm not influenced by it.

Typography became immensely fashionable in the '80s. Notions derived from Tschichold and the Swiss – of appropriateness, clarity and of spareness – were overthrown. It was due for stirring up. It was overthrown largely by rubbish, but rubbish has got its place. It's part of the process of attacking an existing canon. Ever since the '60s men and women have dressed the way they feel like dressing. Maybe in typographic design we may learn to do the same thing.

03 The competitive nature of the business can help raise standards. I have tried to leave the economic anxieties to the accounts department, spending time and effort on projects as they require. This has not always been embraced when I worked for larger design groups as they try to keep tight financial control on projects. Two years ago I co-founded a new company called Openmind and have had one or two sleepless nights wondering where the next project's going to come from, but somehow they keep coming.

Ken Garland

Peter Smith

Cover and openers from the identity manual for Enjoy England, 2004, part of VisitBritain. This exercise in persuasion aimed to encourage autonomous local regions to promote their areas positively.

Ken Garland

Garland points out that he has been design consultant to a variety of commercial companies, for example Butterley Bricks. However, he has acquired a reputation as a politically aware designer too. This material for the Labour Party and CND was designed in the mid-1960s.

05 There are far too many graphic designers so it is a buyer's market now. In 1962, when I started my practice, there were perhaps six, seven or eight groups already there. We didn't realise what a privilege it was to be among so few. It was enviable. Now, for God's sake, there is the matter of pitching for accounts, which I have never ever done. If it ever was hinted at, I shrank from it, I moved away. I cannot imagine how an uncompetitive person like me would tackle the situation now.

I wanted to have clients I liked. When I set up my practice I already had one client whom I had acquired while I was at Design magazine: Galt Toys. We had the most wonderful 20 years working together. I acquired six more clients very rapidly. By the end of my first year I was already working for a number of clients on retainer.

It seems to me to be absurd to have lasting differences of opinions with clients. They are the people who are paying you, they are the people whom you are commissioned to satisfy. But your client is not just the person who pays you. Your clients are also the buyers of the goods and services, the users of the information. In the same way that for a doctor the National Health Service is not the only client. The patients are. I don't pretend to say that my users are the equivalent of a doctor's patient, but I do sense them to be as much my client. I do have a certain independence of mind about this.

I didn't feel any great difficulty from clients preventing me from doing what I wanted to do. I don't remember any compromises that resulted in work I wasn't proud of. However, there's never been a job that when it was done I didn't think I could have done better. I wouldn't say I felt guilty about it, because I just realised that we have a certain amount of time, of money and energy. Given a little more time, a little more energy, a little more thought, you could do better. It's part and parcel of the graphic design business: time and cost constraints, and we shouldn't grumble about it and I don't. That's the nature of the beast.

IT'S A
CLEAR
CHOICE
VOTE
LABOUR
MAY 10

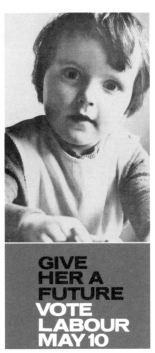

GIVE
HER A
FUTURE
VOTE
LABOUR
MAY 10

Hand
made

Butterley
Bricks

march

Campaign for Nuclear Disarmament 2 Carthusian St EC1

06 Most of my work is commercial. I have a political reputation, which to some extent is undeserved, because it didn't occupy that much of my time. I have been a member of the Labour Party since 1957. I've been a member of CND since 1958 and yes, I've had some political convictions, it's true. But I would say as far as my graphic design work is concerned, it's only occasionally been overtly political.

I turned down work by sort of tactful evasion from IBM, Ilford Films and one or two other quite big clients, mainly because they were big. I didn't like big clients. I managed to dissuade IBM by pointing out a sentence in my book, in which I talked about my unhappiness with multinationals, so we cancelled our appointment.

There were two recessions whilst I was running my practice and neither of them bothered me at all. I went on with the same clients through both. Big clients were the ones who were dropping. Throughout my whole working life I've never felt insecure in this way. It's just pure luck.

I loved being a small outfit, being one of the designers. There was not one job that went through here that I wasn't part of. Had I grown I might have become the manager. Instead we all did our own clerical work, letters, phoning, making arrangements, we never had a secretary, we all did it.

Ken Garland

I was always aware of Ken's diverse and broad range of interests. He had an endless ability to talk and give illustrations on a wide range of subjects. His influence is therefore about much more than pure aesthetics. Like him I resist adhering to a particular design ideology. I like to keep my mind open and produce solutions that are appropriate to needs rather than being based on a particular style or trend.

I am also particularly gratified when end-users respond well to my work, but it's also good to be recognised by your peers. I have from time to time entered design competitions, but I try not to make a habit of it! I like to be aware of what's happening by reading the design press and going to as many exhibitions and lectures as I can.

Alistair's Day: 2nd Stalk 1980

Peter Smith

Whilst working at Dialog Smith developed its identity, 1995. The logo uses the 'g' as a symbolic representation of the name; the speech bubble was then used to carry titles and messages on covers, brochures and signs.

Ken Garland

Garland has never adhered to one 'style' as demonstrated by these posters for London's Hayward and Serpentine Galleries and Science Museum, all from the 1980s. Appropriateness is the key.

Hayward Gallery, South Bank, London SE1
31 October 1980–11 January 1981
Closed 24, 25, 26 December 1980 and 1 January 1981

Michael Andrews

Opening hours: Monday to Thursday 10-8 Friday and Saturday 10-6 Sunday 12-6

Admission: £1.50 Children, students and OAPs 75p
75p all day Monday and 6-8 Tuesday to Thursday

Admits also to *Camille Pissarro*

Arts Council
OF GREAT BRITAIN

07 I never felt envious of my peers. The only people I ever felt any envy for were Samuel Beckett, Harold Pinter, Frank Auerbach…

My social fellows were political, artistic, all sorts, but they weren't confined to a sort of graphic design society although of course I knew about the work of my fellow designers. Some contemporaries ate, slept and drank graphic design. I never did. I never have. It's not to say you can't do the most wonderful, stimulating and excellent work in our trade, but it's not enough to found the whole of one's life on.

I was a founder member of British Design & Art Direction [D&AD], but I only exhibited once. I never sent anything in to any annual except maybe in the early '60s. I never had that desire to achieve the approval of my peers. It's a quirk. If I ever could have a novel published I would seek every possible prize that novel could achieve. That says something about where my priorities must lie, I suppose.

Here's the most splendid accolade I ever received. I'm in somebody's house and they say 'your name sounds strangely familiar'. They ask what I've done and I mention Galt Toys. They go into a cupboard and pull out an old box of Connect and say 'I played with this as a child and now my children play with it. It's been going on 30 years now and we value it so much'. For most of us our graphic work has such a short life, you know, a month, a week, a year. That Bob Chapman and I designed this game, which has proved so satisfying to so many generations is absolutely wonderful.

08 Graphic design contains some very important artistic sensibilities. Having a client doesn't make a difference – Michelangelo was commissioned to paint the ceiling of the Sistine Chapel. I know quite a few painters and sculptors who prescribe briefs for themselves that are every bit as exact as any client has given me.

Of course in graphic design sometimes all you are doing is being an interpreter for someone else's wishes. That's not an unworthy thing to be, but it's not the only thing I've ever been in graphic design. When I've done covers for catalogues I've sometimes indulged myself in exactly the same way as anyone with an open brief might do. The client is prepared to accept my indulgence. There are degrees. I'm not keen to find some absolute that divorces graphic design from other forms of art. I think there are always mitigating factors.

MEANING LIES NOT IN THINGS BUT IN THE RELATIONSHIP ESTABLISHES BUT IN THE RELATIONSHIP BETWEEN THEM

Ken Garland

09 I'm fascinated by the openness and design skills of my grandchildren. It reminds me that skill can be very quickly acquired, even when very young, and that we diminish our ability to absorb artistic skills by the distractions of secondary school. There it is suggested that subjects are self-contained: that mathematics doesn't have art in it and so on.

I started teaching in 1958 at the insistence of Jesse Collins who virtually dragooned me into it, thank God. Within the first couple of weeks I realised how much I enjoyed it. I found that I could talk to people of my own age, which they were then, and that all they wanted to do was to be locked in helpful debate about their work. It seemed suddenly not to be such a difficult job. I didn't know what I'd been so afraid of – and that's the way it's been ever since.

The teachers who impressed me were incisive. I felt I could rely on them to tell it the way it is. I think I too was able to talk about almost any aspect of graphic design with some knowledge and authority. Students could see that I knew my subject well.

10 Perhaps I've been important not so much in the graphic work that I have done, but more in the opinions and attitudes I've taken up. I do seem to have influenced people. To some extent this is because of the work, but it's also from things that I've said, articles published, books written, and yes, I think I have made a mark there of some sort.

To be groundbreaking in my work has never seemed particularly important to me. All I wanted to do was satisfy a brief. Sometimes the invention that went into the work was quite mysterious, unspoken and I didn't really care to explain it to people. What is invention and innovation? It's only rediscovering something that was well-known to cavemen. I don't rate that ground-breaking business very much.

Peter Smith

Smith produced these puzzling Christmas cards for Q-Search, a market research company, 1984. A role reversal that sets the recipients a problem, the message only becomes clear when each card is placed in a particular order.

Ken Garland

Cover and spreads from Metaphors: A Portfolio of Text and Image, 2001, a book of Garland's writing and photographs.

05 I have tried to emulate the good tutors that taught me, especially Ken.

I tell students that they have to be passionate about the subject and see it not so much as a career but more a way of life. In order to be successful you need to be committed and put a lot of time and effort into learning about all the different aspects of the subject.

Graphic designers have a responsibility and can play an important role in society. Anyone starting on a career in graphic design needs to understand that it's not only about aesthetics. It requires an inquisitive mind in order to produce conceptual ideas that are accessible, appropriate and reflect a deep consideration of the subject and audiences.

06 After a few years working as a graphic designer I remember getting a Christmas bonus. My father was amazed, it was more than he had received in bonus payments during the whole of his working life. It was a humbling moment and made me realise how lucky I was getting paid well for doing something I really enjoyed. Needless to say, despite my initial expectations, I have never illustrated an album cover!

11 I think that those of us who ought to take it seriously, because we have the ability to express our feelings about it, don't take it seriously because we have other interests. I don't think it's big enough to absorb us. Right from the beginning it seemed to me I didn't want to be constrained by graphic design as a subject, but to seek reference elsewhere and that's always been the case.

It's been good. I always went down to the studio eagerly and left it reluctantly. I always loved doing everything that I wanted to do and the only disappointment I had was that every time I did something, it wasn't as good as I thought it could be. But this drives you on to do the next thing as well as you can. One of the greatest satisfactions in my working life has been the access we have, via our clients, into so many different worlds. I've learnt so much. I cannot imagine a more stimulating and satisfying work.

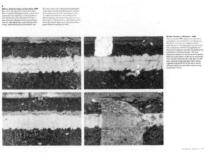

Rosmarie Tissi
self-portrait
'My faithful travelling
companion.'

Sabina Oberholzer

Rosmarie Tissi

Rosmarie Tissi
soundtrack

Luis Bordon
India
Carretaguy
Lamento Indio
Canto de Pajarito
Pajaro Campana
Rodrigues Pena
Malvita
on
Harpa Paraguaia
em Hi Fi

Sergio Cuevas
Lamento Paraguyo
Caballito
Lagrimas
on
La Harpe Indienne

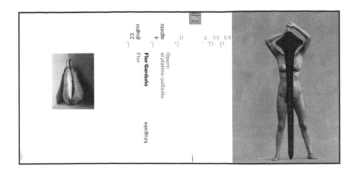

Sabina Oberholzer
biography

Sabina Oberholzer (born 1958, Locarno, Switzerland) studied under Bruno Monguzzi at CSIA in Lugano. In 1983 she founded the Studio di Progettazione Grafica with her partner Renato Tagli. Based in Cevio in the minority Italian-speaking region of Switzerland, Oberholzer and Tagli are alive to the relationship between na[...] and creativity, and sensit[...] to their responsibility wit[...] the small community in which they live and work.

Rosmarie Tissi
biography

Although Swiss, Rosmarie Tissi is not a 'Swiss designer' in the narrow sense that this title might imply; for over four decades she has maintained a playful, intuitive and undogmatic approach that is joyful in its celebration of form, colour and design. Tissi is seduced neither by showmanship nor prevailing fashion, but is driven by the desire to make good work and experience the world; she is notable for her consistently principled approach and her varied and finely crafted graphic art.

Born in Switzerland in 1937, Tissi studied at the School of Design, Zurich (1954–58), including four years as an apprentice in graphic design studios; for two of these she worked as an assistant to the designer Siegfried Odermatt. In 1968 they began sharing a studio as a partnership and Odermatt + Tissi was formed. For the last 37 years both Odermatt and Tissi have enjoyed a unique design relationship; they work without assistants, sharing a studio and intellectual space while each retains independence in project work and working practice.

They rarely work on projects together, but work alongside each other sharing advice and opinions. This equilibrium affords each partner the freedom to work to their individual rhythms; crucially for Tissi it allows her the opportunity to spend time out of the studio, her experiences of foreign travel feeding her open approach to design.

Odermatt + Tissi has a reputation for uncompromising, independent, quality design and graphic art that is functional, informative and elegant. Choosing clients carefully, Tissi has worked on many projects in the cultural and industrial sectors, including the identity and graphic products for textile manufacturer Mettler (1969–72), internal publications for Holderbank cement factory (1975–85), and the chemistry textbook for high school level study (1988–89). In 1991 she won second prize in the competition to design the new Swiss banknotes. Perhaps best known for her striking poster design, Tissi has won numerous distinctions including first prize and gold medal at the 11th International Poster Biennial, Warsaw (1986), the Henri de Toulouse-Lautrec silver medal at the 6th International Poster Triennial, Essen, Germany (1990), and the bronze medal at the 4th International Poster Triennial in Toyama, Japan (1994).

Driven not by economics but rather by a belief in quality and clarity of message, Oberholzer's design philosophy is based on appropriateness and generally results in the elimination of the superfluous, ornate or artificial.

Joint winners of the competition to design a graphic identity for the City of Locarno (1985), Oberholzer and Tagli were also responsible for the design for the Museo Comunale d'Arte Moderna Ascona (1999), resulting in an on-going collaboration with the local authority. They designed the newspaper il Quotidiano, for which they won first prize in the Eidgenössische Stipendien für angewandte Kunst.

Nominated by Rosmarie Tissi, Sabina Oberholzer is a member of the Alliance Graphique Internationale (1997) and is the holder of two federal scholarships for applied arts from the department of culture, Berne (1988 and 1990).

An active member of the international design community, Tissi has delivered typographic workshops at Yale (1991), the University of the Arts, Philadelphia (2000), Elisawa in Barcelona (2001) and Tongji University, Shanghai (2002). She has given illustrated lectures at several international design conferences, most recently at the American Institute of Graphic Arts conference in San Diego (2000), the Society of Typographic Designers, London (2002), and the Tehran Poster Biennial (2004); she has also sat on competition juries around the world. Odermatt + Tissi has exhibited in New York (1992), Essen (1996, 1997) and Tokyo (1998). Tissi is a member of Alliance Graphique Internationale (1974) and the Art Directors Club of New York (1992).

Sabina Oberholzer

Oberholzer and Tagli have worked for the Museo Comunale d'Arte Moderna Ascona since 1999. They have developed a simple, elegant and modern identity applied here to the posters for two exhibitions of the work of Flor Garduno in 2002.

Rosmarie Tissi

A characteristically strong poster for an exhibition of Odermatt + Tissi's posters held at Reinhold-Brown Gallery in New York, 1992.

Sabina Oberholzer

01 **impressions of Rosmarie Tissi**

01 Renato Tagli and I have been working together for 25 years now. We met at college and both of us knew and were influenced by Odermatt + Tissi's work as students. We also have the same initials as they do, this seemed very funny to us and a nice thing.

I met Rosmarie after we won a prize in the late '80s. She came to see our exhibited work and was so enthusiastic. It was such a good meeting. She is very kind and open-minded and there was a real sympathy between us. It was really great. We seem to have a real empathy, it's a proper human contact. She proposed me as a member of AGI and now I call her to hear about what's happening in the German speaking part of Switzerland and tend to refer more to her than younger designers.

Rosmarie Tissi

01 **early career choices/ training**

02 **post-war optimism/ politics and design**

01 I studied drawing at school and had some talent, but actually for a long time I wanted to study chemistry – as a chemist it's possible to really invent something. However, I had some terrible teachers in my last years at school and so in the end I thought it was best to leave and learn something through experience of the real world. I had a sister who was a graphic designer. Hers is not my style at all, but it was still hard to say I was interested in joining the design profession – she wasn't happy that I wanted to do the same thing.

In Switzerland then you could learn partly at school and partly in a studio, like an apprenticeship. I think this was only possible in Switzerland. The principle is good because you learn practically, you have to be quick, you cannot linger for months on one project. It was hard to find an apprenticeship but I found one in Winterthur. This was 1954. After several weeks I realised that I wasn't really learning anything; their taste was awful. I was so disappointed and unhappy, but I didn't feel I could tell my parents because it had already been hard following my sister into the same profession. I felt alone, anxious and unsure what to do, but I decided I had to resolve this on my own.

Sabina Oberholzer

'We put our personality into the work, but I suppose we try not to reveal this too strongly.' Quietly witty promotional material for Ottica Stiefel, an opticians in Locarno, 1992.

Rosmarie Tissi

Tissi's early work from the late 1950s and later cover for the architecture and design journal Domus, 1992, all demonstrate a clarity of vision and economy of means used for maximum effect.

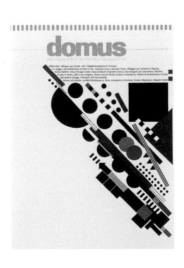

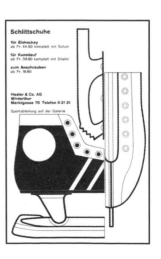

For two lost years I was at this company. Whilst there I went with my work samples to see other studios. I was not even 20 and was very shy. I went from studio to studio. I looked in magazines and saw Siegfried Odermatt's work and decided to try with him. At first he said he was not so sure that he would like to have an apprentice. But he took me on in the end. So until '56 I didn't learn a thing and then learnt a great deal in the following two years.

02 Switzerland was neutral during the war so we didn't have to rebuild our country afterwards. It made us a little bit self-satisfied and I think that designers here were less political as a result. You don't see many political posters in Switzerland because we haven't really had to fight for things. This was very apparent to me when I was asked to do a poster for an exhibition about human rights in Paris. The brief was to do something about 'a problem that is affecting you in your country'. It seemed clear to me that we don't really have such big problems here, so I did something to advocate love for each other because I feel that people are often quite selfish in Switzerland.

02 **formative influences/
enduring approaches**

02 The simplicity and clarity of what is referred to as 'Swiss design' did influence us as students. We are typographers rather than illustrators and so this work made sense to us. We also admired the work of Studio Boggeri in Milan and those Swiss designers who worked in Italy – Max Huber and so on. After college we went to London and visited all sorts of studios exchanging experiences with English designers and meeting people whose work we admired like Henrion and Alan Fletcher.

I think Odermatt + Tissi have influenced us because they have a way of doing graphic design that refers less to contemporary aspirations. By that I mean that they work with all their heart in projects. They are not commercially driven. It was this philosophy that was more important to us than anything about form or aesthetics. In Zurich we tried hard to work for them and spoke to Odermatt about it. He always said 'no, I don't take employees'. The emphasis was on the work not the business and so they were role models for us in this way.

This helped us develop a vision of what we wanted, an ideal. We wanted to demonstrate that what we had learned is possible. We were a little utopian and it is easy when you are young to be criticised as impractical dreamers, but we were keen to prove we could make it work. I would say to everyone: follow your heart. If you don't you will lose in a way.

Rosmarie Tissi

03 **formative influences/
enduring approaches/
important years/
catering for mass markets**

Rosmarie Tissi

In 1991 Tissi won second prize in a competition to design new banknotes for Switzerland. Fifteen Swiss designers had been invited by the Swiss National Bank to make proposals and the three initial winners developed their proposals for production as sample 50-franc notes.

A series of posters for the Swiss Poster Advertising Company exhibition of the best Swiss posters for 1996, 1998 and 1999.

03 When I started it was of course a very good time for Swiss graphic design. There were lots of good new pieces to discuss. I also liked Italian and American design so much. Franco Grignani, for example – who I think is not as esteemed as he should be – is really very modern and very unique. Then the Americans, like Gene Federico, who had a very modern style, Saul Bass and Paul Rand of course. I was influenced by design and by painting. Yesterday we went to a preview at Christie's and saw paintings by Kandinsky, Leger, Braque and Schwitters – all these people influenced me.

I have also always travelled a lot. I needed to do this. Every time I return with new impressions, new influences and that's what has kept me a bit more lively, not so rigid like other Swiss designers. Please don't categorise me as part of that closed Swiss design. I don't like it that much. I like its cleanliness and clarity and all that, but it lacks joy.

I don't think I have a rigidly consistent approach to work. When I have an order, I start with a blank sheet of paper because I try to have a fresh outlook for every job. Obviously I have my style. Just recently I did a small job – a logo – and the client said it's 'strict'. I said that's my style, I cannot change that, but I really try to do something special for each client.

I think my best work was produced between '68 and '85 and some also later up to the present. By 1968 Sigi and I were business partners. The best years for me were the 1970s. You could do everything because it had not been done before. All the firms wanted to have something new, something outstanding. They really wanted to have good things and the taste everywhere was very good. Clients were so open and they still had money. Then it started to go backwards. Now I think it's kind of a sport to save money. It's not necessary all the time.

Companies produce things now to appeal to the masses. They want to sell large quantities and satisfy average tastes. Everything: furniture, clothes, cars, television is designed for the masses. I hope this changes so that the quality of things will go up again.

We decided to set up in partnership in 1983 having worked in Zurich for a while. We decided it wasn't a place that was compatible with how we wanted to live – it wasn't as it had been in the great '60s and we had a more Latin approach to life so going to live in the Italian part of Switzerland seemed more appropriate. We were the first graphic designers from our college to do this in the region so it was quite hard, but we have shown it is possible to come to a small village and still make a mark by doing good work.

We generally try not to refer to other designers' work, but come afresh to each project. We don't refer to fashion for this reason. Of course we put our personality into the work, but I suppose we try not to reveal this too strongly. Our motivation is to produce work that is appropriate and not determined by the style of the time. It seems to us to be easier to produce fashionable work because inevitably a great deal of it is derivative.

We think part of the designer's job is to come up with economic, efficient and practical solutions. We use these as determining factors in our design and are keen not to be wasteful. These issues are becoming more and more relevant and important. To achieve these goals, design organisation is vital. We worked on a newspaper for example. It was early in the use of new technology with journalists having to assemble the pages themselves and we enjoyed developing a system that made it easy for them, but that was also aesthetically strong and quite minimal.

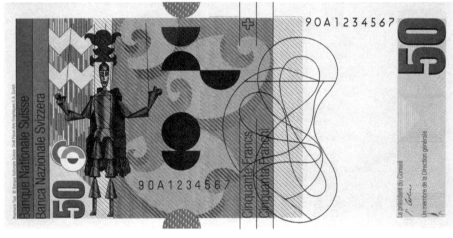

03 I think our clients do understand the value of our work. They know they will get good quality work from us, at a reasonable price. The Museo Comunale d'Arte Moderna Ascona has been a very good client for us. Ours is a particularly empathetic relationship. We are generally happier working for small companies or cultural bodies and hardly ever work for purely commercial clients.

We have designed stamps, newspapers and so on. Our reputation has been established partly by winning competitions and this has really helped in making it possible for us to carry on.

We always work together Renato and me. It is impossible to say this is my work and this his work. We shared ideas right from college. I like to work collaboratively. I like to share – there is less chance of making mistakes! I like to discuss the work, for me it is the only way. Perhaps it is also a more Latin thing and part of my personality.

Rosmarie Tissi

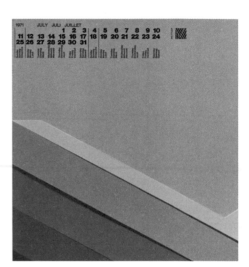

Sabina Oberholzer
Deutsches Plakat Museum and German Child Protection Society's 2002 competition's theme was 'children are the rhythm of the world'.

Rosmarie Tissi
Work for two of Tissi's most receptive clients. The textile firm Mettler (this page); logo, 1969 and calendar, 1971. A poster for open-air concerts for Zurich's Department of Cultural Affairs, 2003 (right).

Poster commissioned for the 1997 UN Conference on Climate Change, under the theme 'the worst case' (far right).

04 On the whole I have felt valued by my clients. In the '70s I worked for the textile firm Mettler. They were great – enthusiastic and happy with what I did. The Department of Cultural Affairs of the City of Zurich was also a very receptive client. Clients have usually come to me on recommendation. I wouldn't like to have a client I had to convince all the time, but I am open to client suggestion. Students sometimes ask 'if a client does not like something, do you change it?' Let's say a client says 'why blue, I would like to have it red': I will change it because this may help the client to see they are wrong, if I hadn't tried it they would always have thought that it would have been better their way. Sometimes of course the client is right, which I am happy to acknowledge. For me this doesn't matter.

I also thrive on constraints. Sometimes if I make a work and have the option of using four colours I will have difficulty in using a third! Work is often much better with less. Because we didn't have computers, we were used to working within technical constraints. This meant we edited our ideas all the time. If anything is possible then you are possibly less discriminating, you try everything and the result is a visually confusing piece of work, which has nothing to do with the client's needs. I use computers now though and I really like it, but I still edit as I would have done working more traditionally.

04 Ours is a profession not an art. As students we felt this strongly. The problem is that there is an art in it too, a sort of craft in a way, but if this dominates rather than the brief then it seems to be the wrong way round to us. I think graphic design is socially important, like architecture – which is more important because it lasts – but graphic design has a role in influencing people too. Communication, without misunderstanding, is vital for our social health.

In graphic design I can say something but the way it is told, the tone and so on, impacts on how it is interpreted. The typography is just as important as the words. This means we have a responsibility.

For example, the Deutsches Plakat Museum set a poster design competition. Each designer had to use the statement 'children are the rhythm of the world' and everyone did something different. This demonstrates how our work can shape a message, change its meaning and emphasis.

100 : 101
drip-dry shirts
discussion 4

05 Sigi and I each have our own clients. Sometimes we initially discuss a project with the client together and it is immediately clear who should do the job. Sometimes we both produce ideas and the client selects which one to use. We are both quite strong. I like to do my own thing and I like to be responsible for my own decisions. I cannot understand those studios where all three names go on every piece of work. How do they work together? Did one have the idea, the other do the layout and the last one choose the colours?

06 Still now, the average person doesn't know what we do. Just recently a woman asked me, 'in what field are you working?' and I said 'I'm a graphic designer' and she said 'mmm, an artist'. I said 'no, I would not call myself an artist' and she said 'I would'.

I was asked once during a discussion round at the Cooper Union School of Design in New York if I thought graphic design was art and when I said 'no' everybody turned against me! I said, 'as long as we have to fulfil a task, it's not'. Making art is a less constrained process, you can do what you feel, but we have clients, their need determines a lot of what we do.

Sabina Oberholzer

05 The female students are always the best, but maybe this changes when they leave. Women still have other things to do in their lives: they are perhaps less competitive than men but it is hard to generalise. I find it hard to be aggressive and to fight in the way that sometimes the business demands, but this can't be true for everybody. Our client at the museum in Ascona is a woman and because of this there is a different approach. As women we are still a little scared of men so if clients are men the relationship is perhaps more strained.

Rosmarie Tissi

Sabina Oberholzer

Oberholzer and Tagli's design philosophy often results in the elimination of the superfluous as this rigorous signage system for the Foundation Monte Veritá and posters for the museum in Ascona demonstrate.

Rosmarie Tissi

Jeans designed in 2004 for a charity project organised by Creation Gallery, Tokyo. All proceeds went to Unicef.

07 In 1975 there was a recession in the whole world. It was the oil crisis. It had never happened like this for me before so I started to worry, but it didn't really change my behaviour. I didn't think, 'I should make money in case that time comes again'.

I have never had to do work that I haven't wanted to do. Some pieces I would not put in a book, they are not attractive enough. But I am happy to show them and say I did this. I have never thought 'oh I hope my colleagues never see this'. Some designers do terrible things just for money. I would say 'no, I'm sorry, I cannot do this'. Of course it sometimes has been financially frightening and I have thought 'how can I continue', but then always something happened to make it ok again.

08 When I was a very young girl I used to make up crossword puzzles, making up questions. I would ask my mother, for example, what's the name of a city in Afghanistan. She said she didn't know and gave me an atlas. I learnt how to read maps and I started to imagine what each place was like. This was the start of my dreams to see the world. I don't go away for long periods any more because I like better hotels and that's expensive, but I used to go on long trips through several countries and would always come back a new person. I have visited 67 countries and all alone. I was never professionally ambitious. My goal was my freedom and with Odermatt I had that freedom. I could go and he would carry on working with the clients. This freedom was very important for me.

I didn't plan my career or anything like that, I just wanted to do good work. When I see some young designers now I can see that they work on their careers. They run around and see important people. I didn't do that. I wanted to have my freedom and I wanted to do good work and to have pleasure in doing it. I didn't think I would be famous or be somebody.

I was also a bit too modest and shy. I am perhaps naïve but I think if you do good work, then reputation should come naturally. Sometimes I think I had so many opportunities, but I just didn't plan ahead in that way. I could have had bigger clients, and I certainly would have more money by now had I taken those opportunities, but I feared feeling trapped... and working all the time... and being responsible for others. No, no, it's okay like this. I need my freedom.

Of course Switzerland is also a very macho country – women only got the vote in '71! Just recently I said to Sigi, 'if I were not as good, my male colleagues would be much nicer to me'. They hate a good woman colleague. I have had a hard time sometimes. I found that clients asked for Sigi and assumed that he did all the work. Even one of our colleagues at AGI said they thought the work was his. It was frustrating. I wonder what happens to all those female graphic design students. When I teach, the women tend to be better. I think it's hard to fight and so perhaps they give up and maybe they are not ambitious enough.

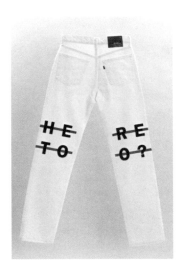

06 I have never taught, but now I think it would be nice as I have experience to share and I think both professors and students would be motivating. I wouldn't like to teach where I studied as most of my colleagues would be the people I studied with and this would seem regressive. Students do come and see us though as I think we have had some influence.

Rosmarie Tissi

09 There were some periods when I wondered 'why does this designer have clients I don't have'. Sometimes I felt this but not all the time. I generally felt confident.

They tell me sometimes that I am part of graphic design history. I hope I am but I would not think of myself like that. Some of my work is groundbreaking, I guess, yes. Like the Summer Theatre poster or the Lichtsatz and Offset portfolio. This was done in 1981 and 1982 and was quite new and the TIPS advertisements in 1968 – I think this was very new at that time.

10 I have only taught short workshops – ten days at a time, at Yale for example. I didn't want to teach more than this because it would have meant I couldn't have been free to travel. I run these workshops on one theme, and mostly centred on typography... free typography. I have found that students have no idea about letters and so I encourage them to play. The project might be to do a cover for a typography magazine. I might restrict them to using four typefaces, but it doesn't matter if it is illegible.

Sabina Oberholzer

Cover and spread from One World, entry for an invited design competition for a new magazine commissioned by the Swiss Agency for Development and Cooperation in 1997.

Rosmarie Tissi

Much of Tissi's work was innovative for its time, particularly her cover promoting offset printing for the printers Anton Schöb, 1982, her Summer Theatre poster for the Department of Cultural Affairs, Zurich, 1981, and the advertisements for TIPS, a Belgian magazine on advertising, produced in 1968.

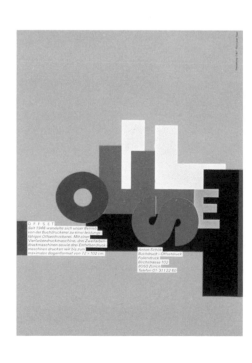

11 I have visited many poor countries where there are terrible problems. This has made me question the value of my work back home. I felt ashamed sometimes, but then I would come back and carry on the same. But when I travelled I really wanted to forget my profession. I had colleagues who wondered why I didn't visit other designers in my travels, but I didn't want to think about graphics all the time.

Graphic design is very important to me now, but when I was younger it was not so important. To see the world, to have my freedom, to go out into nature was. I felt happy outside. Now I like graphic design more and feel defined by being a graphic designer. I cannot help myself although I don't really think it is important in itself. On one level all professionals have to consider their occupation to be important otherwise they wouldn't carry on, and the profession wouldn't exist.

12 I wouldn't like to be starting now with the present economical situation. On the other hand I wouldn't mind starting again if I could remember all I have already learnt and then use the technology of today!

My advice would be not to trust the computer too much, tell it what to do and not the other way round! I would also advocate respect for the work of older generations! When I was young I looked back to see what had been done before and looked at the work of artists. If you study the past you learn how to approach a problem. The other concern I have is that very few designers seem to develop their own approach now, they just follow the trend and in a rather self-orientated way. I have always felt that designers should consider who the client is and what their need is because that is what they are paid to do, not design for themselves. They should want to help the client and not take a job simply to further their own career.

104 : 105
drip-dry shirts
discussion 4

Colin Forbes
self-portrait

Michael Gericke

Colin Forbes

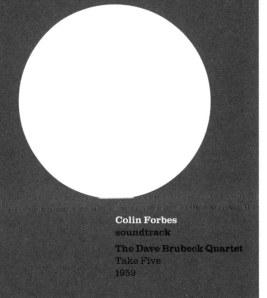

Colin Forbes
soundtrack

The Dave Brubeck Quartet
Take Five
1959

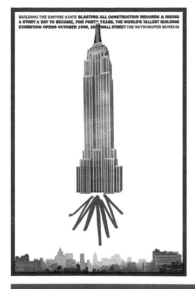

BUILDING THE EMPIRE STATE BLASTING ALL CONSTRUCTION RECORDS & RISING A STORY A DAY TO BECOME, FOR FORTY YEARS, THE WORLD'S TALLEST BUILDING EXHIBITION OPENS OCTOBER 1998, 16 WALL STREET THE SKYSCRAPER MUSEUM

Michael Gericke
biography

Michael Gericke (born Wisconsin, USA, 1956) was educated at the University of Wisconsin, USA (1974–78) and worked for Communication Arts Inc, a small company established by two designers from Charles and Ray Eames's office, before he joined Pentagram New York in 1986. Gericke is now a partner and is responsible for graphic identity, corporate communications and environmental signage programmes.

Colin Forbes
biography

Colin Forbes has been at the forefront of graphic design for over 40 years. Instrumental in developing the professional status of the industry, Forbes has been one of its forerunners. As a co-founder of ground-breaking design groups Fletcher/Forbes/Gill and Pentagram, and through his role in founding D&AD and his enlivening presidency of the American Institute of Graphic Arts, his impact upon the definition and direction of graphic design has been profound.

Born in London in 1928 Forbes attended the Central School of Arts and Crafts, London (1945–46) and (1949–52) where his career-defining friendship with fellow student Alan Fletcher began. They were both students of Herbert Spencer whose teaching, writing and typographic sensitivity proved hugely influential. Forbes worked as Spencer's design assistant (1952–53) before also teaching at the Central School where he became the head of department of graphic design (1956–59).

Forbes established his own design practice in 1960, but it was through Alan Fletcher that he became aware of wider possibilities and his own ambition was awakened; accepting an invitation to visit Fletcher in New York, the pair saw the opportunity for transposing the American model of design practice to London. In 1962 along with American émigré Bob Gill, they formed Fletcher/Forbes/Gill; a dynamic partnership to which Forbes brought his strong graphic sensibility and organisational skills. The first significant British new generation design group of the period, their approach was defined by their belief that the 'solution is in the problem' and clients included global companies such as BP, Reuters, Rank Xerox and Pirelli.

With the arrival of architect Theo Crosby and Gill's departure, the company became Crosby/Fletcher/Forbes (1965) and the firm's activities expanded to include exhibition and architectural design. Exemplary of the group's work were the acclaimed series of posters Forbes designed for Pirelli (1966–69) and his campaign against admission charges to British museums (1970), which display a combination of intelligence, originality and the wittily unexpected.

Gericke designed the identity programme for the FIFA World Cup football championships, USA (1994) and has worked on projects with the American Museum of Natural History and Liz Claiborne.

He has been involved in the regeneration and design for Lower Manhattan following 9/11, including the design of the viewing wall surrounding Ground Zero and the cornerstone for the freedom tower.

Currently Gericke is responsible for the new image and environmental graphics for the embassies and consulates of the United States Department of State worldwide.

Gericke has won many accolades including Fortune magazine's Beacon Award for the creation of outstanding strategic design programmes.

He has served on the Executive Committee of the New York Chapter of the American Institute of Graphic Arts and is a member of the Alliance Graphique Internationale. He is a frequent lecturer and has taught identity design at the Cooper Union, New York. His work is widely exhibited and is represented in museum collections worldwide.

In 1972, with the addition of industrial designer Kenneth Grange, the group metamorphosed once again and became Pentagram.

Pentagram developed an approach that was firmly ideas-based and drew upon associations of subject matter to produce conceptually strong solutions. As the group expanded the structure of the partnership evolved with partners working largely as individuals managing their own creative teams.

In 1978 Forbes made the decision to move to America to establish Pentagram's office in New York. The considerable task of building up a studio and generating clients involved a large degree of risk, yet because of Forbes's initiative Pentagram New York has become one of the most successful and high profile offices of the international syndicate, with clients including Harley Davidson, United Airlines and Citibank. Pentagram now also has offices in Austin, San Francisco and Berlin.

Forbes has played a critical role in developing the professionalism of the industry and has been an influential member of the design community. He was a co-founder of British Design & Art Direction (1963), a member of the British Design Council (1972–75) and elected Royal Designer for Industry by the Royal Society of Arts, London (1973). He served as international president of the Alliance Graphique Internationale (1976–79) and was a galvanising national president of the American Institute of Graphic Arts (1984–86), swelling the number of members and increasing the prestige and regard in which the organisation was held.

In 1997 he received the President's Award of the Designers and Art Directors Association, London for his outstanding contribution to design and in 1992 he was awarded the American Institute of Graphic Arts medal in recognition of his distinguished achievements in the field. He is widely published in magazines and journals and has lectured in the United States, Europe and Japan.

Michael Gericke

Poster for Building the Empire State exhibition held at the Skyscraper Museum, 1998. The design conveys the speed of the building's construction, which rose at more than a storey every day.

Colin Forbes

Poster for Designer's Saturday, 1983, an annual event organised by New York interior designers, furniture retailers and manufacturers. Every year a different graphic designer was chosen to design the publicity.

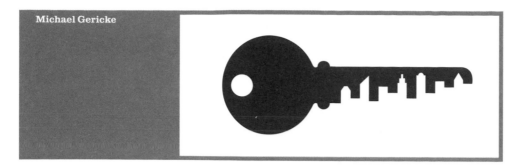

01 **student experiences/
serendipity/
early professional life**

Colin Forbes

01 **early career choices/
getting a grant/
illustration/
the challenges of
graphic design/
early ambitions**

01 In the early '30s my parents moved out to the new suburbs of east London not long after I was born. You can't imagine anything duller! During the Second World War it was no surprise that I left school wanting to design aeroplanes. I should have gone to university to study aeronautics, but instead I was enrolled at a technical college to train as a draughtsman. I had to wait to start and so my father, who worked in public relations for ICI, got me a job through a colleague in a commercial art studio just off the Strand. Geoff White was there with me. We were both working as messengers. I would deliver parcels to illustrators like John Farleigh and designers like Milner Gray. I saw some of what they were doing and it inspired me.

As a result I persuaded my father that I wanted to go to art school. The creative director at ICI knew John Farleigh so I was lucky in being able to go and see him and ask his advice. Farleigh of course taught at the Central School of Arts and Crafts. It was 1945 and I was only 17. It was during the war and fortunately the school needed students.

I then had to do national service, but as my education had been interrupted I got a grant and could go back. It was extraordinary, at the time the Central was the place to be. William Johnstone, the principal, was an unreasonable, egotistical tyrant, but he really had a nose for talent. Reyner Banham, Henrion, Mervyn Peake, William Roberts, Eduardo Paolozzi were all brought in by Johnstone. Terence Conran, Alan Fletcher of course, Derek Birdsall were students – a new generation of designers came out of the Central.

Michael Gericke

Logo for New York's Center for Architecture, 2001.

Colin Forbes

Forbes cites his design of the quarterly magazine Plastics Today, 1960s, as some of his best. The inventiveness of these covers shows that the editor's confidence was well placed. 'No matter what I proposed he was going to support it.'

Invitation, printed on Forbes's own small press, 1954. The influence of his typography tutors at the Central is clear.

01 I grew up in a very small town in the midwest. In high school, my art instructor was an American Indian and I became interested in ceramics. I entered college in the fine arts programme and planned on becoming a university art professor. Then I met a professor who had just retired as the design director of United Airlines. It was via that professor that I became aware of graphic design and visual communication, so this was tremendously good fortune.

Then on graduating from the University of Wisconsin in 1978 I accepted a position with Communication Arts, a young design firm established by two expatriates of the Charles and Ray Eames's office.

I guess it is all a combination of luck, fate and looking for a path. The luck comes from those chance coincidences and the fate is in the many things that are beyond your control. The path is found in recognising those events and the people who interest and inspire you – who hopefully challenge you to look for more.

Because of Farleigh I went back to do book illustration, which fell under the auspices of the book production department headed by Jesse Collins. He was a remarkable teacher. He fortunately insisted that we all did typography because it would give us a skill by which we could actually earn a living. Herbert Spencer had taken over teaching typography from Anthony Froshaug and I went into his class.

I was previously doing a great deal of drawing and illustration and even got a couple of small jobs for House & Garden as a student. But I just couldn't draw well enough. In fact one agent I went to see said 'come back in three years when you've learned to draw'. I got on well with Spencer and gradually I found that I could solve design problems, if I tried hard enough, and found the process intellectually more stimulating. I left art school wanting to do what Herbert and Anthony did – designing catalogues and invitations for exhibitions and perhaps teaching for one day a week alongside this kind of freelance work.

I learnt so much at the Central, and my life was changed forever, but on leaving mine was still a very limited ambition.

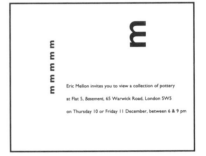

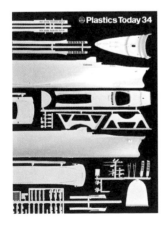

As a student the work of Pentagram – Colin Forbes and Alan Fletcher in particular – had certainly impressed me, but I didn't leave college with any ambition that included becoming a partner there. I wasn't sure of where my career might lead. I'd thought about working for myself. Running my own 'office' was a possibility and something I aspired to do.

I had also been influenced by Chermayeff & Geismar, Robert Brownjohn, Saul Bass, Armin Hofmann, Massimo Vignelli… I graduated feeling very intrigued by graphic design, particularly because it is seen by a wide public and can therefore touch a large audience. The opportunity to create visible commercial work, that becomes a part of popular culture, was very seductive to me.

02 **design influences/
early ambitions**

Colin Forbes

02 **significant people/
pivotal years/
New York/
design connections**

03 **cultural ambition/
the beginnings of
Fletcher/Forbes/Gill**

02 Alan Fletcher and I were close as students. He left the Central and went on to the Royal College. I went to work, as I was married and had my daughter Christine by then. Alan meanwhile, whilst at the RCA, managed to arrange an exchange with Yale for his postgraduate degree and went to America. I got a couple of fairly good design jobs and part-time teaching at the Central. Then Jesse retired and Johnstone offered me the job of head of the department in 1956 and I did that for three years.

In 1958 I was 30. My birthday was the worst day I can remember. I was separated from my wife, I had 100 students, I was supposed to be at the school three days a week so even giving each student one or two hours a term was hard. I thought, I'm going to end up one of those grumpy old buggers, resenting the young.

Soon after that Alan wrote to me from New York, 'if you can afford the airfare, I'll put you up for the summer'. He got me bits of artwork to do there. I stayed with him and Paola in a studio apartment above a cinema on 8th Street and I slept in the kitchen.

Alan had remarkable energy. He was absolutely unabashed, he went to visit Saul Bass, Paul Rand, Herb Lubalin. We visited the design group Brownjohn, Chermayeff & Geismar. They were an inspiration. They were our age and what they had achieved seemed to be just phenomenal. That really marked my change of ambition. I was tempted to stay, but in the end I went back to London and Alan followed. We had become part of a remarkable New York/ London community. From then on most of the leading graphic designers who came to London would visit us and vice versa.

Michael Gericke

The viewing wall at Ground Zero, 2002–03. Intended as a place of reflection, while a permanent memorial is developed, it tells the history of the World Trade Center and lists those who perished in the 9/11 attacks.

Colin Forbes

Insert for Typographica, 1966, demonstrating the potential in representing even the humblest of objects.

The tyre manufacturer Pirelli encouraged creative and sometimes playful design solutions. Cover and pages from promotional booklet for Earl's Court Motor Show, 1963.

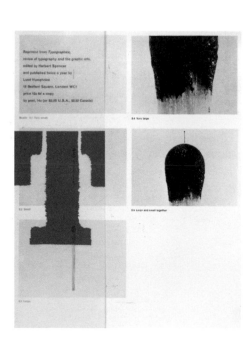

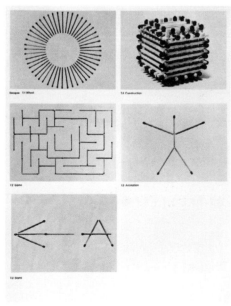

03 Back in London, a group of us organised the exhibition Graphic Designers London. When the American designer Bob Gill arrived in England, he went to see it and immediately identified us as like-minded and wanted to join up with us, suggesting we became partners. Alan and I wanted to think about it.

I had taken a basement apartment in Montagu Square because it was central. It had a fairly large room that Alan and I used as a studio. Meanwhile Bob was working for an advertising agency. Then we had another stroke of amazing luck. Nicolas Kaye, who had brought Bob over from the States, wanted to stay connected with Bob and so invested £5,000/$9,000 (US) in the business. It was quite a lot in 1961.

As Fletcher/Forbes/Gill, we renovated a nice little mews house just off Crawford Street. It took over a year to convert, by which time Bob and Nick had fallen out and he wanted his money back. We managed to borrow the money individually and the end result was a good one.

We owned our own business, just the three of us, as equals. We would never have invested that money if we hadn't been financed in the first place. There we were and we were ahead of the game.

I did feel some anxiety joining up as Fletcher/Forbes/Gill – the night before we started I sat on the bed and thought, 'I'm never going to keep up with those two guys' – wishing I'd gone with a house in the country and a quiet life!

Alan Fletcher and Bob Gill raised my sights. Alan had such a sense of quality and culture and lifestyle – the way he lives is the way that he works. He knows everybody – he's unbelievably sociable. I don't think the present generation actually understands the importance of networking and lifestyle. I don't think their sights are as high as ours were, culturally. There were other people of course, such as Michael Peters, who I would say were more ambitious financially.

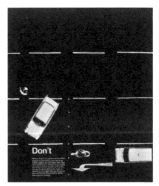

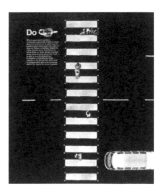

Colin Forbes

Gericke worked with Forbes
to develop the identity
for The Atheneum, a luxury
business hotel in Detroit, 1990.
The logo combines classic
typography with an illustrated
olive branch.

Colin Forbes

Poster for campaign against
admission charges to British
museums, 1970, displaying
a combination of intelligence,
originality and the wittily
unexpected.

Logo for Zinc Die Casting
Conference, 1966. The date
was nothing short of a gift.

04 The period was phenomenal.
Absolutely phenomenal. The
sense of changing ambition was
extraordinary. Previously it had
been very difficult to get out of
one's background. Labourers breed
labourers and middle managers
breed middle managers. Alan and
I absolutely broke that mould. The
timing with Fletcher/Forbes/Gill
was fantastic, we were the first
of a new post-war generation. The
heady experiences of that period
gave me the courage to go to
New York on my own in the '70s
and start Pentagram in the US.

05 Generally the economy was not that
important to us. It can be absolutely
fantastic, yet you can be out of work,
then you can get one good client and
the rest of the world can be going
to hell. The '70s was a hard time.
There was Edward Heath, the coal
miners' strike and the three-day
week but we were very lucky. Getting
Lucas Industries is an amazing story.
I went to Birmingham to pitch and
we didn't get it, it went to Allied who
then made a presentation that the
chairman hated. He said he wanted
to go and see Fletcher/Forbes/Gill.
By then we were Pentagram, but the
chairman still came to see us.

He asked me 'do you remember my
daughter Suzie Scott?' It transpired
that eight years before she had been
an intern with us and had told her
father we were 'the greatest'. The job
was worth half a million pounds a
year. Bernard Scott was remarkable.
He said, 'look, take this recession
as an advantage. You go on working
on your programme, get it all as
well-organised as possible. We've got
to wait for the economy to change
but that doesn't mean you should
stop work'. He became an important
mentor for me. Opportunities are
rare, but when they come you've got
to take them.

03

I joined Pentagram as Colin's senior designer in 1986. I was immediately awe struck, inspired and humbled. His work was widely known. He was smart, articulate, intuitive and had a broad knowledge of design history. He freely collaborated with other designers, illustrators, typographers and photographers; he understood how design can be an asset to business; was knowing, elegant and kind – and exotically European.

We, the undersigned, deplore and oppose the Government's intention to introduce admission charges to national museums and galleries

and Pentagram Design Partnership
—and Lund Humphries

Write in protest to your MP
and send for the petition forms to
Campaign Against Museum Admission Charges
221 Camden High Street
London NW1 7BU

06 I did my best design work in the years prior to and at the beginning of Pentagram. Most people are at their creative best between 35 and 45, you're learning and after that you tend to draw on your previous experience.

I spent an increasing amount of my time worrying about the partnership. I had been working on Lucas Industries, a big project for the automotive, aerospace and industrial divisions, which was over five years of work. One day I was sitting on the train coming back from a monthly meeting in Birmingham thinking 'I don't know if I want to continue to do this' and that's partly why the timing seemed right to go to America.

Also, once we had set up Pentagram the basic structure had changed and I was disappointed by the lack of collaboration across the disciplines. As Fletcher/Forbes/Gill we'd meet every Monday morning to go through all the projects, nothing would go out of the office that hadn't been discussed by all three of us. Of course, often one person went off and did the job but as we were smaller it felt more collaborative. I also felt nostalgia for New York and everything I'd wanted to do back in '58. One day I said to the partners 'Wendy and I want to go and live in New York, do you want me to open a Pentagram office?' and they were very enthusiastic about it.

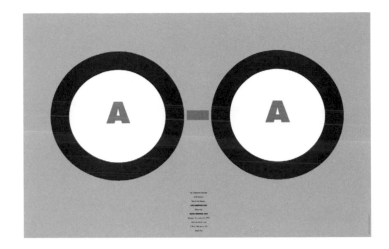

Colin Forbes

Michael Gericke

Poster for the American
Institute of Architects
New York Chapter's 1995
Heritage Ball honouring
Philip Johnson. The image
combines Johnson's
signature round glasses
and the AIA initials.

Colin Forbes

D&AD call for entries, 1963.
Forbes was a co-founder
of British Design & Art
Direction and designed
its logo, which is still in
use today.

07 I planned for a year to go to
New York – burning boats, selling
a house – shooting my mouth off
about wanting to move. I felt very
little apprehension that it wouldn't
all be all right and was full of hubris
from the successful '60s, but it
actually wasn't all all right. It was
very difficult. I had forgotten
about a number of important things,
such as the way business arrives
through a network of connections.
At the time my connections were
all other graphic designers who
were now competitors. I also knew
little about US culture or business.
Peter Harrison an English graphic
designer working in New York then
joined me as a partner in 1979.

It was all initially daunting as I was
making plans and investments
based on the assumption that work
would follow. Fortunately it did.
In New York at the time, half of the
Fortune 500 companies were in
the region and each had to produce
an annual report. Peter had annual
report experience. Gradually this
kind of work began to come our way.
On Wall Street, with the high levels
of American corporate executives, it
wasn't bad to have an English accent.
We got American Express, Warner
Communications and Rupert
Murdoch's News Corporation. I fell
on my feet in the end.

As far as my personal work was
concerned, building Pentagram
New York probably put me back ten
years. On balance I don't regret it.
I'm so pleased I live here. I had felt
that I didn't get enough credit for
what I'd done in London. In the
US I am the person who brought
Pentagram to New York and all
that, to an absolutely exaggerated
degree. Here the influence of Alan
and Bob in creating the partnership
culture is underestimated.

I moved to New York, which was
the biggest market for design
services in the world. I believed that
American Corporations would want
design services in Europe from
a firm with roots in the US and
that multidisciplinary work would
differentiate Pentagram from its
competitors. I believe I was right,
but it took more than a decade for
Pentagram to reap the benefits.

04 Colin's impact on European and American graphic design is enormous. He truly made the AIGA a national body with enormous influence – it (and Colin) has shaped and promoted the profession. Also his work with AGI collegially connected the international design community.

The design and educational community has grown exponentially recently. Being an integral and participating part of the profession can help change its future and influence generations of designers, which is why I too actively engage in this field.

The awareness of graphic design is now very high. More and more businesses understand and utilise it as a tool, or weapon, to differentiate their companies, products and services.

Schools are producing high levels of skilled students, the supporting technologies for design are extraordinary, and the importance of effective, memorable and fresh graphic design, in an overwhelming barrage of images, is more important than ever.

There are downsides of greater awareness but it's mostly quite positive. The speed at which work gets done has changed enormously in the last few years. The good thing is it has let us see, react to and evolve the work more intuitively. The downside is many frequent procurers of design know the technology and expect the work to be completed very quickly – without allowing the time to step back from it.

08 When Alan and I were in Montagu Square we only had one telephone and two extensions. One day Alan answered a call, he put his hand over the phone and said 'it's Henrion'. I picked up the extension and listened. Henrion was an eminent and established designer, he was talking about the professional body, the Society of Industrial Artists and Designers [SIAD] and wondering about ideas to encourage the young to join. He asked if Alan would go round to chat with him about it and added 'will you bring that friend of yours, I can never remember his name!' I was never happy with the SIAD. It was a mixed community, not focused on graphic design. So the upshot was that we were instrumental in setting up British Design & Art Direction [D&AD] in 1963 and Henrion and I became very good friends!

I'm quite proud of my contribution to graphic design as a profession in America. My years as president of the American Institute of Graphic Arts [AIGA] are really quite important to me. Its membership was 900 when I started, when I left it was 5,000 and now it's 13,000. I am also proud of chairing the first AIGA conference in 1988, which truly made it a national organisation. I am not deluded about the significance of this role though. I feel slightly ambivalent about whether I made the right choice or not because future generations won't remember what I did for these associations, in the end what matters will be the work that's left.

05 Colin's work is intelligent and inspired. He believes that design is a tool to solve problems and communicate messages. Ideas are king and they're presented in unexpected and varied ways. Colin's and my work is generally ideas driven rather than stylistic in its approach. I learned from Colin that carefully and thoroughly understanding a client's business – their competitors, situation, market and corporate politics – frees you to be inventive and effective.

I haven't found that clients believe design to be the 'icing on the cake'. Good clients understand the necessity to do something exceptional that is unique to them. The others want to make something they're familiar with, at reasonable quality, but without the courage to truly differentiate themselves.

Quality has many dimensions. For me it means solving a commercial problem for a client with a solution that is uncompromising in its design. Most projects (but not all) have potential if the designer is curious, driven, and has an enlightened client. I believe good work leads to more good work and that great work can only happen with good clients. Colin was always very true to his belief in the value of design and people sought him out for it – because of his work, his confidence and past successes.

Colin Forbes

Colin Forbes

George Nelson book jacket, the first job Forbes designed on arrival in New York, 1978. Forbes didn't have an easy way of producing the artwork so explained the idea over the telephone to David Hillman who put it together in London.

Christmas greeting, 1958. On Forbes's return from his first visit to New York he wanted to send something to everyone he had met. This design marks a change in his approach, less influenced by his mentors this is a graphic image rather than a typographic layout.

09 I think graphic design is one of the biggest expressions of the culture. It always has to be seen in the context of its time and a specific communication purpose. It is ephemeral but I don't think this makes it less important; it is important because it is a reflection of the present.

I see graphic design as a service that can be art by accident. I'm opposed in many ways to the idea that the client is some kind of a patron of the arts. I think if you're taking somebody's money this position is potentially dishonest because most clients think they are purchasing a skill that is focused on their need, not the designer's.

In my experience many clients have been well-educated and are intelligent people who have made a valuable contribution to the design process. Some have been very trusting, open and supportive. In one of my best periods, for example, I did some work for ICI that I am really pleased with. I designed Plastics Today – every quarter. The editor was a real fan. No matter what I proposed he was going to support it.

10 I don't think I was a good head of department. I was at my best when I used to teach a typographic class, but teaching was not for me. It wasn't for Alan either. I didn't want to do my work through somebody else. You get maybe one in 30 – somebody who's really bright and you like and then it's rewarding.

11 Of course we were sometimes influenced by other designers. One of the reasons we did the first Fletcher/Forbes/Gill book was that Gerstner and Kutter had published a book in their first year. I wouldn't say I felt envious of my peers. I always felt I was privileged to be in the design community. I never felt that 'I was the greatest' and had to have followers, I was simply pleased to be able to do what I do well. The previous generation had been more competitive with each other but ours happened to be particularly collegiate. I invited Birdsall to help with the work for Pirelli for example. I think Alan and I always felt fairly relaxed about this kind of thing. Another example is a lunch I organised from New York when I took Woody Pirtle to Zurich when he first joined us. Armin Hofmann, Müller-Brockmann, Ernst Hiestand were all there. We had a nice lunch, about a dozen of us. They thought it was wonderful as they said they never met up like this!

At Pentagram we try to work with clients who appreciate and understand the value of design and how it can be an important tool for their business. There are always economic pressures – high paying jobs with less potential, low paying assignments with enormous freedom and the realities of paying the overheads – and there are many more designers and design firms now, but there are also more opportunities and clients too.

It's very important to me. I really enjoy my work, its challenges, the collaborations, my partners, the opportunity to learn intimately about so many different clients and their businesses, create projects that are seen and used by others and to not know exactly what I'm going to do tomorrow. Design requires you to draw on a wide variety of personal experiences – you have to be curious and explore many things. Remember it's all about design.

12 Herbert Spencer would have called himself a typographer, Abram Games an artist; the idea of graphic design was just taking shape. In retrospect, I think that we were some of the people who actually made it what it is. I believe we were among the first to see ourselves as designers as distinct from artists. Design is a selective intellectual process not a craft. I'm not particularly shy about that. There was a vision and I was part of it.

The transformation of our position in the design community was fast. From '58, that first visit to America... we were already successful by the time we opened the doors at Fletcher/Forbes/Gill. Alan Fletcher will be remembered as one of the ten best graphic designers of our generation internationally. I won't. I think if I do have any claim to be remembered, it is that I helped establish graphic design as a profession. My contribution is that Pentagram has managed to survive with a very similar quality in its second and third generations.

Suddenly, within the last year, there's been increased interest in our early period. For example, Rick Poynor's Communicate book draws heavily on the '60s. The inclusion in books on the history of graphic design influences future writers, so to a certain extent the work of anyone published in these books becomes historically significant. There are also omissions that become sadly permanent.

13 I think you have to take opportunities and do what interests you. Jesse Collins said, 'sooner or later you'll get the kind of work you've got in your portfolio and that's both good and bad'. Everything is cumulative from the beginning. I was lucky going to the Central School with such inspirational teachers and talented fellow students. Then I was lucky to meet Alan with his no-limits ambition. My advice is don't be frightened of failure. If you don't try you're going to regret it. The funny thing is that some people would say, it's not that bad going to New York, if you fail you can always come back. But, that wasn't true. What was I going to do? Go back with my tail between my legs? Once I'd done it, I had to make it work.

118 : 119
drip-dry shirts
discussion 5

Geoff White
self-portrait
In a bedsit, early 1950s.

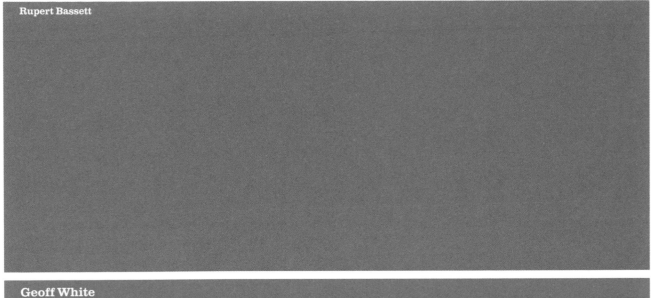

Rupert Bassett

Geoff White

Geoff White
soundtrack

Beethoven
Piano trio in B flat
Opus 97
The Archduke

Rupert Bassett

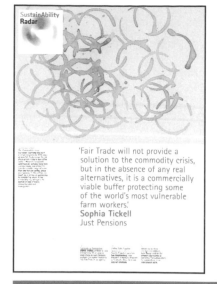

**Rupert Bassett
biography**

Rupert Bassett (born 1965,
Southampton) studied at
Ravensbourne College of
Design and Communication
(1985–88) and the Royal
College of Art (1988–90),
before setting up his own
design studio specialising in
corporate information design.
Committed to the aesthetics
and principles of modernism,
Bassett's structured and
rational design is typified
by the axiom 'consistency
is authority'.

**Geoff White
biography**

Geoff White is a designer and
educator notable for his many years
as a teacher of graphic design and
typography, and his quiet legacy of
influence on succeeding generations
of practitioners. One of the first
British designers to acquire and
utilise the typeface Helvetica, White
has remained a fervent advocate
and life-long disciple of modernism,
still practising and enthusiastically
instructing on the beauty and
possibilities of modernist principles.

Born in London in 1928, White's
early interest in art and design was
interrupted by national service
before he was accepted by the
Central School of Arts and Crafts
(1949–51). He entered the school at a
vibrant time in its history. Painters,
sculptors and architects taught
students across a variety of courses;
Eduardo Paolozzi taught textile
students, Peter and Alison Smithson
taught in three-dimensional design,
and young new designers Herbert
Spencer and Anthony Froshaug
were teaching typography. With
this calibre of tutor, student morale
was high and this rich experience
helped White find a life-long love
of learning.

After leaving college, White worked
as a typographer and layout artist
for a number of agencies including
the National Cash Register Company
Publicity Department (1956–57) and
the Central Office of Information
(1960–62), before joining Dewar-Mills
Associates, a graphic and exhibition
design group (1962). From 1969
he worked as a freelance designer
with clients including Bedfordshire
County Council, where he was
design consultant (1975), and the
Architectural Press for whom he
designed five special issues of
Architectural Review magazine,
two of which were in collaboration
with Mike Burke (1978–88).

White had started teaching evening
classes at the London College
of Printing (1961–63), followed
by a part-time lecturing post at
Ravensbourne College of Design
and Communication (1966–71)
before accepting a full-time position
as first-year tutor at Ravensbourne
in 1971. Keen to keep alive the
typographic legacy of the course,
and strongly influenced by the
teaching methodologies of the
Bauhaus and Kunstgewerbeschule
Basel, White introduced a series of
graphic workshops into the first
year. These rigorous and thorough
exercises explored colour, design
and letterform, and included talks
on the influence of significant art
movements, proportion in
painting and architecture, and
Gestalt psychology.

Bassett has worked on a number of high profile visual identities, including GlaxoWellcome (for Square Red Studio, 1995–96), the RAC (for North, 1997) and the BT Talk Zone exhibition at the Millennium Dome (for Imagination, 1998–99). He has taught typography at Ravensbourne College of Design and Communication (1990–95), the London College of Printing (1996–2002) and currently at Bath School of Art and Design.

Bassett has been the designer for SustainAbility, an independent international think-tank advising on corporate responsibility and sustainable development since 1992.

This relationship of over 13 years has fuelled Bassett's own investigation into sustainable design and its implications for typography in particular. He is currently working on a project seeking to explain to designers the opportunities of global sustainability for the design industry at large.

His egalitarian approach, enthusiasm and unpretentious delivery fostered skill, appreciation of craft and understanding of modernist design principles in his students. The first-year course was driven by White's firm belief in the necessity of the mastery of basic skills and played a pivotal role in establishing Ravensbourne as one of the leading graphic design colleges of the period.

White both attends and delivers numerous lectures and has given talks at Central Saint Martins, the Royal College of Art and the London College of Printing. He has had work published in Graphis magazine (1966), Typographische Monatsblätter (1980), Octavo magazine (1986) and Typographics 1, a review of international typographic design (1995).

In addition to his years at Ravensbourne, White has taught at many design schools including Camberwell School of Arts and Crafts (1969–71), where he was also external assessor (1977), Nova Scotia College of Art and Design, Canada (1980) and Surrey Institute of Art and Design where he continues to this day.

Rupert Bassett

Bassett has been the design consultant for SustainAbility for over 13 years. This is one of a series of posters announcing the publication of its Radar magazine. The image is part of a diagram showing the relative proportion of fair trade to non-fair trade coffee consumption.

Geoff White

Poster announcing a talk by designer Rolf Müller, early 1990s. Throughout his time at Ravensbourne College of Design and Communication White's posters promoting college events exemplified his rigorous and modern approach to design, serving to inspire many of his students.

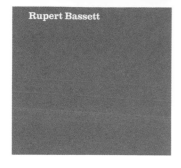

Rupert Bassett

01 **selecting a college/
first impressions of
Geoff White**

01 I visited all the other London art colleges, but applied to Ravensbourne out of pure instinct. I had never seen anything like it before. I immediately loved the Miesian architecture, rigorous signage system and clean white open-plan studios. It looked more like a factory than an art college. But mostly I loved the close similarity of the student work, which looked like it had been made by machines. It was also obvious that the teaching team shared a modernist design philosophy.

I hadn't heard of Geoff White before, but I met him in the first-year seminar room on 23 September 1985, my first day at Ravensbourne. He seemed very quietly spoken and unemotional for an art teacher, much to my relief, but he also seemed to know something very important. I wasn't sure exactly what it was, but I wanted to find out.

Geoff White

01 **early career choices/
getting a grant/
college experiences**

02 **breadth of learning/
the new typography/
painting and drawing**

01 I dropped out of grammar school when I was 15. The school was very sports orientated, but I knew I was more of an aesthete than an athlete and wanted to try 'something creative'. In the local library I found the Artists and Writers Year Book. I wrote to some of the studios listed and thought myself very clever to get a job as a junior and messenger for 30 shillings a week.

The best part of this experience was that we did one day a week day release at Regent Street Polytechnic, at the time the only art school I knew in London. I had been impressed by the work of the Design Research Unit during the war – clever government advertising and exhibitions – and so I went along to see if I could study graphic design at the Polytechnic, but they didn't do it.

I eventually went to the Central School of Arts and Crafts, almost by accident really. Colin Forbes had been a junior with me and it was he who told me about it. I did my national service prior to going, but as my education had been interrupted I was entitled to a grant of £3 a week plus fees. All this may never have happened as Colin and I narrowly missed being blown-up one lunch hour by a 'doodlebug' that fell in the Aldwych. We dived into a doorway and the only injury I sustained was made by a tiny particle of glass that I dusted off Colin's jacket!

Rupert Bassett

Series of posters announcing the publication of issues of SustainAbility's bi-monthly Radar magazine, 2003–05; themes covered include terminology, HIV/AIDS and the increasing consumer power of children.

Geoff White

In these recent Christmas cards White continues to explore modernist principles.

Karl Marx poster, late 1970s. White seized the opportunity to produce this appropriately angular piece of lettering.

In the mid-1950s White went to three evening life classes a week. An exponent of the Euston Road School he learnt how to control paint to achieve correct tonal values.

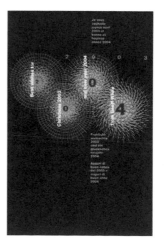

'HIV/AIDS is like a mirror. It shows everything that is problematic about Africa — and it holds these problems right up to your face.'
Angela Wilkinson
Shell / UNAIDS Project

'We are at the early stages of what I call a mental environment movement, that will be every bit as powerful as the physical environment movement that started over 30 years ago.'
Kalle Lasn
Founder, *Adbusters*

'The boom in CSR, corporate responsibility, human rights, sustainable development and the like has created a proliferation of silos in the worlds of activism, government and investment.'
Jed Emerson
Creator of 'blended value'

02 I was interviewed by Jesse Collins and said I wanted to do graphic design. Officially he was head of the department of book production, but I remember he'd address us as 'designers', which was good. Jesse Collins had real influence on me. He went around the studio with an armful of books and introduced us to everything... to designers we'd never heard of like Paul Rand, and to painters like Klee and Picasso.

He also brought in Anthony Froshaug and Herbert Spencer to teach typography. Apart from Hans Schleger these were probably the only two people in Britain at that time who were doing what they called new typography, or continental typography.

Froshaug wasn't there for very long. It was his first job. Years later he told me at a party that he was really nervous when he talked to us for the first time. He fixed his eyes on one student so he wasn't intimidated by talking to 15 people, this student turned all squirrelly, trying to avoid Anthony's gaze! That was the first I had seen of typography.

In the first year I got really interested in life drawing and used to do evening and day classes. I found it confusing in that I really liked the current way of painting that was taught in the school – the Euston Road School – and at the same time I really liked the work of people like Max Bill and El Lissitzky, which was totally different. I wasn't a good student at all in graphic design because I used to sneak off and do life drawing. I was a lousy student really.

124 : 125
drip-dry shirts
discussion 6

Rupert Bassett

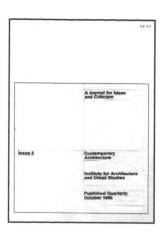
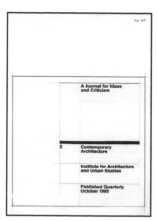
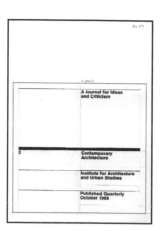

Geoff White

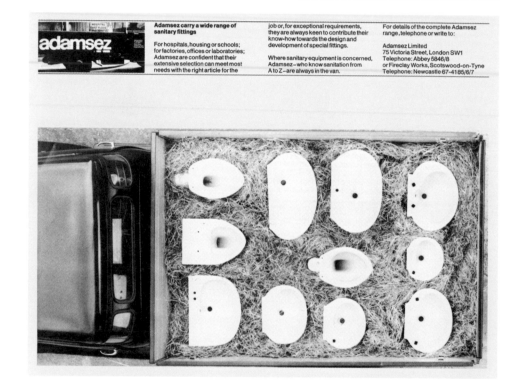

Rupert Bassett

A selection of White's
basic typography exercises
taken from many hundreds
of examples, 1985. These
investigate the use of rules
for emphasis.

Geoff White

In the early 1960s White was
influenced by ideas-based
American design and Swiss
modernism, as the cards and
advertisements produced at
DMA demonstrate.

By the mid-1960s his
allegiance to the latter was
clear, as shown by the red
and black spread, which uses
typographic devices sparingly
and maximises the abstract
potential of images.

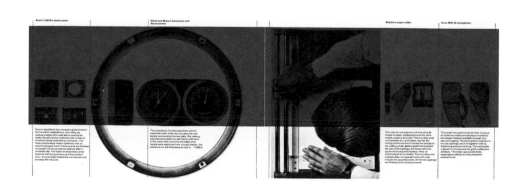

02 Geoff was never dogmatic in the sense of being arrogant or intolerantly assertive. However, he was dogmatic in the sense that he followed a system of teaching with a religious intensity and dedication.

It was immediately obvious that everything he was asking us to learn was going to be useful. He showed us that the same basic design exercises had been taught at other design colleges. It felt like being part of something important. So when he asked us to spend week after week on laborious repetitive exercises we just trusted him and got on with it.

Most of this work was purely formal because Geoff's primary concern was to show us how to make things look good. We spent weeks making simple compositions with points, lines and planes; then we spent weeks doing asymmetric typography exercises; then we spent weeks doing basic colour theory exercises and so on.

It was explained that we were learning elements of the design process in isolated modules because that was the most effective method of learning the subjects. It was also clear that what we were learning would all come together later in the course. To give any specific commercial function to these formal exercises was inappropriate. Geoff's painterly approach to colour and composition were exactly right in this context.

03 Victor Pasmore, the artist, also taught at the Central and had a great deal of influence on me. He used to do a class in basic design. We learnt about fundamentals like colour, proportion, balance and so on. He was in his constructivist phase, doing collages at first and then various perspex and plastic constructions – he used to say that he hoped it would help someone who was designing an electric oven. He was very down to earth about design. He was also sometimes quite anti-painting.

In the Festival of Britain he thought that the best murals were done by designers, not painters, because designers were used to working on a large scale as they were often involved in exhibition design. He used to say 'don't think that just because there's a gold frame round it that it's superior' or he'd say that a lot of advertisements in newspapers were better designed, better composed, than the paintings in the Royal Academy. He taught us that it's no good doing something approximately right, you have to get it precisely right – anybody can do it approximately right.

The trouble is applying this way of thinking to commercial practice. You can't really. You just try and do the best you can, I suppose.

04 After leaving the Central I did think of applying to the Slade School, but I knew I wouldn't have been able to pay for it so I took a job in an advertising agency. For about four or five years I used to go to painting and life drawing evening classes.

My job was as a 'typographer', which just meant filling in the space that the visualiser left. I was sharing a flat with another ex-Central student Ken Briggs. I used to bring my work to show him, to ask his advice. He'd ask 'why are you doing stuff like this, why aren't you doing things like we were taught at the Central?'

Eventually I got a job in a design group called Dewar-Mills Associates. The group had been set up to handle the advertising that was in the journal the Architectural Review... to improve it. It was a really good idea and I could do work there that I couldn't have done in the advertising agency. I found I was thinking about or working on the jobs in the evenings so I gave up the evening class, which was a pity really, because I've never done any painting since.

03 Modernist ideals are sustainable and have been applied throughout the twentieth century all around the world. Unfortunately British commercial design has often suffered from crippling conservatism and nostalgia, especially in the '80s and '90s when Ravensbourne was an oasis in an appalling post-modern Thatcherite design landscape.

Fortunately twenty-first-century business practices must be socially equitable and environmentally benign as well as economically viable (the triple bottom line of sustainability), a situation that restores modernist values to the avant-garde.

I don't think Geoff considered commercial success as a worthwhile personal goal. He wouldn't have been seen dead driving a red Porsche or even entering for a D&AD award. It is a shame that he never sought clients who could really appreciate him and employ his particular skills. I think his modesty stopped him approaching the people he would have liked to work with.

Geoff White

Geoff White

By the mid-1970s White was experimenting typographically as shown in this dynamic spread from an issue of Architectural Review, 1978.

White designed the house-style for Bedfordshire Council, 1975, producing a rigorous identity manual. He brought a contemporary slant to the design of the crest and allied this with modern lettering to produce a strong and flexible logo.

05 When I was working freelance I don't think there was one client that gave me freedom. I also ran out of time because I'm a slow worker. I remember Jesse Collins saying that I usually got there in the end, but that he was worried about how I'd get on outside! Actually, Architectural Review were good. I designed one issue when there was bags of time. They had a guest editor and he had the whole issue written weeks before it was needed, captions and everything. So I had all the copy, I could cast it all off properly. John Hastings, who was the director at the Architectural Press, wrote me a really nice letter afterwards, what was it he said – 'Congratulations... a really sparkling issue'.

When I designed the Bedfordshire Council house-style – a fairly big job – there were lots of problems. The county architect was responsible for it so he had to persuade all the other departments to implement it properly. These kinds of negotiations make the design process often impossible because it's as much about internal politics as it is about the actual design.

As a freelance designer I also discovered that I'm not always a good judge of my own work. When I was teaching at Ravensbourne I would seek the opinion of my colleague Mike Burke who was often referred to as 'the type doctor'. He could look at something I'd done and say 'why don't you just move that over there, make that a bit bigger' and the whole thing would come together.

06 When I was at the Central the student union was run by left-wingers and I too was fairly left-wing. On leaving I worked briefly for CWS, working on the advertising for the Co-operative Society, but I learnt pretty quickly how creatively limiting it can be not to have any decent budgets. It was a worthwhile cause, but when I moved on I appreciated what seemed like real luxuries: getting good quality typesetting and having jobs printed well. I'd lost all the social satisfaction of doing work for the Co-op but gained far more design satisfaction. I think I gave up on all that although I admire those who have the conviction to pursue these concerns.

04 I find that most clients lack a clear understanding of the typographic design that they are responsible for commissioning. They often need to be handled as carefully as students. However, they frequently develop interest and even enthusiasm for typography, especially as they are now increasingly required to produce items of graphic design work for themselves.

I have recently been asked by one of my clients to run my basic typography workshop as an evening class.

In my experience compromise will be avoided by working hard to establish a good trusting relationship with a client in the first place. If they have to impose anything on a project it suggests that their relationship with the designer is all wrong.

05 Geoff's teaching projects usually involved social, political and cultural subjects. They never used overtly commercial content. I had considered his commercial work as supplementary to his teaching activity and never thought of it as in any way representative of his beliefs.

I am primarily interested in social, political and cultural subjects for my design work. I have, I think, been more active than Geoff in my application of design in these areas. This interest has been developed over the past 12 years as a direct result of my relationship with my main client SustainAbility, part economic think-tank, part political pressure group.

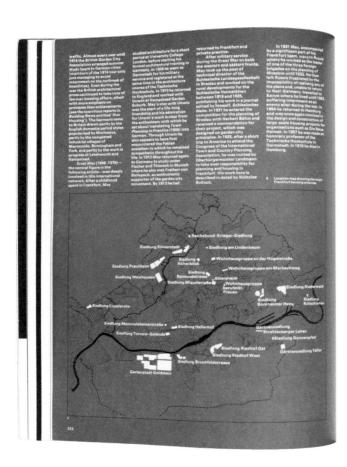

06 Geoff's work has always focused primarily on the purely visual aspects of the design process – typefaces, composition, colour – he just never seemed that interested in the other non-visual elements. I don't ever remember talking about planning or costing. Because of this I prefer to think of Geoff as an artist rather than a designer. This is not true of me: my commitment to sustainable design requires that I am involved in every part of the process.

06 **White's interest in form/ sustainability and design**

Geoff White

07 **Swiss and American typography/ design ideology/ modernism/ post-modernism**

08 **the relationship of form to meaning/ function**

09 **technology/ minimalism**

07 In the late '50s and early '60s there were two big influences on typographic design; the 'typo-images' of American designers like Herb Lubalin and Gene Federico and the classic Swiss typography from the Basel and Zurich schools. You could say that the American approach evolved in advertising and that the Swiss was more apt for print and information design. Swiss typography was quite controversial. Its critics called it antiseptic, austere, bland, boring, clinical, cold, insipid and sterile. Its supporters said it was clean, clear, coherent, direct, lucid, objective, organised, rational and structured. Then in the early '70s Weingart's work began to appear in Typographische Monatsblätter. It was more active than the existing Swiss typography. He used big indents and varied the number of typesizes used, even in one word.

I suppose I would say that I'm still influenced by Swiss design. It was consistent. I remember one of the things that Pasmore used to say was that if you look at Renaissance architecture, the decoration is naturalistic and is consistent with the paintings at the time. In modernist architecture if you have any decoration it should be consistent in the same way. I felt like there should be a consistency across product design, architecture, furniture and graphic design. Just as de Stijl tried to create, I suppose.

For this reason I don't like post-modern architecture. I can see that it happened because many buildings were being constructed in a routine and uninventive way, and that it introduced the use of lots of different materials and colour so that subsequent modernist architecture has become more varied. I also recognise that Weingart shook up graphic design in a similar way, introducing devices like extreme letterspacing. Instead of treating a word as one unit, he'd space it widely so that each letter became an element in the design positioned according to the grid or relating to other typographic elements. The trouble is that people often apply these things insensitively before they've understood enough of the basic stuff.

Rupert Bassett

Illustrating a possible future for information technology these iReport interfaces, 2004, demonstrate the presentation to the consumer of social and environmental values of a product or service.

Geoff White

Wolfgang Weingart's experiments with indentation and typesize broke with the minimal Swiss typographic tradition. These posters from the late 1970s also demonstrate White's interest in dynamic layout.

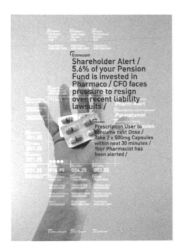

08 People say critically that designers just see words as a grey mass; but they do form a grey mass – that's what I always think. A line is a line of words with a meaning, but it's also a line of a certain length and a certain height.

Jesse Collins used to do this exercise with his students before they did any basic typography. It was called nine lines. You just had to arrange nine lines in a rectangle. I can't remember if they were all the same length and thickness. The idea was that you would start to see type in the same way, as a number of abstract elements. The Germans have a word, Satzbild I think it is, which means the texture of type. There isn't a word for this in English, which means that it is harder for us to embrace the concept. But, it is true that you can make a dark rectangle by using bold type that is tightly leaded or a paler one by opening up the leading. What's important is getting the meaning and aesthetics to work together.

I remember years ago Ken Garland talking about his pleasure in useful things – manuals and so on. I can understand that, but I also think that one of design's functions can be to give pure pleasure. It is great when you pick up a piece of design and it is life enhancing. That seems to me to be quite important. Then there are jobs like hospital signage systems that are functionally important and can be aesthetically pleasing too – that would be an extra plus, the best of both worlds.

09 I didn't have a computer until I retired and now I use one every day. I still do little sketches and drawings before I do something properly, but it is so much easier to experiment and make trials. I can do lots of versions much more quickly than I could by hand. The question is whether that's a good thing – I don't know. Despite the possibility for infinite change, I am more comfortable limiting my choices – number of typefaces and so on.

The Czech architect Eva Jiricna was knocked out when she came to London and discovered that formica was actually available in 350 colours and patterns, but after a year she realised that she wouldn't use more than 12 of them anyway. It's like that with typefaces isn't it?

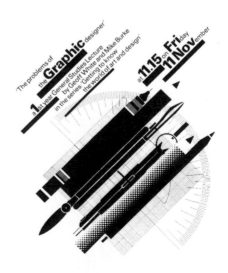

  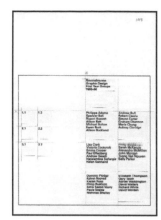

Geoff White

Rupert Bassett

A selection of Bassett's
basic typography exercises
taken from many hundreds
of examples, 2005. These
investigate the use of
grouping for emphasis.

Geoff White

Much of White's work
anticipated the computer;
however, the type on this
poster from the late 1970s
was applied as Letraset
and the proportional merge
was hand-drawn.

White set various colour
exercises to increase
his students' understanding
of the subtleties of colour
harmony and tonal contrast.

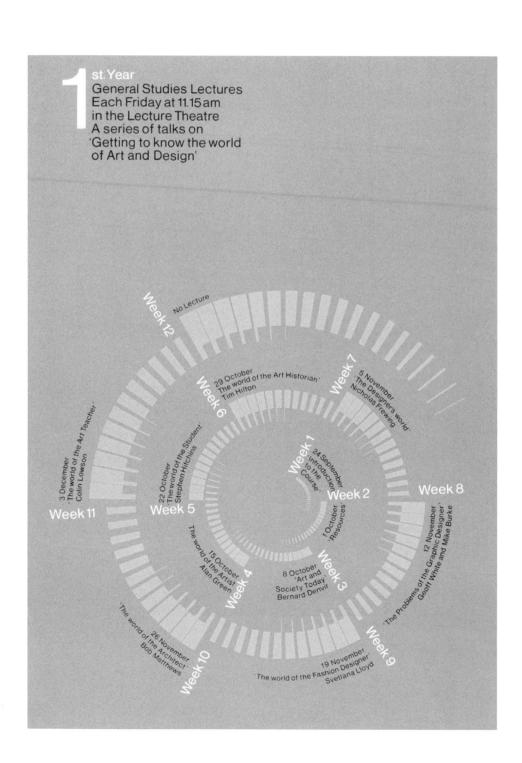

07 Geoff gave us an excellent series of lectures on the history of design and was always careful to connect design developments to social, technological and cultural changes. He invested an enormous amount of time and money, visiting exhibitions and collecting books and magazines. He seemed to consider it his responsibility to pass on this knowledge.

Geoff always managed his classes so that he had the maximum amount of personal contact with students, creating an exciting working environment with a professional studio culture. This does not seem to be happening today because of impossibly high class numbers and overwhelming administrative demands. This is the direct result of colleges being taken over by bureaucrats instead of designers, and this usually means there is no studio culture at all.

08 After leaving Ravensbourne I spent two years at the Royal College of Art. I had applied because one of my other heroes, Gert Dumbar, was supposed to have been teaching there, but instead I spent two years fighting with media darlings and fashion victims. I was shocked by the total lack of teaching philosophy at the RCA. I was quite content to continue to apply sustainable modernist typographic principles in my work but this was regarded as desperately unfashionable.

Since graduating I have regularly taught typography and feel a sort of responsibility as one of Geoff's students. Geoff's basic typography exercises were without doubt the single most valuable part of my education, and my reinterpretations of these are the cornerstone of my teaching. I love the fact that these are clearly based on those of Emil Ruder and Armin Hofmann at Basel and I like to think that I am playing a minuscule part in a tradition of modernist typography.

10 I was teaching from 1971 and full-time teaching seemed very secure. I worry now for the students. There are so many graduates. Where are they all going to end up?

They don't get such a good deal anymore. At Ravensbourne a couple of heads of department advocated 'distance learning'. I still think that in our subject one-to-one teaching is the best way.

Students now are told to be 'original', it's all about individualism. It's similar in life drawing. People come from foundation courses with huge drawings of a knee or something. You can't see the proportion of the body but 'it's really creative'. They draw with their eyes shut, their left hand, the hand of the person sitting next to them. It seems to me to be 101 ways of avoiding something difficult, which is just to try and draw something correctly and to train the brain to estimate distances.

11 I wasn't ambitious enough, probably. I spent too much time socialising and was not sufficiently focused on graphic design. I wasn't really driven and no, I don't think I was envious of my peers.

It's nice when you feel that you've helped somebody to appreciate something or to produce some good work. That's one of the things that makes teaching enjoyable, isn't it? Actually I was looking at some of my students' work and was thinking they've produced some bloody good things.

We were lucky in having good designers to teach in the first year. Over the years we had Peter Wildbur, Simon Johnston and Hamish Muir of 8vo, Dave Ellis from Why Not, Russell Warren-Fisher, Rupert Bassett, Phil Rushton and Colin Maughan as a permanent part-timer. When I retired Patrick Burke, the acting head of graphics, ensured some continuity by making Rupert first-year tutor with Colin as his right-hand man.

The piece about me in Octavo was quite an accident. The magazine was published by the design group 8vo. They were English but had been trained in Basel. One of them, Simon Johnston, said they came back to London thinking they would be the only people that had ever heard of Swiss design. They were really surprised to find me. They could have picked dozens of people for that article. It's just that I had contacted them and given them teaching work. In a way it was sheer fluke because I'm just one more foot soldier… slogging along.

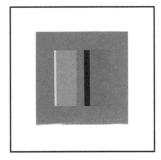

Karl Gerstner
self-portrait
Colour Fractal 4.10
unfinished
Acrylic paint on aluminium
1500 x 1500mm
2003

Helmut Schmidt Rhen

Karl Gerstner

6'00"

Years ago in Chicago I was asked to accompany two dancers who were providing entertainment at a business womens' dance party given in a hall of the YWCA. After the entertainment the jukebox was turned on so everybody could dance: there was no orchestra (they were saving money). However, the goings-on became very expensive. One of the arms in the jukebox moved a selected record on to the turntable. The playing arm moved to an extra ordinarily elevated position. After a slight pause it came down rapidly and heavily on the record - smashing it. Another arm came into the situation and removed the debris. The first arm moved another selected record on to the turntable. The playing arm moved up again, paused, came down quickly, smashing the record. The debris was removed by the third arm. And so on. And meanwhile all the flashing colored lights associated with jukeboxes worked perfectly, making the whole scene glamorous.

7'00"

After he finished translati ng into German the first le cture I gave at Darmstadt, Christian Wolff said, „The stories at the end are very good. But they'll probably say you're naive. I do hope you can explode that idea."

8'00"

Down in Greensboro, North Carolina, David Tudor and I gave an interesting program. We played five pieces three times each. They were the Klavierstück XI by Karlheinz Stockhausen, Christian Wolff's Duo for Pianists, Morton Feldman's Intermission No. 6, Earle Brown's Four Systems and my Variations. All of these pieces are composed in various ways that have in common indeterminacy of performance. Each performance is unique, as interesting to the composers and performers as to the audience. Everyone in fact, that is, becomes a listener. I explained all this to the audience before the musical program began. I pointed out that one is accustomed to thinking of a piece of music as an object suitable for understanding and subsequent evaluation, but that here the situation was quite other. These pieces, I said, are not objects but processes essentially purposeless. Naturally then I had to explain the purpose of having something be purposeless. I said the sounds were just sounds and that if they weren't just sounds that we would (I was of course using the editorial we) - we would do something about it in the next composition. I said that since the sounds were sounds this gave people hearing them the chance to be people, centered within themselves where they actually are, not off artificially in the distance as they are accustomed to be, trying to figure out what is being said by some artist by means of sounds. Finally I said that the purpose of this purposeless music would be achieved if people learned to listen; that when they listened they might discover that they preferred the sounds of everyday life to the ones they would presently hear in the musical program; that that was allright as far as I was concerned.

Karl Gerstner
soundtrack

John Cage
Indeterminacy
1958

Gerstner is uncomfortable with the idea that music could form an atmospheric backdrop to another activity, and instead has chosen to show part of his visualisation of American composer John Cage's Indeterminacy.

Cage wrote a series of paragraph-long anecdotes, thoughts and jokes, and delivered them to accompany a Merce Cunningham dance. He read them aloud, quickly or slowly as required so that one was read per minute.

Helmut Schmidt Rhen
biography

Helmut Schmidt Rhen (born 1936, Cologne, Germany) is an artist, graphic designer, typographer and teacher. His work clearly demonstrates a belief in the interdependency of art and design. He places emphasis on experimentation in both his design work and his serial constructive paintings, believing that when rules and chance are allowed to interconnect, countless permutations are possible.

He studied design and painting at the Staatliche Werkakademie in Kassel (1957–60), then worked as a freelance designer before moving to Basel and starting work at Gerstner + Kutter advertising agency (later to become GGK) as a graphic artist and art director (1961–65).

Karl Gerstner
biography

Karl Gerstner is a typographer, graphic designer and artist of considerable status and influence. Motivated by his belief in freedom and inspired by the inclusive philosophy of the Bauhaus, which proposed multi-disciplinary practice as an ideal, Gerstner's visual investigations have spanned the worlds of applied and fine art. Through his practice and writing, he has passionately advocated the concept of systems, most notably the grid, as a process of constructing meaning and aesthetic clarity. His precise, intricate and often complex structures originate in mathematical calculations and logic, but are utilised expressively and with aesthetic ingenuity.

Born in 1930 in Switzerland, Gerstner attended a preliminary course in art and design at the Allgemeine Gewerbeschule (1944–45), followed by a three-year apprenticeship in Studio Fritz Bühler; where he met Armin Hofmann. During this period he took complementary classes and was taught typesetting by Emil Ruder. Both Hofmann and Ruder were pioneers of the Basel School in graphic design, the principles of which Gerstner found highly influential.

After a short period working as designer in the Basel Ethnographic Museum, Gerstner became a freelance designer at Geigy pharmaceutical company (1949–53) and then established the Büro Basel design studio (1953–59), where his ambition was to adopt a broadly Bauhaus approach to design.

Gerstner developed connections with a wide-ranging group of artists and designers including Max Bill, Josef Albers, George Vantongerloo and the architect Alfred Roth, editor of the Swiss architectural and design journal Werk. Gerstner proposed, designed and edited a special issue of the magazine on Swiss graphic art (1956). A year later he published the book Kalte Kunst? to promote an understanding of the Swiss post-constructivist school that advocated absolute purity and simplicity – and of which he considered himself to be a representative. In the same year he exhibited his paintings for the first time in Zurich.

In 1967, upon Gerstner's suggestion, he became art director of Capital magazine in Cologne (1967–68). After leaving the magazine he continued to run his design practice producing several projects on behalf of Stadt Köln (Neue Zentralbibliothek, Lik), the corporate identity for Fachhochschule Düsseldorf and working for clients that included the Bank für Gemeinwirtschaft and the Kunstverein Hannover. He became a member of the Alliance Graphique Internationale in 1976.

Schmidt Rhen was appointed professor at Fachhochschule Dusseldorf in 1976, a post he held until 1993. In 1984 he co-founded the Forum Typographie.

In 1994 Schmidt Rhen moved to Hamburg, setting up Labor Visuell in 2001, which is dedicated mainly to art and painting.

Throughout his career he has exhibited widely in Europe. He has participated in group exhibitions such as Schrift und Bild (Baden Baden/Amsterdam 1963), Ein Plakat ist eine Fläche die ins Auge springt – Plakate der Kasseler Schule (Frankfurt/Kassel 1979), BUKS Buchkonstruktionen (ZKM Karlsruhe, Berlin, Paris 1999) and Die Poesie des Konkreten, Plakate & Grafik der Kasseler Schule (Berlin 2000).

His solo exhibitions include Poesie der Systematik – Design: Schmidt Rhen (with an accompanying book, Dusseldorf 1996) and An/Aus/Sichten (Galerie Hoffmann, Friedberg 2004).

His work has been shown in a variety of books and publications. These include Typografie – Wann, Wer, Wie (Cologne 1998), Zwei2 by Jörg Stürzebecher (Milan 1999) and Die Poesie des Konkreten (Berlin 2000).

In 1959 Gerstner founded the advertising agency Gerstner + Kutter with his Geigy colleague Markus Kutter. In the same year they published New Graphic Art, a seminal text surveying the history of the modern movement in graphic design. In 1963 Gerstner published the more theoretical cult volume Designing Programmes, advocating a methodological approach to design and the use of 'integral typography' – analysis of text, image and hierarchy to inform the development and structure of ideas and layout. The book inspired MOMA's didactic show Think Program in 1973.

Architect and electronic music pioneer Paul Gredinger had joined Gerstner + Kutter in 1962 and the agency became Gerstner, Gredinger and Kutter (GGK) in 1963. GGK underwent an ambitious programme of expansion and took on an increasingly international client list that included large multinational companies such as IBM, Nestlé, Volkswagon and Swissair.

Gerstner left GGK as managing director in 1971 and concentrated on his work as an artist. He had had his first show in Paris in 1962 and regular exhibitions in New York, London, Caracas, Buenos Aires, Tokyo, Berlin, and Zurich have followed to the present day. In 1981 The Spirit of Colours, the Art of Karl Gerstner was published, followed in 1986 by Gerstner's own book The Forms of Colours.

Gerstner's espousal of quality extends beyond the realm of graphic design to include quality of life, and in 1990 he published Karl Gerstner's Avant Garde Küche, in which he adapted his methodology to the art of the kitchen. Most recently Gerstner published a review of his life's work in two volumes: Review of 5 x 10 Years of Graphic Design and Review of Seven Chapters of Constructive Pictures.

Although he retired from GGK as a director, Gerstner remained with the company as a freelance designer and undertook significant projects including the redesign of the Parisian newspaper France-Soir (1975), the iconic corporate identity for Swissair (1978) and in the 1980s, his consultancy and design for IBM.

Gerstner happily accepted the commission to design the catalogue and advertising for the Kurt Schwitters exhibition at Centre Georges Pompidou in Paris (1994). The parallels between the two men played a part in persuading Gerstner to accept the job; both had founded advertising agencies, were passionate typographers and had successfully oscillated between art and design.

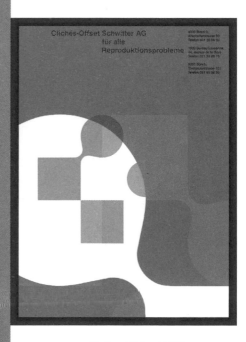

Helmut Schmidt Rhen

Poster, 1974, announcing a group show at the Kunstverein Hannover. Schmidt Rhen designed a typographically arresting identity for this gallery and implemented it on a variety of items, 1972–75.

Karl Gerstner

The identity for the repro firm Schwitter was Gerstner's first. This advert ran for several years. Each time the same plates were used but inked with different combinations of the full colour set to demonstrate the variety of overprints that could be achieved.

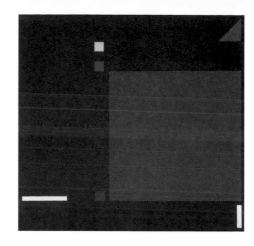

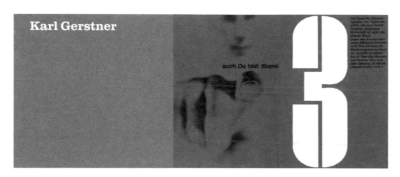

Karl Gerstner

Helmut Schmidt Rhen

Carré Rouge
Acrylic
behind frosted opal glass
34 x 35.3cm
1956–57

Karl Gerstner

A poster advertising Basel's Liberal Party for the elections of 1956. Gerstner's goal was to give the party a strong new image. The party's ballot paper number, used large and combined with an arresting photograph, achieved the desired result.

Geigy chemicals celebrated 200 years of existence in 1958. Gerstner designed all the necessary printed matter including this book, Geigy Today.

01 At the age of 14 – the cruel bloody war was still on – I had to take a decision about my future, which turned out to be a real stroke of luck as for one year I took an introductory art and design course at the Allgemeine Gewerberschule in Basel. After that I was hired by Fritz Bühler for a three-year apprenticeship in his advertising studio. There I met Armin Hofmann, a young designer responsible for 'strong graphics' – ideas expressed in his writing, typography and so on. Besides the practical work in Bühler's studio I was obliged to take complementary courses at the school, where I was instructed by Emil Ruder and learned typesetting – still in the lead epoch.

Hofmann and Ruder were a fruitful pair to whom I'm much obliged. They were leading in the avant-garde and became the main exponents of the Basel School. Hofmann was – and is – a great graphic designer and a teacher recognised worldwide. When he showed me how to design a letterform I learned much more than this. Ruder was a dedicated typographer, with a profound sense of general culture, and always placed his specialist knowledge in its historic context.

Above all Ruder transmitted his enthusiasm for the 'new typography' of the '20s and '30s, showing and explaining Tschichold's and Bauhaus' books. That was the basic orientation of my beginnings.

A few years later I learnt to appreciate the Zurich scene with – among others – Richard P Lohse, Max Bill and the photo-pioneer Hans Finsler. These people were even closer to the Bauhaus tradition – Bill was a student of that school who laid the foundations for so many developments in modern design. Its criteria – concepts instead of decoration, ethical and aesthetic standards, truth to materials – are valid in every creative field. No wonder that Bill was active as an architect, industrial designer, sculptor, painter, typographer and advertising designer – and also an effective politician and theorist. My goal was more modest. I wanted to become a general communication designer and a picture-maker. This double activity, using similar elements for different impact, lasted all my life: making everyday things like works of art and works of art like everyday things.

When my apprenticeship ended I took a modest but highly interesting job in the Basel Museum of Ethnology: redesigning the prehistoric section. Then, in 1949, Max Schmid, an old tutor of the Bühler time, asked me to join him as a freelance designer working for Geigy chemicals, where he had ended up as a one-man design department.

01 I became inadvertently aware of modern graphic design practice when I was a boy. I joined the Jungenschaftsgruppe – a radical boy scout group – and one of the tenets of this free-thinking organisation was the use of all lower case typography.

My interest in modern art also started early when a school friend showed me an album of cigarette cards he was collecting and I was immediately drawn to the ones that showed early twentieth-century paintings. They were quite a revelation and very different to the oil paintings hanging in my parents' house. I began to find out about movements like cubism and the theoretical approaches of artists like Paul Klee.

I partly embraced these ideas because I could see that they represented alternative ways of thinking – in opposition to the political ideas apparent in my youth.

I have always wanted to connect art and design. To me they are interdependent, like day and night. Because of this my role models are Mondrian, Arp, El Lissitzky, Max Bill and, from younger generations, Gerstner, Wolfgang Schmidt and the early Diter Rot. I also very much admired the work of Dutch design practitioners like Hendrik Werkman, Piet Zwart and Willem Sandberg.

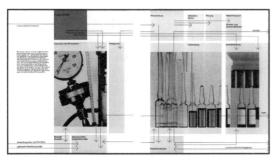

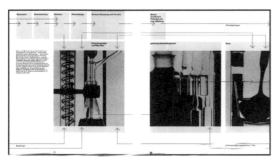

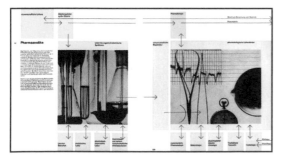

02 Of course I was as happy as everyone else in Switzerland that my country wasn't overrun by Nazis. It would have been a catastrophe, especially for my native city Basel on the border of Germany and occupied France.

Switzerland was mentally reasonably prepared to resist Nazi ideology. In 1939, just before the war, there was a great effort made to organise a national exhibition. This enforced the Swiss identity and helped to strengthen national unity, raising confidence and self-assurance. The end of the war brought not only happiness but also shock when all the Nazi crimes came to light. It's no wonder that this awareness produced a great deal of idealism, among young people in particular. I was 15 and also wanted to contribute enthusiastically towards building a more humane world.

But progressive ideas were not much in demand. The precious coin of the national exhibition showed its less positive side. Switzerland's self-image had become too cosy and nostalgic with a focus on sentimental things that encouraged a kind of protectionist conservatism. Another unexpected threat showed up in the east – communism. Didn't Stalin forbid progressive artists in the same way Hitler did – Kandinsky, Malevich, El Lissitzky and so on?

The post-war years were in many ways very troubling – the cold war followed for decades – and yet the battle for freedom and acceptance also had a positive side: when you fight against something, you sharpen your criteria.

Karl Gerstner

Helmut Schmidt Rhen

One of a series of abstract
and minimal posters
for Leverkusen's museum,
Schloss Morsbroich,
early 1960s.

Karl Gerstner

Schmidt Rhen cites
Gerstner's design of Leser
gesucht für die Zukunft des
Werks/Gebrauchsanweisung
für das Werk der Zukunft as
having a profound impact
upon him. This book with two
beginnings and no end, was
written by Markus Kutter.

02 I became aware of Karl
Gerstner in the late 1950s
because of his newly
designed magazine Werk,
and especially because
of his book Kalte Kunst?
I found it in a bookstore and
used my last Deutschmark
to buy it. I was astonished
by it; the relationship between
the content and the design,
and the fundamentals that
it covered.

I still have that copy – it's
sacred to me because it
marked the beginning of an
awakening for me. I went
on later to admire his and
Kutter's books Die Neue
Grafik and Zukunft des Werks.

I first met Gerstner in 1961.
I lived in Mainz where it was
impossible to find progressive
clients so I drove in my Deux
Chevaux to visit Gerstner in
Basel. My goal was to work
with him and no one else. He
already knew my Morsbroich
posters and liked my work,
so the upshot was that I moved
to Switzerland with my
young family and stayed for
four years.

I remember how impressive
Switzerland was. Germany
had been devastated in the
war, but having been neutral
everything in Switzerland was
intact and seemed luxurious –
the quality of signage and
so on. The possibilities were
thrilling to me; I was very
active producing art in that
period and I got to know lots
of interesting people.

03 These early years were formative.
Looking back I can see a clear
development from the beginning,
but it didn't feel like that at the
time. In a relatively short time I had
established the basic principles of
my future work as a typographer and
graphic designer. But constantly
I was broadening my experience. For
instance I developed the Bauhaus
concept of the grid, making grids
that were less rigid and more flexible
to adapt to the needs of the job.

My typography has always been
strictly related to the purpose, to
the content. It was never formalistic.
I always felt most comfortable
when I was not only the typographer
but also the author. My book of 1957,
Kalte Kunst?, is the first where
I conceived the content and design
in conjunction. It is split into
three parts – history, present and
future – each on a different coloured
paper. The historical part is
divided horizontally into copy and
illustrations, and every spread
is related by theme and so on. There
is unity, which makes the content
as clear as possible for the reader.
Or have a look at the book of Markus
Kutter's writings Leser gesucht für
die Zukunft des Werks also titled
Gebrauchsanweisung für das Werk
der Zukunft. Maybe it's the only book
that not only has two titles but also
two beginnings and no end. It seems
very free, but is based on a strong,
but variable grid.

Whatever I'm doing applies
conclusions arrived at through
logic – in typography as well as in
pictures. If someone asks me where
the emotion resides I like to make
a comparison with music. If you
play a scale on a piano and hear
a dissonance, you can be sure the
interval between notes hasn't
the right oscillations. This can be
expressed in numbers. Numbers
are inherent to perception, even if
there is no dissonance. I call it
precision of perception.

Gerstner himself was quite a difficult person to get to know personally, retaining some distance as an employer. However, when I left GGK, he suggested that we address each other using the more informal 'du'. We went on to stay in contact and he later recommended me as art director for the magazine Capital.

I don't necessarily advocate 'simplicity' – for example the use of elemental geometric forms – as an aim in design. Chairs on which you can sit comfortably, or fonts that you can read well, need much more varied, complex and organic forms.

However, I admired Gerstner's systematic methods and learnt a great deal from him in this respect. This was not competitive in any way – I never tried or wanted to catch up with him! I consider my work to be organised but joyful. Spontaneity alone is not enough. I research and experiment, using theoretical ideas combined with serendipity. The name of my studio, Labor Visuell, reflects my approach. It is a laboratory for the visual arts.

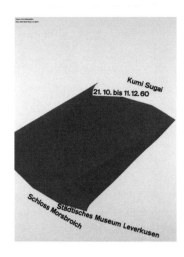

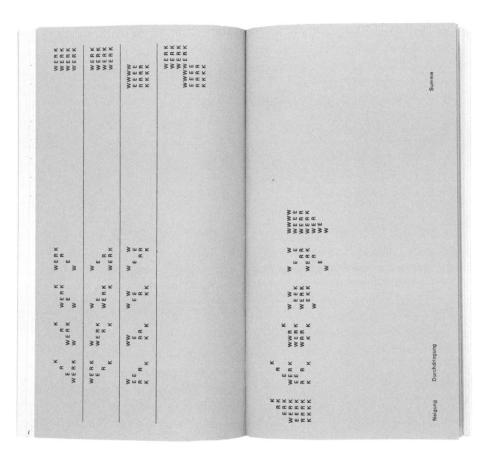

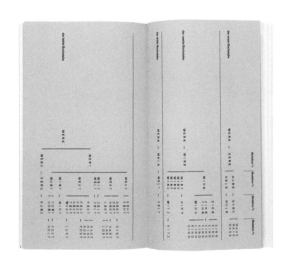

03 Generally I found clients to be trusting, appreciative and understanding of my approach to work. If not, we parted.

Obviously my work as an artist and as a designer has fed into each other. I often used ideas developed for fine art in design solutions. This is a continual process and can happen either way round and then back again. For example, because of my experience using fonts, I developed my Ich-pictures or I-pictures. These were exploring the ideas of the self, the ego, at a time when using 'Ich' too much was considered immodest.

These ideas were later appropriate for a rather provocative campaign I developed for a co-operative bank. The 'Ich' is ambiguous, does it refer to the viewer or the organisation? I was lucky to work with a very courageous promotions manager at the time who supported the idea and so the client was happy to go with it.

Karl Gerstner

04 Apropos Markus Kutter – historian, PR manager and avant-garde novelist – at this time we had a free and inspiring relationship, which in 1959 led us to found the advertising agency Gerstner + Kutter, without knowing anything about advertising.

In this period advertising had a rather bad reputation – above all in Switzerland – and for good reason. In spite of that, or perhaps because of it, I was interested in this new field of activity. Here was something to improve and I was fascinated by these two arts coming together, the visual and the textual. Also I had seen examples from the USA, especially from the early DDB, which convinced me that advertising had indeed the prerequisites of a true art. In the beginning graphic design and typography had been the most crucial elements in our work, but after a short time something became more important: the generation of ideas.

To implement our ideas properly we were more or less obliged to found a photographic department and later even a movie studio. We really wanted to penetrate the whole creative domain and dreamt of becoming a sort of Bauhaus, but as a business, not as a school. In the pursuit of this aim we planned to add an industrial design branch and so we hired an architect – he'd never built a house but was – and is – a pioneer of electronic music. He is one of the most unconventional and thus creative spirits I've ever met: Paul Gredinger, who became the second G of our new name GGK.

In a relatively short space of time the company had grown and was expanding into other countries. The first GGK abroad was in Dusseldorf, where at that time our biggest account by far was with the Ford company.

Ford Germany was, in 1967, in serious trouble and the management had asked permission from Detroit to change agency from JW Thompson – who served Ford worldwide – to our small Swiss agency that nobody there had heard of. After two years of internal fighting the German board who engaged us was changed and we were fired with it. Of course for GGK it was a catastrophe, but still it was a challenging experience.

For me it was the right moment to quit. The bigger GGK grew, the more I transmuted from a designer to a manager – not my hottest vocation. I handed over the business to Gredinger who shaped GGK Dusseldorf into one of the most creative teams. I was happy to have more time for my pictures and continued to make graphic design, but only for projects that I could do on my own.

Helmut Schmidt Rhen

Black and green poster from the campaign for the Bank für Gemeinwirtschaft, 1969–70, which both built on and influenced the Ich-pictures. Shown here are two silk-screened limited edition prints, 1982. Mit Sich Selbst. 45° (left) and Ju's Besorgungen.

Karl Gerstner

Poster and rough from Gerstner + Kutter's first advertising campaign, Rheinbrücke department store, late 1950s.

The Swissair logo, 1978. A typographic solution combined with the Swiss cross in a rhomboid that refers to the tail of a plane.

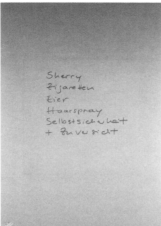

05 The essential basis for cooperation is trust. Mutual respect and understanding make the process easier and more fertile. The smaller the client the more feasible this is. One of our first clients was a German office furniture producer who was not only the owner but also the sales manager responsible for the marketing and advertising budget. Our pleasant partnership lasted for decades. It is a different thing with the big shots. Too many people are invited to express their precious opinions – not so much to improve the advertising concepts, but to demonstrate their unique wisdom.

It's a different situation when you are developing a corporate identity. It's necessary to deal with a number of panels because the top executives are the ones who will have to get behind the new identity.

In the case of Swissair I chose to convince them step by step. Firstly I wanted to get an agreement on my logo proposal. I argued for a typeset logo, instead of the existing drawn logo, and presented a number of alternatives. When the choice was made everybody thought the decision was their own. Secondly I considered the symbol, a more difficult task because the staff loved the old 'arrow wing' they'd grown accustomed to over many years.

The breakthrough came when I proposed rejecting any symbol and replacing it with our national emblem the Swiss cross – which was already used and visually dominated their planes. That was the solution: the Swiss cross in a kind of rhomboid that made a reference to the plane's rudder. This communicated the typical Swiss characteristics of reliability and punctuality much more strongly. Everybody was excited and the arrow wing was forgotten immediately.

Of course there are always accidents and you are defenceless against them. For instance I wanted to paint the planes a glossy dark umbra. The models I presented looked terrific and a large majority opted for this design. But a tiny group was furiously opposed. Someone came up with the argument that the Allegheny Airline once had black planes, called 'flying coffins' by the public. Nobody else had heard of this, but my proposal was dead at once. The fear that this could also happen to Swissair was too great regardless of the validity of the argument.

Am I confident? What should I say? I always had conviction about my work. That helped me to convince others – without luxurious presentations. Maybe I tried more than designers usually do to develop and communicate the rationale for what I did. I never just said how beautiful something was, I always convinced clients using reason. If I made a mistake – and it happened – I didn't argue but just accepted that something went wrong and went back to work.

Karl Gerstner

06 When the PC was invented and marketed by IBM, the company had to address a broader public. The consequence was that their corporate identity needed to be strengthened. This was not only an essential but also an extremely complicated task. IBM cooperated with 75 agencies worldwide and wanted to establish a corporate typeface.

This was at the beginning of the '80s when ITC – the International Typeface Corporation – ruled the typesetting market and strictly guarded copyrights. Although the lead epoch had ended, working with fonts was still in a faraway future.

After some preliminary reflections I made the proposal to design a type especially for IBM. Happily I was commissioned to do it. The result, carefully developed and even registered as IBM original is now known as Gerstner Original and can be used by anyone who wishes to. So what happened?

Concurrently the IBM US mother company had hurriedly made a decision on the corporate font and chosen the classic Bodoni. Unfortunately nobody was aware that Bodoni exists in about 200 different versions, some of them hardly recognisable as Bodoni. The decision was irrevocable. But I was commissioned to do a new job: to make the definitive choice, resolve the copyright problem and produce a manual to clarify usage. IBM generously also made me a gift of my own type design.

Helmut Schmidt Rhen

No 1.12 and 2.12
Acrylic
behind frosted opal glass
both 72 x 60cm
1996

Karl Gerstner

Poster, catalogue cover and spreads for Kurt Schwitters exhibition, Centre Georges Pompidou, Paris, 1994. All items use the typeface Gerstner Original.

Gerstner has always been interested in making art accessible. In the 1960s he organised Poster Art Action. Five hundred signed copies of six artist's prints were displayed, without additional commentary, on advertising hoardings around Zurich for 14 days.

04 Max Bill distinguished between design and art defining them as the production of 'objects for physical versus psychic use', in other words 'objects for practical versus spiritual use'.

Generally I find considering graphic design as distinct from art rather redundant. I would draw one important distinction though, which is that graphic design is aimed at predetermined audiences whilst art is searching for its target groups. However, this shouldn't lead to making presumptuous judgements of either: I like smart advertising better than I like dumb or boring art.

Fine art is very important to me, but writing and reading are as well. It is a totality of more literal and abstract thinking that is vital. Our task as designers and artists is communication. A way to avoid becoming dilettantes is to start being a true amateur (by which I mean the original definition of 'connoisseur') in many disciplines.

07 Graphic design is a matter of solving problems, art is a matter of inventing problems.

08 Graphic design is as important a task as one makes it. Everything can be done consciously and seriously – or not. I confess I'm confused when I look at recent developments. I see the predominance of big brands taking the decisions away from consumers. People are encouraged to buy the latest of everything. Only if they do can they feel integrated into the current social context. Evidently advertising – including graphic design – plays a leading role in this game.

Life has become short-term. If someone creates a new hairstyle I have to hurry to adopt it. If a new mobile phone is introduced I have to have it the next day. I observe this from a distance and I'm worried that it will result in horrendous superficiality. I guess I'm too old to have an objective understanding of this fundamental change in social behaviour. For as long as I remember, I've bought as though it were to last a lifetime, after careful consideration – even clothes.

Of course I'm not blind to the fundamental connections between consumer and producer. There are more people studying and inventing and producing things and somehow the two sides manage to create a kind of equilibrium. I don't know how, it's a wonder to me, but this makes me hopeful that also the art of graphic design – and art itself will have a fair future.

144 : 145
drip-dry shirts
discussion 7

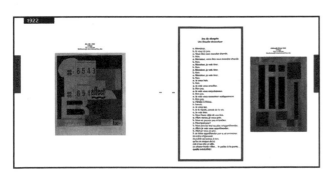

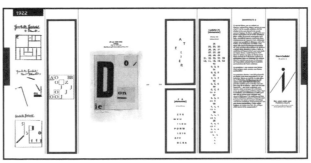

05 When I left school I wanted to train to be an art teacher but my father wanted me to be an apprentice kunstschlosser, an artisan working in metal. It wasn't for me and so I sought an apprenticeship at a publishing house. It was there that I did my first design job, which led many years later to my realising my wish to teach design. I have loved it, working with students, engaging them by explaining my interests in modern thinking.

I always advised my students that there is more than one solution to each problem so avoid comfortable routine. It is important to question yourself continually, why you do something in this way and not another, so that you develop criteria for decision-making. My personal slogan is to have more in the shop than is shown in the window.

Karl Gerstner

09 Becoming part of history – a great ambition in whatever field. Before I guess what the future may bring I'm very busy with the present. Every morning when I wake up I feel how much it is unbelievable chance that I was born and am still alive. There is an obligation to make the best of my existence.

It is true that I have had some recognition as a graphic designer and as an artist. I'm not so ambitious to become famous, but I'm ambitious to make respectable work in both graphic design and picture-making. That's my satisfaction. Of course I'm proud to see my pictures in collections and museums, but this is also a relative pleasure. How many artists have I witnessed at the summit of a splendid career, and how many of them are now totally forgotten, their pictures somewhere in a dark stockroom? Twenty or 30 years later a few of them are rediscovered – and that's how things go on. It's a long, long journey to get a place in history.

10 I only taught for one year, 1955, when I replaced Armin Hofmann who had been offered a chair at Yale. It was just long enough to become aware that teaching was not my gift. I'm very impatient with myself as well as with others – a bad attitude for a professor. In my defence I mention some of my books – among others Designing Programmes and Compendium for Literates – which were quite often useful as educational material.

Helmut Schmidt Rhen

Schmidt Rhen both taught at Fachhochschule Düsseldorf and designed the identity. This poster, 1983, announces a Type Directors Club show.

Karl Gerstner

Cover and spread from the issue of the Basler Zeitung magazine, 1996, honouring Gerstner and his work.

Colour Sound 69a AequiVersion, 1999

Colour Sound 39 IntroVersion, 1975 (initial idea), 1977/78 (realised)

Colour Sound 69 ExtraVersion, 1998

Relief pictures in 12 layers Nitrocellulose lacquers on phenolic resin panels 1190 x 1190mm

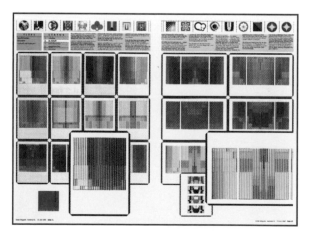

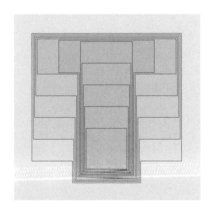

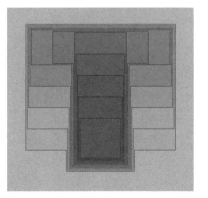

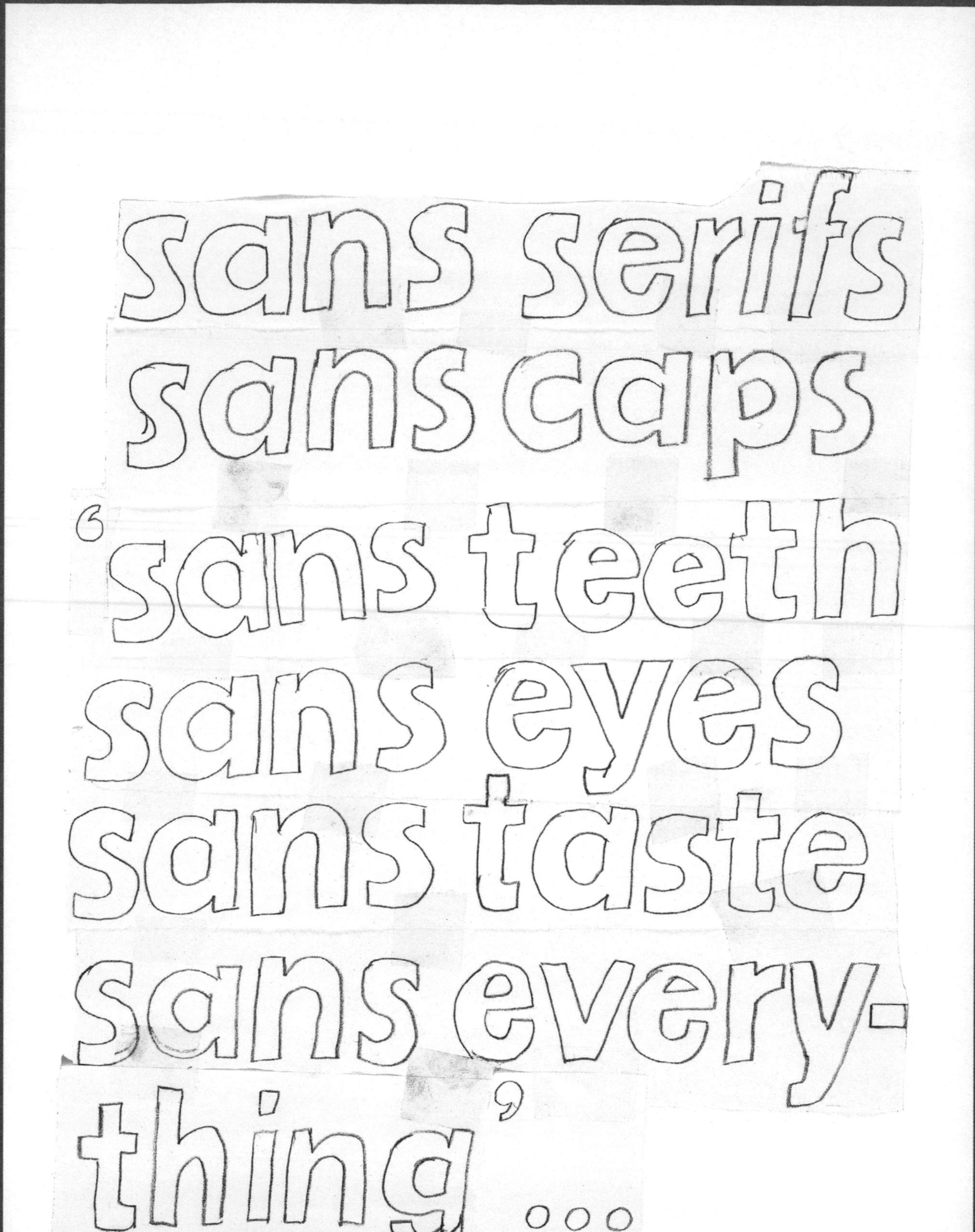

sans serifs
sans caps
'sans teeth
sans eyes
sans taste
sans every-
thing'...

Margaret Calvert
self-portrait
As You Like It
Act II, scene 7, line 167

Kerr Noble

Margaret Calvert

Margaret Calvert
soundtrack

The Beach Boys
Good Vibrations
1966

C

BEAUTY AND THE BEAST

New Swedish Design
18 November 2004–6 February 2005
Crafts Council Gallery. Free Entry.

Crafts Council, 44a Pentonville Road, London N1 9BY
Tuesday to Saturday, 11am–6pm, Sunday 2–6pm
Nearest/Resource Centre / Local Wharfar
Disabled Access. Three minutes from Angel Tube.
Telephone 020 7278 7700 www.craftscouncil.org.uk
The Crafts Council is an educational charity
registered in England 201396 + Help Crafts Council. Come in Exit.

Kerr Noble
biography

Kerr Noble was founded in 1997 by Frith Kerr (born 1973, Surrey) and Amelia Noble (born 1973, London). Kerr studied at Camberwell College of Arts and Noble at Central Saint Martins College of Art and Design before they met at the Royal College of Art (1995–97) where they established their studio.

Margaret Calvert
biography

Margaret Calvert's career encompasses both design and education. Through her long and close association with the Royal College of Art she has been an important link between generations of designers and has played a role in developing emerging graphic design talent for the last four decades. Her work has entered the public consciousness mainly through her collaboration with Jock Kinneir on the design of the signing system for Britain's road signs. The system, despite later modifications, is still in use today.

Born in South Africa in 1936, Calvert came to England in 1950 with her mother and sister. After two years at St Paul's Girls' School, she studied at Chelsea School of Art (1953–57) and then, having started as assistant to Jock Kinneir, attended evening classes in typography at the Central School of Arts and Crafts (1957–58). Kinneir had taught Calvert at Chelsea and initially she assisted in the design of lettering and signs for Gatwick Airport.

In 1958 Jock Kinneir was appointed design consultant to the Anderson Committee set up to advise the Minister of Transport on the design of signs for Britain's new motorways. By 1964 a completely new signing system incorporating the all-purpose roads was implemented.

Significant design factors included lower case sans serif lettering (Transport medium and Transport bold) and colour-coding designating different road classifications. Calvert was mainly responsible for drawing Transport and working out an integral spacing system. She also designed several of the pictorial warning signs including 'men at work' and 'school children crossing'. Kinneir devised the brilliant system, based on the width of the capital 'I', for the diagrammatic layout of the signs. The radical scheme pioneered new standards of consistency and clarity for signing and was influential worldwide.

In 1963 Kinneir Design Associates was established. Individual projects of a more ephemeral nature included a set of adhesive luggage labels and a pack of souvenir playing cards for the P&O Orient Lines, an opera score cover, forms and brochures for Rymans (1963) and a building systems book for the construction company Tersons (1964).

In 1966 they became Kinneir Calvert and Associates, and then in 1972 Kinneir Calvert Tuhill Limited, undertaking major lettering and signing projects for National Health hospitals, British Rail, the British Airports Authority and the Army.

Kerr Noble's work is less defined by a style than their research-driven approach; their inventive interpretation of material is often playful and is characterised by idiosyncratic flair – the imaginative use of image, type and ornament.

Kerr Noble's work has spanned brand and identity design, editorial, exhibition, and interactive design. Their clients include the British Council, Channel 4, Laurence King Publishing, Liberty, Pentagram, Tony Kaye and the Design Museum, London for whom they work regularly designing graphics and exhibitions.

In 2003 they won an Arts Foundation award to develop their self-published magazine Lost But Not Forgotten. They were featured in the recent exhibition Communicate: Independent British Graphic Design since the Sixties held at the Barbican Art Gallery (2004).

Other projects included stamps for the Royal Mail (1970), the signing of Melbourne and Sydney airports, and the design of the large facia sign for the World Trade Centre, Brussels (1972). Calvert also designed lettering for the Tyne and Wear metro in Newcastle, which she subsequently adapted as a typeface for Monotype. Named Calvert it was Monotype's first Lasercomp digitised font (1981). In 1992 Calvert used it to sign the outside of the Royal College of Art. In 1994 she designed A26, a font based on traffic signs, for Fuse.

Since 1966 Calvert has taught at the Royal College of Art where she has held the positions of head of graphic design (1987) and acting course director (1989–91) after the resignation of Derek Birdsall. She was conferred as a senior fellow in 2001.

Calvert has contributed to several publications and broadcasts. Recent exhibitions include Communicate: Independent British Graphic Design since the Sixties, at the Barbican (2004); Designing Modern Life and You are Here, both at the Design Museum, London (2005). She is an honorary fellow of University of the Arts, London (2004) and a member of the Alliance Graphique Internationale.

Kerr Noble

Kerr Noble created the typeface Timber Type for the exhibition Beauty and the Beast: New Swedish Design, at London's Crafts Council in 2004. Inspired by the presence of nature in the Swedish way of life, it was made by hacking into simple shapes and is reminiscent of wood chopped for winter.

Margaret Calvert

As a member of the Alliance Graphique Internationale Calvert was asked to submit a poster, on the theme of a personal portrait of Paris, for inclusion in the exhibition and book celebrating the AGI's fiftieth anniversary, which took place in 2001.

Kerr Noble

01 **breadth of learning/ formative influences**

01/K I studied graphic design at Camberwell. At the time no distinction was made between graphic design, illustration, photography, advertising, fashion... we were interested in the idea of 'communication' and finding different and individual ways of exploring it. With the exception of some visiting lecturers who were designers – such as Scott King and Dirk Van Dooren – we were mainly taught by artists and film-makers.

The mix was very exciting, although initially I was apprehensive. I came from a graphic design orientated foundation course, my father was a graphic designer and I struggled at first to see how what I was being taught added up to what I thought graphic design was. I was bewildered by the lack of teaching 'proper' graphic design, but I was also excited by the potential of what it could be. Darren Lago, who is an artist, taught me in my third year and influenced me a great deal, giving me a new perspective – that still I'm really grateful for.

This set the tone for the work that I was to continue to do at the RCA – research led, conceptual pieces that were often audio-visual. Although there were lots of design groups whose work I liked and respected, I couldn't see where I could fit in when I left college.

Margaret Calvert

01 **art and design training/ breadth of learning/ discovering typography/ formative influences**

Kerr Noble

For the book No More Rules: Graphic Design and Post-modernism, 2003, Kerr Noble designed a typeface based on Neville Brody's font Pop. The result, a serif version of the classic 1980s' face, reflected notions of post-modern graphic design practice.

Margaret Calvert

Early 1960s, range of adhesive labels designed to complement Jock Kinneir's baggage labelling system for P&O Orient Lines.

Calvert scribbled a rough, using the then new felt pens, for the cover of the last edition of the art and design publication Motif, 1967. It was so liked that it was used as the final artwork.

01 My art mistress at school was Winnie Pasmore – the sister of the painter Victor Pasmore. She had been to Chelsea School of Art and so she suggested that I studied there. I was 16 or 17 and knew nothing about London art schools, but Chelsea was fantastic from day one. I was terribly naïve, a real schoolgirl. The other students seemed so sophisticated. The painters looked great with shirts tied round their middles, caked in paint. Some wore flat ballet shoes and black stockings – very bohemian... I was once called a beatnik, because I walked round with a guitar – a classical one – but you couldn't tell the difference really, in its case.

I did the two-year intermediate course first. This was basically a fine-art based foundation course. It included life drawing and anatomy – which I loved. For the first time I organised a series of marks on a sheet of paper and combined them with notations in columns round the drawings. This wasn't about grids or anything like that. It was to make things clear for me – a piece of communication for myself.

If you passed intermediate you were invited into this lovely large staffroom for an interview. In my case the head of illustration, Brian Robb, asked a few questions and then said, 'well, I think you're a born illustrator'. I thought, 'fine, OK'. I'd always drawn as a child, it was my passion, or one of them. It was certainly in me but it had to be encouraged. However, now I know that you're not born to be anything unless you are a genius.

I wasn't totally happy with the illustration course. It seemed far more glamorous to be a painter or sculptor. But the thing about the course that was good was being introduced to all the print media – lithography, etching, lino-cutting – and a designer, Hans Schleger, came in one day a week to give us an insight into graphic design. That was my first contact with someone who worked both for advertising agencies and ran his own design practice. I had immense respect for him – nobody had told us how to go and look and think before. He said ideas come first and don't even think about the typography, just suggest where it could go as that would be done by people who really knew about it.

My parents are both painters and my foundation course was fine-art based, which had a big impact on me. Then at Central Saint Martins I was taught by Phil Baines whose logical, detailed, historical and respectful approach to typography had an enormous influence on me. I started to work typographically and developed a research-based approach prior to going to the RCA – what I developed there was a more experiential dimension to this work.

When I met Frith, and saw the great work she was making, it seemed a perfect opportunity for us to join forces and create our own studio.

I had to look up the word 'typography' in the dictionary. It had a wonderful definition – organising words to get a meaning across. Years later I was teaching it. I would never call myself a typographer, but I always tell students 'you're not going to get anywhere in graphic design unless you have a really sound foundation in typography', which I still believe to be true.

I was disappointed with Chelsea in some respects – it was too laid back in the final two years. I suppose I needed someone to give me a problem. When Jock Kinneir walked into the studio – he replaced Hans Schleger – there was just something about his manner, his directness, which got my attention. He gave us a very simple project to do about Battersea Fun Fair, a cover or something, but it involved lettering, which was a problem – spacing it, deciding how it should relate to the image – it had to be thought out. So I was beginning to think. I just took off from there, really.

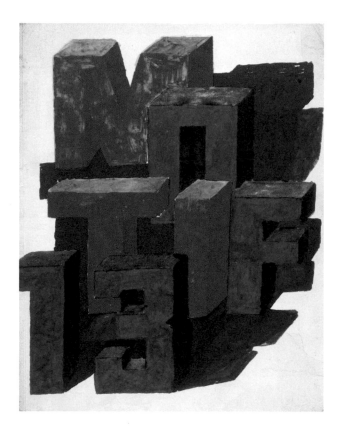

152 : 153
drip-dry shirts
discussion 8

I try to encourage students to be open because some of the key moments in learning come when you least expect them. Going to college is about getting an education – not a job.

I remember one particular project in my third year. I had just started to feel like the experiments I had been doing were coming together when I was asked to do a slide show on 'anything'. Reluctantly I went away and pondered if it was possible to meaningfully answer such a brief. In the process I discovered how beautiful and luminous the projected image is and that my ideas could translate easily to audio-visual. This was a simple discovery, but it was also very thrilling and underpinned much of my work at the RCA.

02 **the relationship of student to working life**

Margaret Calvert

edward samuel and partners chartered architects 23 old burlington street london w1 regent 1742

02 early working life/ Jock Kinneir/ learning typography

edward samuel MA ARIBA AA dipl stella samuel ARIBA AA dipl

Kerr Noble

Report covers, 2001, for TWResearch, a market research agency specialising in media, leisure, youth and cultural trends. To reflect their ideology, a 'world' of characters was developed in collaboration with illustrator Paul Davis.

Margaret Calvert

A hand-rendered letterhead for an architect, early 1960s, demonstrating the influence of the typography classes Calvert had taken at the Central School.

The fishmonger Burkett approached Calvert, having seen her work on the signing of Britain's motorways, asking for an identity that was similarly modern and clean.

My advice to students would be:

Don't pick graphic design thinking it's easy – it's not!

Struggling and failing helps you to develop.

Remember it's a delightfully big field with lots of areas to choose from.

Be prepared to work with people – you can't be too autocratic, but you need to be able to maintain your own personal creative values.

Learn some typographic skills – it is impossible to pretend with type.

It is not a career that will make you rich, but no one ever tells you this!

Document your work continually and thoroughly. I never photographed my Central Saint Martins final show and I regret this. In this industry, people judge you on your projects and experience, rather than qualifications.

02 After Chelsea often the good students went to the Royal College of Art, but I never had the slightest interest in going on. I was in limbo in terms of what to do and was accepted to do a one-year teaching qualification at London University. It wasn't really me. It meant doing things with puppets and so on and no way could I have faced 40 children or whatever.

I remember Jock asking if I would like to work for him, not 'with' because it was an apprenticeship in some respects. I was absolutely over the moon. I asked, 'what does it involve?' and he said 'nothing like you do here, it's design'. Design. He had just got the job to do all the signing for Gatwick Airport. I have kept a copy of my letter to London University saying that I could no longer accept their place.

Next thing I knew I felt like my whole world had fallen apart because he wasn't sure the project was going to happen. It had been delayed or perhaps he got cold feet. I lived in North Ealing then with my mother and sister and I was coming back from Chelsea one day and bumped into him on Ealing Broadway station. I think the shock of seeing me on that platform made him ask if I was still interested in working for him. Of course I said 'yes'. It was 1957.

I went to see him the next day. He explained more of what the work for Gatwick involved. I obviously needed to brush up my typography so I enrolled on an evening class at the Central. Colin Forbes was running things then, but I was taught by George Daulby. He took me to the library and showed me an amazing book that was very thick, quite small, and showed several typefaces all in different sizes. I suddenly realised, 'OK, that's what it's about' – it just got me very excited, the differences, the look, the lot.

We were set a simple design brief, like a compliments slip, organising a few lines of information very beautifully. I just happened to look at what one student was doing with a pencil and wow – 'Oh, so that's typography!' The typographer Anthony Froshaug was also an influence, in a very distant sort of way. I got hooked on working with one size of type – 8pt.

Jock paid me very little but that didn't matter. I was learning. If you are being employed you are there not for yourself, but to make it work for whoever's employing you. The first job I did was to design the front of some Schweppes machines that soft drinks came out of. I was very influenced by painters like Matisse and Picasso. I know this was far removed from that, but I wanted an excuse to put down some colours in a messy seductive way. I had these enormous sheets of newspaper and then offset colours to get lovely overprints and layers. The client seemed to like it and they were all over the West End.

154 : 155
drip-dry shirts
discussion 8

Kerr Noble

03 information design

Margaret Calvert

03 **signing projects/
politics and design/
font design**

Kerr Noble

The delivery of information
need not preclude inventive
design. This London General
Assembly leaflet, 1999,
uses the poem A Description
of London, 1738, to map the
journey down the Thames.

Margaret Calvert

(left to right, top to bottom)
Signing for Heathrow and
Glasgow Airports, the NHS
and the Tyne and Wear metro.
The font Calvert, issued in
1981 and used for the RCA sign
in 1992; the drawing shows
its development. The font
A26, designed for Fuse, 1994.
Signing for Britain's roads,
1960s and '70s, and lettering
for Saint Quentin-en-Yvelines,
France, 1972.

03/K A lot of what we do is
'information design', but the
interpretation and delivery
of the information hopefully
means that we also produce
something beautiful and
thought provoking.

For example, the map
we did for Channel 4. We
were asked to produce
a leaflet listing the details
of sightseeing spots along
a boat trip down the River
Thames. These appear at
the bottom of the piece, but
in addition to that we wanted
to set the journey to a poem
and our investigations led
us to the fantastic poetry
library at the Royal Festival
Hall. We found a magical
description of London in
the eighteenth century and
used the font Caslon, which
was a contemporary of
the poem – with all of its
magnificent flourishes!

03/N Information design is
fascinating because it is
absolutely necessary.
It's about life and people –
the designer has to be
responsive and responsible,
which is an exciting and
challenging prospect.
Information design can be
thought provoking too, a
comment on its surroundings
and function, so signs for
example communicate on
many levels.

03 In 1958 we started work designing
the signs for Britain's roads. It was
an enormous job. We wanted to
keep it minimal, to focus on clarity
and of course costs were important.
The changeover took five years and
the budget was about £22 million.
Our work was first tested on the
Preston bypass, then the M1 and
then we had a further chance of re-
thinking things. After various tests
we wanted to amend the medium
weight of the lettering to increase
legibility. I redrew it with a slightly
larger 'x' height and tightened the
letterspacing, but it was considered
to be less legible than the original.

Generally there was a tremendous
belief in the Government and
in the various departments and
institutions commissioning
British design. I was in my element
designing for the public at large.
It's a tremendous responsibility to
get it right.

Signs should be functional and
beautiful, appropriate and
economical. I think in the end as
much creativity and innovation
can be applied to working on signs
as a magazine cover or whatever.

For years I wasn't particularly
associated with road signs. Then
Jock was approached by Channel 4.
A very enlightened producer
wanted to do an arts programme
on typography and asked Jock
to talk about the road signs.

It was called Signals. Jock was
60 then and wanted to pull
the blind down on graphic design –
to concentrate on more personal
projects – so I did the programme.
I was head of graphic design then
at the Royal College of Art. I think
the students were quite impressed.
Jock once said, 'signs are round
your neck for life Margaret' so he's
left the legacy to me to handle!
Jock died in 1994.

We worked internationally on
signing projects too. In 1972 we were
commissioned to produce a report
on visual communications for a new
town in France, Saint Quentin-en-
Yvelines. I designed some seriffed
lettering for the project but it was
considered too English. I thought
this was a rather nice criticism so we
then used it for signing on the Tyne
and Wear metro in Newcastle. It
seemed appropriate in a very richly
endowed town, architecturally – we
didn't want to use another sans serif
face. I worked on various weights
and Monotype issued it as a font in
1981, called Calvert. I would never
have chosen that name. The sign for
the Royal College is designed by me
and uses it. Then in 1994 I designed
A26, a font based on the traffic signs,
for Neville Brody's experimental
digital typography project Fuse.
The name is the best thing about it!

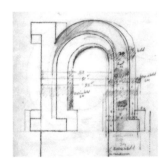

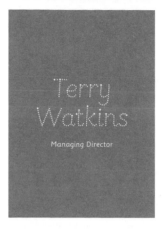
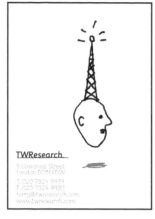
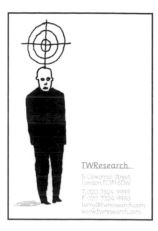

Margaret Calvert

04 Compromise can make something better, but I think clients have to be challenged. I did a job for a multi-storey building systems company in the '60s. The entire setting was in 8pt Univers – it only looked good at that size. The fine-line architectural drawings were beautiful. It was set in hot metal and proofed, and then the client decided that the type wasn't big enough. It was all changed to 9pt. I said it would look hideous, need more pages and would throw the whole balance out. The setting came back and of course it looked terrible. Only after a tremendous amount of persuasion did the printer agree to reset it.

I advise students to find a client with whom they can build up a relationship. You've got to be interested in that client and their problems and their work. The ideal is to develop your approach through working with the right clients. They educate you and you educate them and if you've got a bastard, and there are several, don't get involved. Graphic design is a team effort and that includes the client.

This is the difference between a fine artist and a designer. Somebody comes to you with a problem to solve. Every job has constraints whether it's the budget or the audience or a plot of land or a road or whatever, but constraints should be a springboard for your ideas. You can have more fun with limitations, don't you think? Establishing constraints gives you many more possibilities. Like a grid does. It is ultimately order out of chaos. It's quite nice to turn it the other way round of course, chaos out of order. I do think if you've been thinking in straight lines then you need to start seeing some curves, metaphorically speaking.

Kerr Noble

At TWResearch each person receives a set of 12 business cards, two of a set are shown, designed in 2001. Handing these out becomes a more bespoke experience as individuals decide which of Paul Davis's characters is most appropriate.

Margaret Calvert

Calendar, 1971, for a design competition. The light of the day changed the length of the shadows, denoting the passing of time.

A spread from the book for Terson's, 1964. After some persuasion Calvert's restrained typography was retained.

Convincing some clients to trust our instincts is not always easy and takes time. People commission us for our way of thinking because we don't have a repeatable 'style' to our work. Our work is concept driven so we do a great deal of investigating before we even start to design. A successful project for us combines high quality research, ideas and design.

Tony Kaye never wanted to see our portfolio. He rang one day in 1999 and said he wanted to meet us, Phil Baines had recommended us and so he didn't need to see any work, he just wanted to talk to us. We've been working for him ever since.

Being female is not really an issue in the same way that it was – not now that we are a bit older and have a good portfolio of work. We've shown that we can make interesting work, and this is all that matters.

05 The bigger we got the more we had to get jobs that would last two years at least. We rarely had quick turnover jobs, and of course we did live in times when designers were paid retainers. Both the British Airports Authority and British Rail paid us retainers so that we would give their work priority. You were paid your hours on top of that – a very good arrangement.

As a woman working in graphic design you were hardly acknowledged. Jock always made sure that I was credited. The first real acknowledgement came in Derek Birdsall's book 17 Designers London in 1963. By '64 things had changed. We got busier and busier and took on more people to help. At that time I said that I should be on the letterhead. So we became Kinneir Calvert and Associates.

Now I quite like to call myself an independent designer. I don't like the word freelance.

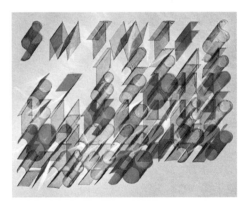

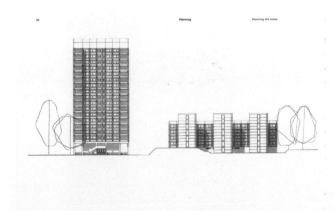

I think of Margaret as a perfectionist. I knew of her as a good tutor prior to going to the RCA, so I was thrilled to discover she was to be my personal tutor there.

My first impression was that she was interested in people and life. She is very open and this is what makes her a good teacher. Lots of people can teach technique, but teaching ways to think is what is important. Margaret shared her experiences with us – as a pupil, designer, tutor – and shared stories about past students, which were fascinating and useful to hear about.

Her advice to us has always been to be yourself and do it your own way as she has done. Margaret loves to mimic people's mannerisms – her own, her colleagues, friends... I'd love to know how she mimics us two goody-two-shoes!

Margaret Calvert

06 When I was aged 29 I thought I knew it all, but when I started teaching I was destabilised – in a good way. I was probably just 30 then and some of the students were older than me. The problem with teaching of course is that as I have grown older they've stayed the same age, but the fact that we're all alive at the same time, and share common interests, makes the difference in age inconsequential, I like to think.

I was at a crossroads after Jock retired. I was teaching two days a week by then and the rector of the Royal College, Jocelyn Stevens, called me in and I became more involved. Two years later I ended up running the graphic design department.

The Royal College is very competitive for students. They're always in a critical arena, having to prove themselves, it's very difficult for them. I do try to think of myself at their age, when I first went to Chelsea. I was treated as someone, by people I thought were very famous and I had great respect for. I like to encourage everybody to have the confidence to be who they are, but they must be interested in what they're doing.

Art school is a playground to explore possibilities, make connections and be creative. As a tutor you're there to encourage and inspire and to give an informed opinion based on experience. I think I've always been a natural rebel, questioning things. You could get really bored in institutions if you become repetitive. I don't like platitudes. I don't like settled cosiness, particularly in education.

Margaret Calvert

Calvert's contribution to the exhibition organised by Pentagram, 2004, to celebrate the artistic potential of an everyday communication tool, the ballpoint pen.

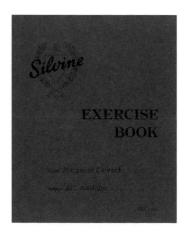

I will always remember going to Margaret's house for lunch on a Friday – leaving the studio at 12.30 and saying to our work colleagues that we'll be back in a couple of hours, but six hours later calling to tell them to go home!

Although Margaret wasn't my personal tutor at the RCA, I used to join her weekly crits and would enjoy talking to her in the studio – she always seemed to have time for you. I thought she was smart, funny – and sassy! She taught me about the importance of detail and encouraged our conceptual approach to design.

In some ways one could say that graphic design is not a very important part of life because it is seen as a transient, throw-away commodity. On the other hand, because graphic design – in all its many forms – is everywhere, then really it should be great, inspiring, funny, meaningful and challenging: it should intelligently reflect the world it is a part of – even if it is only a bus ticket, a sign, or a paper bag.

The significance of graphic design for us lies in its potential to deliver messages with character and difference to an increasingly visually homogenised world. We can improve people's quality of life through graphic design, if we care to do so.

07 I've never thought I was important. Honestly not. If I'd thought that, I couldn't enjoy myself. I couldn't enjoy my relationship with the students. I've also never felt envy for my peers although I've certainly admired different approaches to mine. I would say that I have never felt totally confident, I struggle with every project, but occasionally I like what I've done, in retrospect.

08 As such graphic design is not important, but it's become my life. It's a way of being, discovering who you are and believing in yourself. It's a confidence thing. When work becomes too easy or too facile you're in a rut and you have to change things. The idea that you get better towards the end, it's not true. You can do your best work on the very first job. As you get older, you compete against yourself because you don't want to get up in the morning and bore yourself.

I'm now extremely selfish in terms of work. I am invited to do this or that. Not commercial projects, not paid. That's my luxury now. I do not do work for money. I do not want to repeat myself. I think Alan Fletcher said that graphic designers don't just disappear or stop, they fade away. I like to think that I'm one of those blank sheets of paper in a magic painting book where you get a brush, wet it and see what happens.

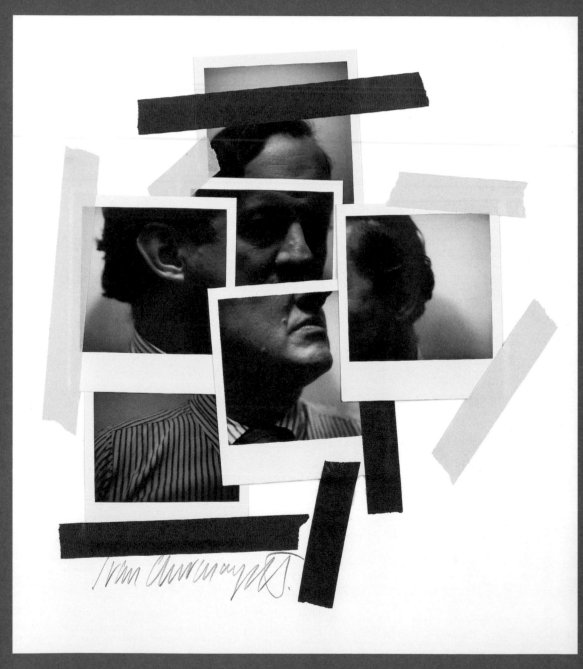

Ivan Chermayeff
self-portrait

Dirk Fütterer

Ivan Chermayeff

Ivan Chermayeff
soundtrack

Igor Stravinsky
L'Histoire du Soldat

Dirk Fütterer
biography

Dirk Fütterer (born 1967, Dinslaken, Germany) attended the University of Essen, Germany (1989–96) where he studied under Professor Dr Heinz Kroehl and Professor Dr Norbert Bolz. He worked as a freelance designer (1991–96) at companies including Claus Koch CC and Verb, and independently for clients such as Biochemisches Institut, Zurich and Morphosys, Munich before joining Büro Hamburg (1996–98).

Ivan Chermayeff
biography

Ivan Chermayeff is an imposing figure in American graphic design; designer, artist and illustrator, he is a founding principal of one of America's leading practices Chermayeff & Geismar Inc, and has been responsible for many of the most recognisable and enduring corporate identities of the last five decades. Intelligent and professional, Chermayeff's approach to design is pragmatic and based upon clarity and common sense; yet what makes his work memorable is the poetic relationships he conjures with words, images and meanings to create resonant visual communication.

Born in London in 1932, son of Serge Chermayeff the distinguished architect, Ivan Chermayeff grew up in a rich cultural environment, surrounded by art and artists. A young man of confidence and conviction he began his studies at Harvard, but left after two years to study graphic design at the Institute of Design in Chicago. In the mid-1950s he joined the School of Art and Architecture at Yale University where he met Thomas Geismar. After graduating Chermayeff worked as an assistant to Alvin Lustig and designed record covers for CBS before setting up in business with Robert Brownjohn and Thomas Geismar in 1957.

Brownjohn, Chermayeff & Geismar Associates produced work that reflected their shared knowledge of typography, art history and visual culture through bold, intelligent manipulation of image and symbol. Significantly the group chose to describe themselves as a design 'office' rather than a studio, a clear indication of their business-like approach. Their work included book jackets and record covers and the United States pavilion at the Brussels World's Fair (1958), where they represented the American urban landscape through an ambitious three-dimensional typographic environment. In 1960 Brownjohn moved to England and the company reformed as Chermayeff & Geismar Associates later to become Chermayeff & Geismar Inc. In 2005 the firm metamorphosed again into Chermayeff & Geismar Studio where the pair continue their practise of graphic design and identity consulting and also pursue more personal interests in art and design.

In 1998 he became senior designer at Chermayeff & Geismar Inc where he worked for clients including Siemens, AT&T and the Shinsegae Department Stores, Seoul. He left in 2000 to become design director at Enterprise IG, New York where his projects included the corporate identity for Ford Motor Company, Spencer Stuart and DuPont Textile & Interiors.

In 2003 Fütterer founded his own design studio in Dusseldorf. Based in Berlin since 2004, Fütterer:id specialises in identity design and allows Fütterer the independence to accept smaller challenging commissions alongside his work for larger companies and corporations. He is motivated by the desire to communicate content through original ideas and fresh thinking; an approach he also applies to his teaching. Since 2004 he has been professor of typography at the University of Applied Sciences in Bielefeld, Germany.

Fütterer has been an associated partner of Chermayeff & Geismar Inc, a member of WestWord Group, Chicago and a partner of Logo Projektagentur, Dortmund. He has won awards from the Art Director's Club, New York (2000) and Critique magazine, having won the Troisdorfer picture book award (2000), the Finest Books award from Stiftung Buchkunst and a Certificate of Design Excellence from the Print European Design Annual (1997).

Chermayeff & Geismar placed their emphasis on problem solving and clarity of communication. They gained widespread recognition for their comprehensive corporate design scheme for Chase Manhattan Bank (1960), the abstract logo they designed becoming an influential prototype for corporate symbol design. They planned, designed and supervised the corporate graphic programmes for multinational companies ranging from Mobil Oil (1964) and Xerox (1965), to the Museum of Modern Art, New York (1970) and Time Warner (1990). Allowing each solution to evolve from its problem their work has included everything from logos, annual reports and posters to aeroplanes, T-shirts and television titles. They have designed important and innovative exhibitions including US government pavilions at Expo '67 in Montreal and Expo '70 in Osaka, and the Nation of Nations exhibition for the Smithsonian Institution (1976).

Chermayeff's illustration work has included advertisements and posters for the Public Broadcasting System and the Museum of Modern Art, New York. A respected artist, Chermayeff's playful graphic collages have been exhibited throughout the United States, Europe and Japan.

Chermayeff is a member of the Industrial Designers Society of America, the Alliance Graphique Internationale and is a former president of the American Institute of Graphic Arts. He has served as the Andrew Carnegie Visiting Professor of Art at Cooper Union and is a Benjamin Franklin Fellow of the Royal Society of Arts. He was a trustee of the Museum of Modern Art for 20 years and has received numerous awards and accolades, among them gold medals from the American Institute of Graphic Arts (1979) and the Society of Illustrators (2002).

Dirk Fütterer

Front and back catalogue cover for the stock black-and-white photography library Ibid. Fütterer worked on the identity whilst at Chermayeff & Geismar, 1999–2000.

Ivan Chermayeff

Illustration for the New York Times after the 9/11 attacks in 2001.

Ivan Chermayeff

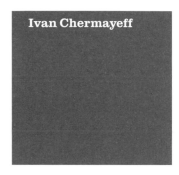

**01 Serge Chermayeff,
architect and father/
early career choices**

**02 breadth of learning/
diverse college experiences/
design mentors/
collaboration**

Dirk Fütterer

Identity for Eli's, 'probably
the grocery store with
the highest quality foods
in Manhattan', 1998–99.
Fütterer worked on this
project whilst at Chermayeff
& Geismar, using a typeface
that resembled handwriting
'to convey the idea of
absolute freshness, like a
European marketstand'.

Ivan Chermayeff

Book cover, 1957 and dance
festival poster, 1993. Almost
40 years apart but both
demonstrate Chermayeff's
immense flexibility and
ability to achieve maximum
impact through an economy
of means.

01 My life is about seeing. Learning
how to see and learning that
seeing is something that has to
be learned. It's partly a matter of
talent but mostly it's a matter of
looking. My father could see pretty
well and was articulate and very,
very supportive of anything I or my
brother Peter wanted to do. He
always encouraged us.

I was brought up surrounded
by artists. My father's friends were
artists, writers, poets, creative
people. They were around constantly
and always introducing me to new
things and new thoughts. It was
very heady, very exhausting, very
argumentative and very stimulating.

Despite my father being an
architect I didn't want to work in
this field. It requires tremendous
patience and a lot of good luck
and leads to an enormous amount
of disappointment. As a graphic
designer you work on 100 projects
in a year and 95 of them are
actually produced. In architecture
you work on four projects and
maybe one is produced. There's
also a tremendous amount of
up-front work in architecture before
you get to the creative end of it.

At the age of about 16 or so I wanted
to be a designer. That doesn't
mean that I knew what one was,
but I felt that there was the
possibility of having more control
working in visual communication
than architecture as it's a direct
response to a prescribed need.

02 I learned more from looking than
from classes or school really,
and more from artists than from
anyone else – Klee, Miro, Picasso;
the great contemporary artists of
our time and the twentieth century.

I did all kinds of stuff as a designer
at high school; the yearbook,
literary magazines. I even put my
hand to calligraphy when I was a
freshman, doing all the diplomas for
Harvard University and the Law
School. At 50 cents a piece, it was a
very good way to make some money!
I left Harvard after two years as
they had never heard of design, and
went to the Institute of Design in
Chicago. I spent two years there. In
terms of exposure and knowledge
I was ahead of people my own age.
All the people I was really close to
were older than I was and graduated
and moved on whilst I was there,
so I too left and went to Yale, which
was great. Yale gave me a fellowship,
so that was helpful, and it was
only the second year that design
was taught there.

01 I was most impressed by the designers that I met during my time studying at the Universität Essen, in Germany. People like Adrian Frutiger, Hans-Rudolf Lutz, Steff Geissbühler (principal at Chermayeff & Geismar), April Greiman, Gert Dumbar and David Carson. I had been under the impression that applied art was somewhat inferior to 'real art'. These encounters with some design heroes made me realise that design could be a real art form in its own right.

As a student I strived to be a 'good' designer. The idea of working for mediocre agencies and boring clients seemed unbearable. I was very impressed by Steff Geissbühler's lecture and I imagined how it would be to work for a company like Chermayeff & Geismar one day. At that time it was more like a dream, I was lacking the self-assurance that I could survive in such an environment.

02 Two or more good minds with a common goal can change the world. If you find partners like that, marry them, or at least chain them to your office and keep the partnership for the rest of your life! But it can be difficult to find as most good designers like to work freely on their own because in a team you have to compromise. Many are not open-minded and self-assured enough to become good team players.

I had already had a summer job with the graphic designer Alvin Lustig before I went to Yale. He was very important to me because of the opportunities he gave me. My design mentors include Müller-Brockmann; I would consider him one of my fathers and the same with Paul Rand. I felt as close to Ikko Tanaka as anybody else that I can think of too. I just found his work to be very close to that which my own hands could produce. My Japanese is zero and his English is zero but we became friends. We would meet and have lunch, taking along somebody else to help translate. We'd send each other everything that we did: books, articles, this and that.

Of course Tom Geismar and I are both very sympathetic to each other. We don't do the same work, we don't have the same hand, but we sure like and understand the same things, whether it's graphic design or movies or art. We have been partners for damn near 50 years. That's a long time. Most married couples don't spend as much time together as partners do. He's here right now in the next room. We are both very much believers in the co-operative nature of design. It's not just about doing your thing, it's a matter of solving problems efficiently and intelligently, and that requires different attitudes and minds.

TOWAARD A SANE NUCLEAR POLICY

Dirk Fütterer

03 In 1998 I started as a senior designer at Chermayeff & Geismar. I had read and heard a lot about Ivan but I hadn't met him before and although I liked him from the start, I was a bit intimidated by his experience. I had never worked with anybody who had been in the design business that long. As a student I was under the impression that any designer over 60 must be retired or dead!

I owe him a lot. He destroyed my former appreciation of hip styles and cool surfaces. He made me realise that design without an idea is in most cases arbitrary and meaningless. Ivan's notion of design seemed warm, likeable, emotional and human; this was a contrast to a great deal of work that I suddenly recognised as mechanical and shallow.

Although he appreciated my German obsession for details, Ivan was always interested in the big idea, the big picture. He shocked me once or twice by telling me to stop fooling around endlessly with minor details that could only be seen by a designer with a magnifying glass. Ivan looked at design from the perspective of an artist, not a craftsman.

Ivan Chermayeff

03 I was at Yale for just a year and worked for Alvin Lustig for a few months afterwards, before starting the office with Robert Brownjohn, whom I'd known for a long time. He was a little older than Tom Geismar and I, who were classmates at Yale. Tom was in the army, I wasn't, so Brownjohn and I started with the understanding that Tom would join us when he got out of his service.

We had the very beginnings of our office and we did whatever we could to survive. We'd swap our services with other people to avoid paying bills. So we'd design a letterhead for our doctor or our lawyer, we'd do business cards for this person or that, little invitations or announcements and so on. We turned out dozens.

Brownjohn had worked with George Nelson, I had worked with Lustig. I had also worked at Columbia records and so between us we had various connections.

I inherited a client from Lustig for example. I used to work on this project for Lustig which was for a little brush company. The man who owned the company was an enthusiast about it. I used to have lunch with him three times a week at the bar at the Ambassador Hotel. I was his surrogate family. He was a self-made Jewish man who was intense and terrific. He put his older brothers and sisters through college and never went himself. He had decided to promote his company well and had come to Lustig when I worked there. I happened to be the one put in charge of this unimportant little client. Later on, after Lustig had died, it became my job.

I had also worked for Edward Larabee Barnes, the American architect. He had a connection to Pan American World Airways and was doing the standards for their ticket offices. He didn't know anything about graphic design so I was working there in his office, helping on that side of things. But my major contribution to the whole thing was proposing that they call themselves Pan Am. That saved my salary many thousands of times over. At say 50 dollars to produce each letter, the difference when you have ticket offices the world over really comes to something. Anyway Pan Am became a client of ours later too.

Dirk Fütterer

Identity designed whilst at Chermayeff & Geismar for South Korean department store chain Shinsegae, 1999. The target audience was mostly women 'apparently many men never find the time to leave their desks'.

Ivan Chermayeff

Menu covers, inaugural Pan American World Airways flight of the Boeing 747, 1958. Pan Am became a long-term client – one of Chermayeff's major contributions having been his suggestion that they shorten their name.

Ivan and I worked on the identity for Shinsegae, the Korean department store chain. The design process was relatively intuitive. Ivan didn't think much of a strategic approach to design and didn't believe that focus groups and so on inevitably lead to good solutions.

He judged everything using common sense and was an advocate of pragmatic, straightforward, honest and sometimes even undiplomatic communication. It became clear to me that good visual communication does not need to be explained by a lot of words.

Because of my prior connection to Columbia we also did dozens of record album covers, usually re-released recordings using whatever we could find to generate imagery. We were paid nothing to speak of. But we had the time and didn't have a lot of people to worry about on the payroll. We were learning. There's a lot to be said for learning on your feet. I had to be resourceful. Making images as collages, quick and fast – it was visually very entertaining, exciting stuff. That's what we started doing.

I didn't worry about whether it was going to work or not. It worked successfully, probably because of the broadness of what we do. It goes back to connections. We do a lot of work with architects partly because of my upbringing. I have an interest in art and artists – they're part of my circle. This gives me a connection to the creative world, which makes new connections possible and these generate new opportunities. Our profession is different all the time, which is what's stimulating about it.

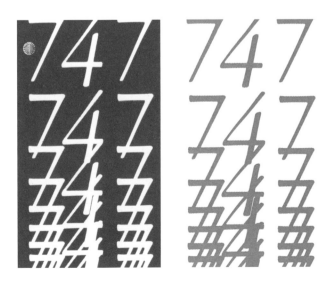

Dirk Fütterer

04 Ivan was uncompromising and unwavering when he presented our work. He did not accept any foul compromise when marketing people tried to interfere. This proved to me that good design is rarely the result of a democratic process. These lessons influence my way of thinking still today.

Chance connections have been important to my success, although most of them cannot be related to lucky circumstances alone. I tend to think that the more active you are, the greater the chance that at some point you will be at the right place at the right time.

04 **compromise/
making connections**

Ivan Chermayeff

04 **affinity with clients/
making good work/
long standing clients**

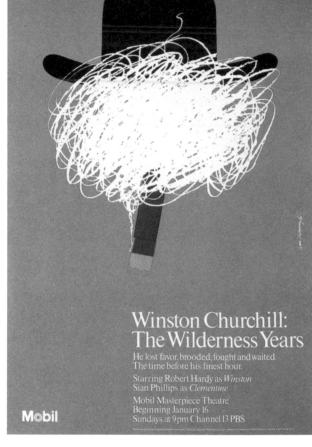

Dirk Fütterer

In 2003 Fütterer founded his own design studio Fütterer:id. The identity system for Wilo, an international manufacturer of pumping systems, has clarity and rigour and took two years to develop and implement.

Ivan Chermayeff

Chermayeff & Geismar were consultants to Mobil for 38 years, designing all manner of literature, their forecourts and the logo, with its distinctive red 'o' seen here in three-dimensional form. Mobil also sponsored a series of television screenings, for which Chermayeff designed an extraordinarily broad range of posters throughout the 1970s and '80s.

Onc of the things that we usually had was six, seven or eight clients who really wanted good work. I mentioned before the guy with the brush company, Joe Schick. He was a marvellous and supportive person, he loved what I did and encouraged and criticised properly. It makes all the difference: clients who respect you and admire your work. These relationships can make you want to work harder.

I was on the board of an insurance company. You can imagine how much I might know about that, but anyway I was. This wasn't because I was expected to pay attention to all the figures, but because they also had communication problems and every once in a while I would make a contribution about this that they valued.

Graphic design as we think of it is a reasonably long-term proposition. Our clients have been with us sometimes for decades. Mobil, for example, despite having 25 designers on their staff chose us as their consultants for 38 years, before Exxon swallowed them.

170 : 171
drip-dry shirts
discussion 9

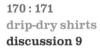

Dirk Fütterer

05 About 15 years ago the
introduction of the computer
seemed to threaten everything
dear and holy to the design
community. It's true that a lot
of people started to work as
designers who had never
heard of any design rules nor
understood the concept of
good typography. But can
we really talk about a general
decrease in design standards?
Can we really say that in
general in the '60s there were
higher design standards
than today?

To my mind there's more
good design today than there
was ever before. Because
of technology, a lot of good
designers produce a lot more
good design in much shorter
time. However, the opposite
is true too. There's also more
mediocre and bad design
than ever before, because
of technology. I would
guess that the ratio between
good and bad design stays
relatively constant over time.

Ivan Chermayeff

Dirk Fütterer

Fütterer worked on the
identity for the black-and-
white stock photography
library Ibid. whilst at
Chermayeff & Geismar,
1999–2000.

Ivan Chermayeff

Chermayeff is clear that
'graphic design's not art'.
However, his design and
illustration skills are
multifarious as these record
covers for Gramavision,
1989–90, demonstrate.

Ibid. colour cover,
showing Chermayeff's
later development of
the identity.

05 Graphic design's not art. Somebody
else may determine it's art, but that's
after the fact. You're not making
art. It very rarely turns out to be art,
it sometimes does, and that's just
fine, but it's beside the point. It is
however just as important as art.
This is not about elevating art – most
art is terrible. The great is great and
the rest? Well, bad art isn't even art.
In my opinion, it's nothing and the
same goes for most design.

Design solves a need. Somebody
who gets out an old can of
paint and writes 'used tires' on
an old board and hangs it up has
a communications need. It's a
real need, and this kind of solution
is often really direct and intelligent.
It's usually done at a size that's
legible and readable, it uses contrast
like white on black or black on
white, there's nothing cute and
personal and stupid about it, it's just
there. That's most of what design is
all about, cutting the crap aside,
slicing off the gangrene and getting
down to common sense.

An inordinate amount of time
is spent in design defining what
the task is and working on the
conceptual end to make it more
interesting than just writing 'used
tires'. Making it rich and interesting.
But making it rich and interesting
and irrelevant is stupid, which is
an awful lot of what goes on. You
often have to redefine the problem
because it's very rare to get a brief
that's entirely thought through and
accurate and appropriate. If it were
everybody would be a designer and
they wouldn't need us. Even now
clients hardly know that they need
us sometimes. We put some order in
the chaos of communication and
make a strong and memorable visual
connection with people. One that is
appropriate to whatever the product
is and to whoever is the audience.

06 I opened my own office in 2003. In the first year my goal was to survive. In the second we moved to Berlin and my goal was to maintain design standards, no matter how desperately we needed business. Now it is time to remember why I initially wanted to be a designer. I need to think more about our profile and become a bit more selective about new projects.

I think my professional ambitions are now what they were when I was working for Chermayeff & Geismar: I would like to be a designer who is good at what he does. I am positive that this is an achievable goal.

In this business you cannot make money a priority because you would have to compromise on quality – good design takes time and time is money. I still believe in the romantic idea that a designer will become successful sooner or later just by doing good work consistently over time. This is very hard to do, but a good and solid reputation always pays off in the long run because the best contacts and most of the really good jobs come by referral anyway.

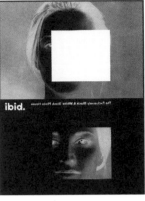

172 : 173
drip-dry shirts
discussion 9

06 After working for more than 50 years one knows a hell of a lot about how things get done. I was lucky enough to start at a certain time when things were open and there were economic possibilities. By the '70s and '80s, we'd been working for a long time and were spoilt by having a reputation.

The technology has kind of messed it up a bit now so graphic design has some challenging problems. Computers speed things up, obviously, but they don't make design any better. I generally think that real excellence has dropped in the last decade, not increased. I think it will increase again, but it will take a long time. Now, when a little company decides they want a newsletter, they hire a kid and buy a computer program. They don't have to do it properly, so the result is acceptable but ordinary. This goes on everywhere you look. Europe, Japan, everywhere. There's also a lot of excellence of course, but as a percentage of the grund total of things I don't think it's greater, it's probably less.

07 Naturally there were periods that were slower. It's busy again now for example, but you know for many years before that it was pretty quiet for everybody. In Britain, here, France, everywhere. It was pretty slow. But we didn't let anybody go or move to a smaller office. It was just tighter. We made less money. But we've never been in the business of making money as a priority. I'm comfortable, I'm not complaining. But if money-making had been a priority we would have been less discriminating about our work and probably better off. But we never cared about that and we still don't. All we want to do is pay the rent and bring up our children and our grandchildren. That's all.

08 I am only ambitious to do good work. I'm never satisfied, if that's what ambition means, yes. I am.

Alan Fletcher is one of my colleagues that I admire tremendously. We've been pals for 40 odd years now. Massimo Vignelli too, we're all about the same vintage. He doesn't turn out anything terrible ever. Sure, from time to time we have run up against good people who are after the same opportunity. Massimo, for example, is a competitor every once in a while. It's good to have creative people around who are competitors, I see it as a blessing, not a problem.

Dirk Fütterer

07 Today I get bored easily by design that is all about surface and not about content or ideas. As a professor this is what I ask my students to remember and I too am working hard to meet these standards.

It might sound a bit strange, but I am not generally interested in graphic design in itself anymore. It is ideas and concepts that fascinate me and of course graphic design is a fantastic means of expressing these visually. Everybody knows that one image can say more than 1,000 words, this means that a graphic designer can have power and influence. Every graphic designer hopes to accomplish something, some day – I always wanted to do something relevant with my life.

I do believe that you have to live and suffer for it to create something relevant. Personally I like graphic design that satisfies cultural needs, that entertains and inspires, that surprises you and makes you think, that stimulates communication, that changes the way we look at things and that changes our world.

Ivan Chermayeff

09 Way back in 1959 before Brownjohn went to London, we did a little booklet for fun, about words, playing with words. It was done over one weekend and was reprinted in Typographica by Herbert Spencer. Well, it has sort of re-emerged. There has recently been a major exhibition of our work at Cooper Union, a big school here. We were digging around for some old things and we came up with this booklet. We decided to reprint it to give away to every visitor to the exhibition. We hadn't looked at it in 45 years, but it's great. An art director in a publishing company who came to the show remembered the book, it had been instrumental in his deciding to be a designer. So, now it's being re-published this fall, this Christmas by Chronicle Books. We did it 45 years ago and it's coming back out and it still looks pretty fresh, I must say. It doesn't look like an old thing at all.

Ivan Chermayeff
Brownjohn, Chermayeff & Geismar came up with this little book, Watching Words Move, 1959. It was published as an insert in an issue of Typographica. A recent reprint, to give away at a Chermayeff & Geismar exhibition, attracted a publisher and 45 years on it is to be re-published.

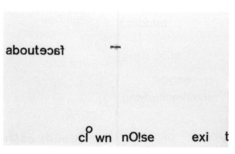

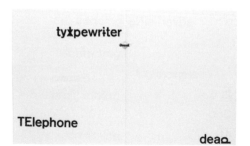

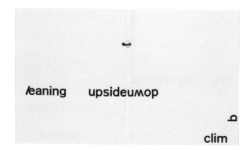

08 Don't do it if you want to become rich – there are many easier ways to accomplish that. Don't do it because you think it is cool – it is not cool to work like a chicken with its head cut off to meet crazy deadlines. Don't do it if you are very sensitive – you will get hurt, because literally everybody has an opinion on graphic design.

Do it if you're curious about anything in life – you will get in touch with weird people and strange things. Do it if you have something to say – if you're lucky, you might get heard. Do it if you like to make yourself and others feel good – you might improve or sometimes even save lives.

And never trust your teacher! This was good advice that I got from Gert Dumbar when I was a student.

10 Graphic design is not heart surgery. In the grand scheme of things it's a pretty small contribution, but I think it can make people think and maybe help them along. It is all about content and ideas and can be part of conveying important messages.

It's consuming and all that but it's not all-consuming. There are other things, I've got three daughters and a son, and work has never got in the way with them. I also think it's extremely important to be culturally aware, going to see movies and theatre, and what other creative people are up to in lots of different spheres. Tomorrow 500,000 orange banners are being unfurled in Central Park. It's the biggest single artwork that this city has ever known. They've spent 20 million dollars putting it together and it has taken the artist Christo and his wife Jeanne-Claude 25 years to make it happen. Thinking of it is cool, it really is. So obviously I'm going to see it from whatever perspective I can when it's unfurled.

11 We really like the young people who have run through our office, some have been with us for a long, long time. We have associates, we have partners who have been with us for decades, we've had people come and go. We enjoy what we get from them and hopefully we give as much back. We believe that two good minds with a common goal are much better than one.

My advice to anyone starting out is work hard, don't believe everything you're told and be open to new things. When you see things that can be changed for the better, do it when you can and be very selective about what you work on and who you work with and for.

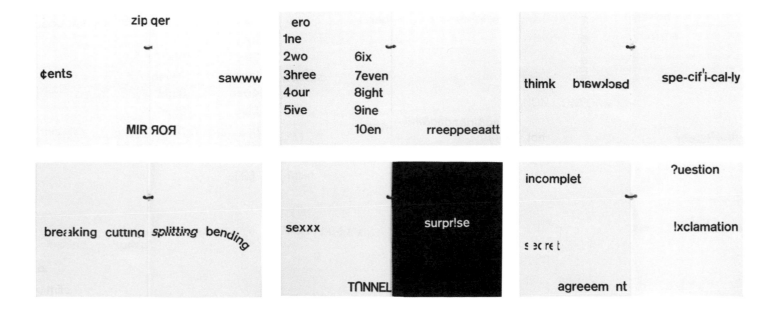

The following **reference section** is made up of an in-depth **timeline** and **index**. If you want to know what our contributors were reading, listening to or sitting on in the period 1945–69 then the first place to look is the **timeline**. Intended to give a flavour of any given year, it highlights events of varying significance from the assassination of John F Kennedy to the invention of Velcro.

The **index** will help you navigate the rest of the book; if you are trying to find a particular reference this is the place to start.

The section closes with **contributor biographies**, **image credits** and some very sincere **thank yous**.

››› commissioned for **Drip-dry shirts** by Lucienne Roberts

››› written + designed by Kelvyn Laurence Smith co-written + edited by Rebecca Wright

››› **Smith's timeline** of twentieth-century influences on visual communication + culture, 1945–69

››› **Introduction**
The primary intention of this timeline is to reinforce the cultural and historical context of the book in which it proudly sits. It is offered as a starting point for reference + research rather than a comprehensive or definitive document but – despite many conflicting sources – every attempt has been made to be precise with the information + accurate with the dates.

The entries are designed to represent an overview of the given year – each entry is relative + therefore often of varying value. The selections made are of course subjective, but reference has been made to most of the important graphic design practitioners of the period. Their work epitomises the significant qualities underlying graphic design of the mid to late twentieth century. Less significant undertakings and events are scattered alongside these pioneering happenings to portray the full spectrum of achievement + innovation of the period.

Smith's timeline is not necessarily something that is understood immediately – perhaps more of a layered chronicle that the reader can refer + return to over time.

››› **Architects, artists, designers + printers:** the death of the previous generation of pioneers

››› **The international style: European modernism**

››› **The New York School: America + émigrés**

››› **The festival style + British modernism:**

››› **Publishing: books, journals + magazines**

››› **Corporate identity: logos + trademarks**

››› **Typeface design:**

››› **Record sleeve design:**

››› **Image-making: illustration + conceptual image**

››› **Photography:**

››› **Education: mentors + philosophical giants**

››› **Architecture:**

››› **Art: sculpture, painting, collage + installation**

››› **Cinema:**

››› **3D design: industrial, interior + product**

››› **Literature: fiction, non-fiction + poetry**

››› **Music: jazz, avant-garde, rock + pop**

››› **Happenings: influential cultural occurrences**

››› **Invention: technological development + process**

››› **World events: global influences + politics**

››› **Significant deaths: influential figures**

45	46	47
Kathy Kollwitz: dies **Edwin Lutyens:** dies **Hendrik N Werkman:** dies	**László Moholy-Nagy:** dies **Paul Nash:** dies	**Pierre Bonnard:** dies **Frederick W Goudy:** dies
Max Bill: USA Baut poster **Josef Müller-Brockmann:** Jedermann Hermès ad **Hendrik N Werkman:** The Next Call book	**Max Huber:** Arte exhibition poster **Max Huber + Ezio Bonini:** Sirenella poster **Richard P Lohse:** Poetes à l'Ecart book jacket	**Donald Brun:** Balkamp egg-brandy poster **Max Huber:** Triennale di Milano poster **Josef Müller-Brockmann:** The Forest exhibition
Will Burtin: art director, Fortune magazine **Alvin Lustig:** New Directions book jackets **Alexey Brodovitch:** Ballet book	**Lester Beall:** Fortune 33 magazine cover **Lou Dorfsman:** joins CBS as staff designer **Paul Rand:** Knopf + Vintage book covers	**Paul Rand:** Disney Hat ads **Bradbury Thompson:** begins Westvaco Inspirations **Bradbury Thompson:** Mademoiselle + Art News
Tom Eckersley: Don't be an Absentee poster **Abram Games:** Commando Medical Service poster **Stanley Morison:** editor, Times Literary Supplement	**Abram Games:** Displaced Persons poster **Ashley Havinden:** Britain Can Make It poster **Ashley Havinden:** Simpson Daks ad	**Abram Games:** Olympic Games poster **Walter Tracy:** head of type development, Linotype **Jan Tschichold:** Penguin Composition Rules
J Entenza + W Smith: Arts + Architecture magazine **Gio Ponti:** founds Lo Stile journal **Oliver Simon:** Introduction to Typography	**R Harling + J Shand:** Alphabet + Image **Paul Rand:** Thoughts on Design **Peter Ray:** Designers in Britain (volume 1)	**Ray Eames:** Art + Architecture covers **Georgy Kepes:** Language of Vision **László Moholy-Nagy:** Visions in Motion
Barnett Freedman: Ealing Studios **Herbert Leupin:** Panteen AG **Richard P Lohse:** Escher Wyss	**Eugen + Max Lenz:** Falken Verlag **George Nelson + Irving Harper:** Herman Miller M **Hans Neuberg:** Voetroflex	**Hans Hartman:** Gerüst GmbH **Marcello Nizzoli:** Olivetti **Jan Tschichold:** Penguin Books
Jan van Krimpen: Spectrum **Imre Reiner:** Stradivarius **Bradbury Thompson:** Monalphabet	**Frederick W Goudy:** Goudy Thirty **Eugen + Max Lenz:** Profil **A Overbeek:** Studio	**Roger Excoffon:** art consultant, Fonderie Olive **Jan van Krimpen:** De Roos **Hermann Zapf:** art director, Stempel
David Stone Martin: art director, Asch Records **David Stone Martin:** Mary Lou Williams Trio **Meggs:** Songs by the Dinning Sisters	**Jim Flora:** Kid Ory and his Creole Jazz Band **Alexis Steinweiss:** Joseph Szigeti: Prokofiev **Alexis Steinweiss:** Music of Jerome Kern	**Robert Jones:** Boogie Woogie **George Maas:** Bebop: Keynote Album 140 **Alexis Steinweiss:** Beethoven: Concerto
Mervyn Peake: Capt Slaughterboard . . . book **Paul Rand:** Coronet Brandy ad campaign **Luigi Veronese:** Biblioteca Cinematografica cover	**Dick Elfers:** Defensible Democracy poster **Frank R Paul:** City of the Future **Ettore Sottsass Jr:** Cocktails recipe book	**Edward Bawden:** The Arabs book **John Minton:** Treasure Island book **George Salter:** Tower of Babel book jacket
Yevgeny A Tschaldey: The Reichstag **Shoji Ueda:** Schoolgirls **Weegee:** New York Crowd	**M Bourke-White:** Mahatma Gandhi . . . **Cosette Harcourt:** Edith Piaf **Arnold Newman:** Igor Stravinsky	**Berenice Abbott:** Designer's Window . . . **Werner Bischof:** Rural Tavern, Puszta **Ernst Haas:** Homecoming Prisoners
Josef Albers: professor, Black Mountain College **Gyorgy Kepes:** professor of visual design, MIT	**Herbert Bayer:** professor of design, Aspen Institute **Ernst Keller:** tutor, Kunstgewerbeschule, Zurich **Inge Scholl:** founds Volkshochschule, Ulm	**Abram Games:** tutor, RCA, London **S Rhodes:** founds Cartoonist + Illustrators School, NY **E Ruder + A Hofmann:** join Basel School of Design
Marcel Breuer: The Tompkins House **Charles + Ray Eames:** (CSH #08) **W Smith:** begins Case Study House Program (CSH)	**Arne Jacobson:** Youth Dwellings **Richard Neutra:** Kaufmann House **Mies van der Rohe:** Farnsworth House	**Alvar Aalto:** Baker House dormitory at MIT **Hassan Fathy:** Gourna Village **Richard Neutra:** Bailey House (CSH #20)
Jean Dubuffet: Couple in Grey **Ben Shahn:** Death on the Beach **Yves Tanguy:** The Rapidity of Sleep	**Barbara Hepworth:** Pelagos **Giorgio Morandi:** Still Life **Wols:** The Blue Pomegranate	**Alberto Giacometti:** Man Pointing **Eduardo Paolozzi:** I was a Rich Man's Plaything **Jackson Pollock:** Full Fathom Five
Marcel Carné: Les Enfant du Paradis **David Lean:** Brief Encounter **Billy Wilder:** The Lost Weekend	**Frank Capra:** It's a Wonderful Life **Howard Hawks:** The Big Sleep **David Lean:** Great Expectations	**Edward Dmytryk:** Crossfire **Elia Kazan:** Gentleman's Agreement **Carol Reed:** Odd Man Out
Corradino d'Ascanio: Vespa **Isamu Noguchi:** Coffee Table IN_50 **Sixten Sason:** Electrolux vacuum cleaner	**Ben Bowden:** Bicycle of the Future **Charles + Ray Eames:** Plywood chair **Raymond Loewy:** Scenicruiser bus	**Charles + Ray Eames:** Plywood table **Isamu Noguchi:** Chess table **Gio Ponti:** La Pavoni coffee machine
George Orwell: Animal Farm **Bertrand Russell:** A History of Western Philosophy **Evelyn Waugh:** Brideshead Revisited	**Simone de Beauvoir:** Tous les Hommes sont Mortels **Eugene O'Neill:** The Iceman Cometh **Dr Spock:** The Common Sense Book of Baby . . .	**Saul Bellow:** The Victim **Anne Frank:** The Diary of Anne Frank **Thomas Mann:** Doktor Faustus
Benjamin Britten: Peter Grimes **Lionel Hampton:** All-American Award Concert **Woody Herman:** The Thundering Herds	**Billy Eckstine + Orchestra:** Billy Eckstine **Duke Ellington + Orchestra:** At His Very Best **Igor Stravinsky:** Concerto in D	**Louis Armstrong:** Louis Armstrong's Hot 5 **Charlie Parker:** Bird Lives – Dial Masters **Sarah Vaughan:** Sassy Sings
UK: BBC introduces The Light Programme **UK:** Blackout ends **Tennessee Williams:** Glass Menagerie first staged	**Winston Churchill:** Iron Curtain speech **Charles Eames:** MOMA one-man show **V&A Museum:** Britain Can Make It exhibition	**Rudolf Bing:** first Edinburgh Festival **Christian Dior:** New Look in fashion **Chuck Yeager:** first supersonic flight
P Le Baron Spencer: microwave oven **Vannevar Bush:** develops hypermedia theory	**Ladislao Biro:** Biro pen launched (UK) **IBM:** ENIAC: first digital computer **Earl S Tupper:** Tupperware (released)	**Dennis Gabor:** Holograph **Edwin Land:** Polaroid instant film introduced **US:** scientists discover plutonium fission
Europe: WW2 ends **US:** drops atomic bombs on Hiroshima + Nagasaki **US:** Harry S Truman becomes president	**Charles de Gaulle:** resigns as president of France **Europe:** Nuremberg War Trials **US:** United Nations opens in New York	**Europe:** Marshall Plan: US pledge $20bn relief **India:** obtains independence from British rule **Pakistan:** splits from India
Adolf Hitler: dies **David Lloyd George:** dies **Franklin D Roosevelt:** dies	**John Logie Baird:** dies **John Maynard Keynes:** dies **HG Wells:** dies	**Ettore Bugatti:** dies **Al Capone:** dies **Henry Ford:** dies

48	49	50
Morris Fuller Benton: dies **Joost Schmidt:** dies **Kurt Schwitters:** dies	**James Ensor:** dies **William Nicholson:** dies	**Max Beckman:** dies **Eliel Saarinen:** dies **Karel Teige:** dies
W Dangerter + W Marti: Meyer + Co stationery **Max Huber:** Gran premio dell Autodrome poster **Herbert Matter:** Knoll Chair ads	**Max Bill:** Die Gute Form exhibition **Richard P Lohse:** Bauen + Wohnen magazine covers **Carlo Vivarelli:** For the Aged / Elderly poster	**Franco Grignani:** Bellezza d'Italia magazine cover **Max Huber:** Arbiter + Jazztime magazine covers **Siegfried Odermatt:** opens Zurich studio
Lester Beall: art director, Scope magazine **Alvin Lustig:** Anatomy for Interior Designers cover **Herbert Matter:** Fortune magazine covers	**Doyle Dane Bernbach:** forms **Alvin Lustig:** Invitation: An Exhibition of his Work **Paul Rand:** No Way Out film poster	**Herbert Bayer:** CCA: Great Ideas of Western Man ads **Giovanni Pintori:** art director, Olivetti **Paul Rand:** Weintraub + Co, Morse code ad
Abram Games: United Nations Day poster **Abram Games:** Festival of Britain 4d stamp **FHK Henrion:** founds Studio H	**Anthony Froshaug:** Beltane School forms **Anthony Froshaug:** Faust invitation card **Jan Tschichold:** C Day Lewis, Penguin Poets series	**Misha Black (DRU):** Courage + Co visual identity **Tom Eckersley:** Graphis 31 cover **Imre Reiner:** Typographica 2 cover
Will Burtin: Test tube cover, Scope magazine **Le Corbusier:** publishes Modulor 1 + 2 **Ray Eames:** Herman Miller graphics	**Alec Davis:** Design magazine launched **Hans Schmoller:** joins Penguin Books **Herbert Spencer:** Typographica launched	**Alexey Brodovitch:** Portfolio magazine launched **Edgar Kaufmann Jr:** What is Modern Design? **Ladislav Sutnar:** Catalog Design Progress
Abram Games: Festival of Britain **FHK Henrion:** National Blood Transfusion Service **Hans Schleger:** W Raven Co Ltd	**Erberto Carboni:** Italian Radio **Louis Danziger:** Flax Art Supplies **Helmut Salden:** Van Oorschot	**Ian Bradbury:** Brook Photography Ltd **Charles Loupot:** Nicolas **Hans Neuburg:** W Oertli AG
Dick Dooijes + Stafan Schlesinger: Rondo **Georg Trump:** Forum I **Hermann Zapf:** Palatino	**Alessandro Butti + Aldo Novarese:** Normandia **Jan van Krimpen:** Romanée Italic **Oldrich Menhart:** Monument	**Oldrich Menhart:** Parlament **Bradbury Thompson:** alphabet 26 **Hermann Zapf:** Michelangelo
Jim Amos: Duchin plays Tchaikovsky **Guidi:** Cocktail Capers **Alexis Steinweiss:** develops paperboard LP cover	**Jim Flora:** Jimmy Dorsey: Dixie by Dorsey **Robert Jones:** Doris Day: You're My Thrill **Robert Jones:** Frankie Carle: At the Piano	**George Maas:** Haydn **David Stone Martin:** Bird + Diz **Alexis Steinweiss:** Music of George Gershwin
Henri Matisse: Nice tourist office poster **George Salter:** Doctor Faustus book jacket **George Salter:** Joseph + his Brothers book jacket	**Alvin Lustig:** 3 Tragedies book **George Salter:** The Lonely book jacket **Raymond Savignac:** Monsavon poster	**Charles M Schulz:** Peanuts cartoon strip **Saul Steinberg:** American Fabrics magazine cover **Henryk Tomaszewski:** Cryk poster
Robert Capa: Pablo Picasso + his son Claude .... **Henri Cartier-Bresson:** Pakistan **Bert Hardy:** Gorbals Boys	**Bill Brandt:** Underwear Fashion **Robert Doisneau:** La Dernière Valse ... **George Rodger:** Sudan, The Nubas	**Robert Doisneau:** Le Baiser de l'Hotel de Ville **W Eugene Smith:** The Wake **Otto Steinert:** Pedestrian's Foot, Paris
Anthony Froshaug: tutor, Central School, London **Richard Guyatt:** head of school of graphic arts, RCA **Berthold Wolpe:** tutor, Camberwell School of Art	**Edward Bawden:** tutor, Banff Art School, Canada **Jacqueline Casey + Ralph Coburn:** tutors, MIT **Herbert Spencer:** tutor, Cental School, London	**Otl Aicher:** co-founds Institute of Design, Ulm **Josef Albers:** director of graphic design, Yale **FHK Henrion:** tutor, Royal College of Art, London
Alvar Aalto: Everett Moore Baker House **Charles Eames + E Saarinen:** (CSH #09) **Kemper Nomland + KN Jr:** (CSH #10)	**Buckminster Fuller:** Geodesic Dome **Philip Johnson:** Glass House **William Levitt:** Lake Success, Levittown	**Walter Gropius:** Harvard Graduate Centre **Mies van der Rohe:** Farnsworth House **Raphael Soriano:** Shulman House
l'Art brut + CoBrA: groups founded **André Masson:** Landscape with Precipices **Jackson Pollock:** Action Painting	**Henry Moore:** Family Group **Barnett Newman:** Onement III **Jackson Pollock:** Number 2	**Franz Kline:** Chief **Willem de Kooning:** Excavation **Barnett Newman:** Tundra
Howard Hawks: Red River **M Powell + E Pressburger:** The Red Shoes **Vittorio De Sica:** Bicycle Thieves	**Henry Cornelius:** Passport to Pimlico **Carol Reed:** The Third Man **King Vidor:** The Fountainhead	**Akira Kurosawa:** Stray Dog **Joseph Mankiewicz:** All About Eve **Billy Wilder:** Sunset Boulevard
Unknown: Prestige 65 pressure cooker **Ferdinand Porsche:** Porsche 356 **Eero Saarinen:** Womb chair	**H Blomberg +:** Ericofon **George Nelson:** Tray table for Herman Miller **Harvey Schwarz:** Deccalia gramophone	**Harry Bertoia:** Wire Mesh chair for Knoll **Robin Day:** 661 dining chair for S Hille + Co **Charles + Ray Eames:** Plastic DAR side + armchair
Truman Capote: Other Voices, Other Rooms **Norman Mailer:** The Naked + the Dead **Jean-Paul Sartre:** What is Literature?	**Simone de Beauvoir:** The Second Sex **Arthur Miller:** Death of a Salesman **George Orwell:** Nineteen Eighty-Four	**Graham Greene:** The Third Man **Jack Kerouac:** The Town + The City **Ezra Pound:** Seventy Cantos
Charlie Parker: Complete Benedetti Recordings **Charlie Parker:** The Savoy Recordings **Igor Stravinsky:** The Rake's Progress	**Miles Davis:** Birth of The Cool **Dizzy Gillespie + his Orchestra:** Ol' Man ReBop **Olivier Messiaen:** Modes of Durations + Intensities	**Jean Barraqué:** Séquence **Morton Feldman:** Projections **Oscar Peterson:** Oscar Peterson at Carnegie
Aldeburgh: music festival founded **London:** Olympics **MOMA:** Competition for Low-cost Furniture Design	**MOMA:** Modern Art in Your Life + Good Design **US:** first non-stop flight around the world **Andy Warhol:** graduates	**Lumitype:** launches phototypesetting machine **MOMA:** Design for Modern Use: Made in the USA **Xerox:** first copying machine
L Fender: electric guitar **Peter Goldmark:** 33 1/3 LP record **Haloid Co:** Xerox: Model A	**UK:** manufacture plutonium **US:** test ejector seats **US:** Columbia + RCA produce 7-inch vinylite records	**UK:** BBC transmit first overseas live TV broadcast **US:** introduce credit cards **US:** berkelium, the ninety-third element discovered
Israel: established as an independent state **South Africa:** apartheid begins **US:** Harry S Truman becomes president	**China:** declared People's Republic **Europe:** East Germany created **NATO:** established	**India:** declares itself a republic **UK + US:** send troops to Korea **US:** Senator McCarthy begins communist witch hunt
Sergei Eisenstein: dies **Mahatma Gandhi:** dies **DW Griffith:** dies	**Malcolm Campbell:** dies **Margaret Mitchell:** dies **Richard Strauss:** dies	**George Orwell:** dies **George Bernard Shaw:** dies **Kurt Weill:** dies

51	52	53
››› **Esther Bensusan Pissarro:** dies	**Paul Eluard:** dies	**Raoul Dufy:** dies
		Francis Picabia: dies
		Vladimir Tatlin: dies
››› **Kenneth D Haak:** New York Times poster	**Josef Müller-Brockmann:** Zurich Met Police ads	**Herbert Bayer:** World Geographic Atlas for CCA
Josef Müller-Brockmann: Hermès ads	**Siegfried Odermatt:** Linol-druck ad	**Richard P Lohse:** New Design in Exhibitions book
Josef Müller-Brockmann: Tonhalle concert poster	**Anton Stankowski:** Lorenz baut ad	**Josef Müller-Brockmann:** Automobil-Club posters
››› **Lester Beall:** Diameter (April issue) magazine cover	**Aaron Burns:** director, The Composing Room	**Gene Federico:** Go Out: Woman's Day mag ad
William Golden: creative director, CBS	**Alvin Lustig:** Perspective quarterly magazine	**James K Fogleman:** defines term corporate identity
Allen Hurlburt: designer, Weintraub Agency	**Otto Storch:** art director, McCall's magazine	**Robert M Jones:** establishes Glad Hand Press
››› **Phillip Boydell:** Festival Titling typeface for FoB	**Milner Gray (DRU):** Gilbey house-style + identity	**C Forbes, P Wildbur + H Bartram:** form FWB
FHK Henrion: Agriculture + Country pavilions at FoB	**Milner Gray (DRU):** Tate + Lyle house-style	**Abram Games:** British Aluminium ads
E McKnight Kauffer: To England poster	**Herbert Spencer:** Design in Business Printing book	**Abram Games:** Capstan poster
››› **Walter Allner:** Fortune magazine cover	**Max Bill:** Form book	**Marcel Duchamp:** Dada exhibition catalogue
Alexey Brodovitch: Harper's Bazaar + Portfolio mags	**S Chwast, R Ruffins + E Sorel:** Push Pin Almanac	**Eric Gill:** Essay on Typography (reissue)
Eugen Gomringer: Constellation poems	**Walter Herdeg:** Graphis Annual	**Paul Klee:** Pedagogical Sketchbook (UK)
››› **James K Fogleman:** CIBA	**Rudolf Bircher:** Swiss Air	**Abram Games:** Danish Bacon Co Ltd
William Golden: CBS eye	**Milner Gray (DRU):** Tate + Lyle	**Milner Gray (DRU):** Council of Industrial Design
Jan Tschichold: Typographische Monatsblätter	**Hans Schleger:** MacFisheries	**Art Paul:** Playboy Bunny
››› **Roger Excoffon:** Banco	**Alessandro Butti + Aldo Novarese:** Microgramma	**Roger Excoffon:** Choc + Mistral
Aldo Novarese: Augustea	**Jan van Krimpen:** Spectrum	**Adrian Frutiger:** Phoebus
Hermann Zapf: Sistina	**Hermann Zapf:** Melior + Saphir	**Paul Renner:** Topic
››› **Rudolph de Harak:** Benny Goodman…	**Rudolph de Harak:** Harry James…	**Rudolph de Harak:** Liszt: Sonata in B Minor
Eric Nitsche: Szymanowski: Violin Concerto	**Rudolph de Harak:** Strauss Waltzes…	**Robert Jones:** art director, RCA records
Eric Nitsche: Wagner: Arias + Monologues	**Eric Nitsche:** Richard Strauss: Ein Heldenleben	**Eric Nitsche:** Weber: Sonata No 1
››› **Olle Eksell:** Graphis cover	**Edward Bawden:** mural for Canadian Pacific Line	**E McKnight Kauffer:** CCA magazine ad
Hank Ketcham: Dennis the Menace comic strip	**Abram Games:** See Britain by Train poster	**Giovanni Pintori:** Olivetti poster
Leslie Wood: The Little Red Engine goes to Town book	**Herbert Leupin:** Trix poster	**Tadeusz Trepkowski:** Nie! poster
››› **Emmy Andriesse:** Fashion Designer + Model	**Henri Cartier-Bresson:** Decisive Moment	**Cecil Beaton:** Elizabeth II's Coronation
Ernst Haas: London	**John Deakin:** Francis Bacon	**Robert Doisneau:** Les Chiens de la Chapelle
Franz Hubmann: Alberto Giacometti	**Willy Ronis:** Le Petit Parisien, Mai	**Elliot Erwitt:** New York City
››› **Max Bill:** director, Hochschule für Gestaltung, Ulm	**Jesse Collins:** tutor, Central School, London	**M Bill + T Maldonado:** introduce modernism, Ulm
Muriel Cooper: design director, MIT design services	**Herbert Matter:** professor of photography, Yale	**Nigel Henderson:** photography tutor, Central School
Alvin Lustig: develops graphic design dept, Yale	**Henryk Tomaszewski:** tutor, Warsaw Academy	**Edward Wright:** typography tutor, Central School
››› **CH Aslin:** Hertfordshire schools	**Marcel Breuer:** Ceasar Cottage	**Sven Markelius:** Vällingby Urban Development
FHK Henrion: Festival of Britain pavilions	**Le Corbusier:** Unité d'Habitation, Marseilles	**Eero Saarinen:** GM Technical Centre
Powell + Moya: Skylon + Churchill Estate	**Craig Ellwood:** (CSH #16)	**Peter Womersley:** Farnley Hey
››› **Salvador Dali:** Christ of St John of the Cross	**Independent Group:** formed	**Henri Matisse:** The Snail
Adolph Gottlieb: The Frozen Sounds No 1	**Henry Moore:** King + Queen	**Henry Moore:** Internal + External Forms
Stanley William Hayter: Sun Dance	**Nicolas de Staël:** Countryside	**Mark Tobey:** Edge of August
››› **Elia Kazan:** A Streetcar Named Desire	**Stanley Donen:** Singin' in the Rain	**Yasujiro Ozu:** Tokyo Story
Akira Kurosawa: Rashomon	**Akira Kurosawa:** Ikiru	**George Stevens:** Shane
Vincent Minnelli: An American in Paris	**Fred Zinnemann:** High Noon	**Fred Zinnemann:** From Here to Eternity
››› **Charles + Ray Eames:** Surfboard elliptical table	**Harry Bertoia:** No 22 Diamond chair	**Charles + Ray Eames:** Hang-It-All
Charles + Ray Eames: Wire Mesh chair	**Robin Day:** S Hille + Co: Lounger armchair	**Gio Ponti:** Serie B bathroom range
Edwin Land: Polaroid Land camera	**Arne Jacobson:** Ant / Myren chair	**Dieter Rams:** designer, Braun AG
››› **Samuel Beckett:** Malloy	**Samuel Beckett:** Waiting for Godot	**Kingsley Amis:** Lucky Jim
Marshall McLuhan: The Mechanical Bride	**Ray Bradbury:** The Illustrated Man	**William Burroughs:** Junkie
JD Salinger: Catcher in the Rye	**Ralph Ellison:** Invisible Man	**Arthur Miller:** The Crucible
››› **Chet Atkins:** Chet Atkins' workshop	**John Cage:** 4'33"	**Miles Davis:** Volume 2
Benjamin Britten: Billy Budd	**Nat King Cole:** The Unforgettable Nat King Cole	**Leadbelly:** Leadbelly's Last Sessions
Karlheinz Stockhausen: Crossplay	**Hank Williams:** Moanin' the Blues	**Annunzio Paolo Mantovani:** Strauss Waltzes
››› **Europe:** AGI forms	**Helsinki:** Olympics	**Dr John H Gibbon:** first open heart surgery
UK: Festival of Britain	**Rocky Marciano:** wins heavyweight boxing title	**Hillary + Norgay (Tenzing):** climb Everest
US: first Abstract Expressionist show in New York	**Princess Elizabeth:** becomes Queen Elizabeth II	**ICA:** Parallels of Life + Art exhibition
››› **US:** CBS broadcast experimental colour images	**Photon:** phototypesetting machines developed	**Francis Crick + James Watson:** discover DNA
US: first electric power produced from atomic energy	**R Robinson + E Schittler:** develop first tranquiliser	**US:** introduce colour TV
US: UNIVAC 1 first commercial computer	**M Ventris + J Chadwick:** decipher Linear B script	**US:** DuPont introduce polyester
››› **UK:** troops seize Suez Canal zone	**Jordan:** Prince Hussein becomes king	**Egypt:** becomes a republic
UK: Winston Churchill re-elected prime minister	**UK:** first atomic bomb tests off Australia	**Korea:** war ends
US: Harry Truman signs Peace Treaty ending WWII	**US:** first hydrogen bomb tests in Pacific Ocean	**US:** Dwight D Eisenhower becomes president
››› **William Randolf Hearst:** dies	**King George VI:** dies	**Joseph Stalin:** dies
Ferdinand Porsche: dies	**Maria Montessori:** dies	**Dylan Thomas:** dies
Ludwig Wittgenstein: dies	**Eva Perón:** dies	**Hank Williams:** dies

54	55	56
Henri Matisse: dies	**Fernand Léger:** dies	**Lyonel Feininger:** dies
E McKnight Kauffer: dies	**Alvin Lustig:** dies	**Paul Renner:** dies
Dziga Vertov: dies	**Yves Tanguy:** dies	**Alexander Rodchenko:** dies
Armin Hofmann: Basel Civic Theatre identity	**Armin Hofmann:** Kunsthalle Basel exhibition poster	**Max Bill:** Josef Albers catalogue
J Müller-Brockmann: Tofranil 10mg JR Geigy ad	**J Müller-Brockmann:** Tonhalle Beethoven poster	**Wim Crouwel:** New Acquisitions poster
Willem Sandberg: B Nicholson Stedelijk catalogue	**J Müller-Brockmann:** Bally Arola mural	**Armin Hofmann:** Adam Smith: Great Ideas CCA ad
S Chwast, M Glaser + E Sorel: form Push Pin	**Saul Bass:** Man with the Golden Arm graphics	**Herbert Matter:** Knoll Furniture ads
Cipe Pineles: Charm magazine cover	**Erik Nitsche:** art director, GDC	**Giovanni Pintori:** Olivetti Electrosumma 22 poster
Paul Rand: Radio Corp of America: Morse Code ad	**Erik Nitsche:** Atoms for Peace, GDC poster	**Ladislav Sutnar:** Addo-x business machines logo
Tom Eckersley: Poster Design book	**John Dreyfus:** advisor, Lanston Monotype Corp	**Ken Garland:** art director, Design magazine
Tom Eckersley: Viaduct cover for The Director mag	**Paul Peter Piech:** Avery testing machines ad	**FHK Henrion:** The Complete Imbiber for Gilbey's Gin
Herbert Spencer: British Transport book	**Hans Schleger:** Such Game MacFisheries poster	**Hans Schleger:** Look Before You Shop ad
Rudolf Arnheim: Art + Visual Perception	**Leo Lionni:** Family of Man exhibition catalogue	**Emil Ruder:** Ronchamp
Hugh Hefner + Art Paul: Playboy magazine	**Emil Schulthess:** editor, Du magazine	**Willem Sandberg:** Experimenta Typographica
Hermann Zapf: Manuale Typographicum	**Henry Wolf:** Esquire magazine cover	**Edward Wright:** This is Tomorrow catalogue
Herbert Matter: New Haven Railroad	**John Denison-Hunt:** Clive Development Co Ltd	**Richard Hamilton:** Granada TV
Josef Müller-Brockmann: L+C AG	**Milner Gray (DRU):** W+A Gilbey Ltd	**Paul Rand:** IBM
Marcello Nissolli: Olivetti (Greek spiral)	**Hans Schleger:** Council of Industrial Design	**Albe Steiner:** Ar-flex
Hans (Giovanni) Mardersteig: Dante	**KF Bauer + W Baum:** Fortune[a]	**Freeman Craw:** Craw Clarendon + CC book
Georg Trump: Trump Mediaeval	**Will Carter:** Klang	**Roger Excoffon:** Diana
Hermann Zapf: Aldus	**Ashley Havinden:** Ashley Script	**Emil J Klumpp:** Murry Hill
Jim Flora: Pete Jolly Duo	**Saul Bass:** The Man with the Golden Arm	**Betty Brader:** Cal Tjader Quintet
Neil Fujita: Chet Baker + Strings	**Reid Miles:** Genius of Modern Music (volumes 1 + 2)	**William Claxton:** Chet Baker + Crew
Willaumez: Wagner	**Ben Shahn:** Chicago Style Jazz	**Colonel Tom Parker + Popsie:** Elvis Presley
Hans Erni: No to Atomic War poster	**Jules Feiffer:** cartoonist, Village Voice	**Paul Rand:** I Know a Lot of Things children's book
Norman Rockwell: What Makes It Tick? ad	**Herbert Leupin:** Tribune de Laussane poster	**Ronald Searle:** Have a Good Rum for Your Money ad
Armanda Testa: Pirelli poster	**Kay Thompson + Hilary Knight:** Eloise book	**Henryk Tomaszewski:** spearheads Polish illustration
Werner Bischof: On the Way to Cuzco	**Edouard Boubat:** First Snow . . . Paris	**Cecil Beaton:** Dame Edith Sitwell
Chargesheimer: Konrad Adenauer	**Andreas Feininger:** The Photojournalist	**W Eugene Smith:** Andrea Doria victims . . .
Josef Sudek: A Walk in the Magic Garden	**Willy Ronis:** Le Repos du Cirque Pinder . . .	**Josef Sudek:** Roses
Josef Albers: influential tutor, Ulm	**Wim Crouwel:** begins teaching, Rietveld Academy	**Louis Danziger:** tutor, Art Centre School of Design
Dennis Bailey: finishes teaching, RCA, London	**Alvin Eisenman:** art + architecture tutor, Yale	**J Müller-Brockmann:** tutor, Zurich School of Arts
Alexey Brodovitch: visiting critic, Yale University	**Armin Hofmann:** design seminars, Yale	**Bradbury Thompson:** joins faculty of design, Yale
Craig Ellwood: (CSH #17)	**Le Corbusier:** Chapel Notre Dame-du-Haut	**Lucio Costa + Oscar Niemeyer:** begin Brasilia
Richard Gordon: The Pearson House	**Q Jones + F Emmons:** Jones House	**Arne Jacobson:** Carl Christensen Works
Richard Neutra: Eagle Rock Community Centre	**Mies van der Rohe:** Illinois Institute . . .	**Heikki + Kaija Siren:** Tapiola Garden City
Alberto Burri: Sacking + Red	**Jasper Johns:** Flag	**Richard Hamilton:** Just What is it that Makes . . .
Joseph Cornell: Untitled (Ostend)	**Pablo Picasso:** The Women of Algiers	**Henry Moore:** Reclining Mother + Child
Serge Poliakoff: Diptych	**Maria-Elena Vieira da Silva:** Composition 4045	**Ben Nicholson:** February 1956 – Granite
Federico Fellini: La Strada	**Delbert Mann:** Marty	**John Ford:** The Searchers
Alfred Hitchcock: Rear Window	**Otto Preminger:** The Man with the Golden Arm	**Nicholas Ray:** Rebel Without a Cause
Elia Kazan: On the Waterfront	**Satyajit Ray:** Pather Panchali	**Satyajit Ray:** Aparijito
AAM Durrant + D Scott: Routemaster bus	**Charles + Ray Eames:** Stacking chair	**Charles + Ray Eames:** Lounge chair + ottoman
Charles + Ray Eames: Sofa Compact	**Florence Knoll:** Parallel Bar metal-frame table	**Marcello Nizzoli:** Mirella sewing machine
George Nelson: Steelframe Group storage units	**George Nelson:** Coconut chair for Herman Miller	**Dieter Rams + Hans Gugelot:** Phonosuper SK4
William Golding: The Lord of the Flies	**Graham Greene:** The Quiet American	**Agatha Christie:** The Mousetrap
Aldous Huxley: The Doors of Perception	**Victor Nabokov:** Lolita	**Günter Grass:** The Tin Drum
Dylan Thomas: Under Milk Wood	**Patrick White:** The Tree of Man	**John Osborne:** Look Back in Anger
Irving Berlin: There's No Business like Show . . .	**Judy Garland:** Miss Show Business	**Cole Porter:** High Society
Art Blakey: A Night at Birdland	**Bill Hayley:** Rock Around the Clock	**Elvis Presley:** Elvis + Elvis Presley
Art Tatum: Solo Masterpieces	**Frank Sinatra:** In the Wee Small Hours	**Frank Sinatra:** Songs for Swingin' Lovers
Roger Bannister: breaks the four-minute mile	**France:** Citroën launch the DS Goddess	**UK:** This is Tomorrow exhibition
Ray Kroc: founds McDonald's Corporation	**ICA:** Man, Machine + Motion exhibition	**Melbourne:** Olympics
US: Boeing 707 maiden flight	**Tennessee Williams:** Cat on a Hot Tin Roof premiere	**Elvis Presley:** gyrates on the Ed Sullivan Show
Livingston Electronic: first stereotape recordings	**Narinder Kapany:** invented fibre optics	**Ampex:** video recorder
Photocomposition: becomes commonplace	**Linofilm:** phototypesetting machine	**Bette Nesmith Graham:** typing correction fluid
Dr Jonas Salk: develops polio vaccine	**Sony:** TR-55 first transistor radio	**UK:** Ernie: first premium bond machine
US: McCarthy hearings begin	**UK:** Sir Anthony Eden becomes prime minister	**Hungary:** Soviets crush uprising
US: Nautilus first atomic submarine launched	**US:** Rosa Parks refuses to give up her bus seat	**UK:** troops leave Suez Canal
US: Supreme Court rule against school segregation	**Warsaw Pact:** military alliance signed	**USSR:** Khrushchev denounces Stalin
Lionel Barrymore: dies	**James Dean:** dies	**William E Boeing:** dies
Charles Ives: dies	**Albert Einstein:** dies	**Bertolt Brecht:** dies
Auguste Lumière: dies	**Charlie Parker:** dies	**AA Milne:** dies

57	58	59
WA Dwiggins: dies **Bruce Rogers:** dies **Percy Wyndham Lewis:** dies	**Giacomo Balla:** dies **Jan van Krimpen:** dies **Bart van der Leck:** dies	**William Golden:** dies **Tom Purvis:** dies **Frank Lloyd Wright:** dies
Wim Crouwel: Hiroshima poster **Karl Gerstner:** Schiffnach Europa book **Willem Sandberg:** Jonge Schilders catalogue	**Anthony Froshaug:** Quarterly Bulletin Ulm journal **Karl Gerstner:** JR Geigy Aujourd'hui ad **Josef Müller-Brockmann:** Werner Bischof poster	**Wim Crouwel:** Jean Lurçat poster **Karl Gerstner:** Leser gesucht für die . . . book **Armin Hofmann:** Giselle poster
Brownjohn, Chermayeff & Geismar: forms **BCG:** American pavilion at Brussels World's Fair **Giovanni Pintori:** Olivetti Tetractys poster	**Saul Bass:** Alfred Hitchcock's Vertigo film titles **Will Burtin:** 3D Human Cell exhibition for Upjohn . . . **Bradbury Thompson:** Westvaco's American Classics	**Freeman Craw:** The Journal of Commercial Art cover **Otto Storch:** Patterns for McCall's Magazine **Henry Wolf:** art director, Harper's Bazaar
John Bainbridge: London Transport posters **Alan Fletcher:** designer, Fortune + Time-Life **M Gray + A Ball (DRU):** Guards cigarette pack	**Ian Bradbury:** Bazaar retail identity + applications **John Sewell:** consultant designer, Better Books **Herbert Spencer:** Basis of Growth essay	**Birdsall, Daulby, Mayhew + Wildbur:** form BDMW **Abram Games:** Men who score read . . . FT poster **Ray Hawkey:** design director, Daily Express
Leo Lionni: Fortune: Designs for the Printed Page **George Nelson:** Problems of Design **Vance Packard:** The Hidden Persuaders ad report	**Robert Massin:** art director, Editions Gallimard **J Müller-Brockmann, RP Lohse, H Neuberg +** **C Vivarelli:** publish Neue Grafik	**Alexey Brodovitch + R Avedon:** Observations **Aaron Burns:** The Composing Room: four books . . . **Willy Fleckhaus:** Twen magazine
Ralph Eckerstrom: Container Corp of America **Franco Grignani:** Bellezza d'Italia **Anton Stankowski:** Standard Elektrik Lorenz AG	**FHK Henrion:** KLM (Royal Dutch Airlines) **Romek Marber:** Holland + Hannen + Cubitts **Carlo Vivarelli:** Therma	**Pieter Brattinga:** Steendrukkerij de Jong **Alan Fleming:** Canada National Railways **J Kinneir + M Calvert:** Vehicle MOT
Konrad F Bauer + Walter Baum: Folio **Adrian Frutiger:** Univers **E Hoffmann + M Miedinger:** Neue Hass Grotesk	**Dick Dooijes:** Mercator **JL Renshaw:** News Gothic Bold **Hermann Zapf:** Optima	**RH Middleton:** Record **Ed Rondthaler:** Alphabet Thesaurus No 1 **Georg Trump:** Pepita
Paul Bacon: Mulligan meets Monk **Ian Bradbery:** Ernestine Anderson Sings **Ivan Chermayeff:** Beethoven: Symphony No 3	**Neil Fujita:** The Hi-Lo's . . . **Reid Miles:** Art Blakey: Moanin' **Reid Miles:** Kenny Burrell: Blue Lights 1	**Josef Albers:** Enoch Light: Provocative Percussion **Saul Bass:** Anatomy of a Murder **David S Martin:** Billie Holiday: All or Nothing at All
S Chwast: Devil's Apple for Push Pin monthly **William Golden + Ben Shahn:** The Big Push CBS ad **Dr Seuss:** The Cat in the Hat book	**Edward Bawden:** Vathek book **Tom Geismar:** Common Sense . . . cover **Ben Shahn:** Ounce Dice Trice	**Ivan Chermayeff:** The Wisdom of the Heart cover **Leo Lionni:** Little Blue and Little Yellow book **Bruno Munari:** La Forchette di Munari poster
Peter Keetman: Highboard **Irving Penn:** Pablo Picasso **Willy Ronis:** Lovers of the Bastille	**Cornell Capa:** Bolshoi Ballet School, Moscow **Bruce Davidson:** The Dwarf **O Wilson Link:** Main Line on Main . . .	**Imogen Cunningham:** Pregnant Nude **Ed van der Elsken:** Durban, South Africa **Alberto Korda:** Quixote Atop a Lamp post, Havana
Tom Eckersley: head of design, LCP, London **Anthony Froshaug:** tutor, Institute of Design, Ulm **Edward Wright:** tutor, RCA, London	**Colin Forbes:** head of graphic design, Central School **Mies van der Rohe:** retires, Illinois Institute . . . **Masuda Tadashi:** founds Design Institute, Japan	**Bruce Archer:** influential tutor, Ulm **Frank Overton:** tutor, LCP, London **Cipe Pineles:** publication design tutor, Parson's NY
Craig Ellwood: (CSH #18) **Frederick Gibberd:** Harlow New Town **LCC Architectural Dept :** Roehampton Estate	**Buff, Straub + Hensman:** Bass House **Pierre Koenig:** (CSH #21) **M van der Rohe + P Johnson:** Seagram Building	**Émile Aillaud:** Cité de l'Abreuvoir Estate **Philip Johnson:** Roofless Chapel at New Harmony **Frank Lloyd Wright:** Guggenheim Museum
Philip Guston: The Clock **Mark Rothko:** Light Red over Black **Clyfford Still:** 1957 – D No 1	**Kenneth Armitage:** Figure Lying on its Side **Sam Francis:** Blue on a Point **Eduardo Paolozzi:** Japanese War God	**Peter Blake:** Girlie Door **Mark Rothko:** Red on Maroon **Jiro Yoshihara:** Painting
Ingmar Bergman: The Seventh Seal **Federico Fellini:** The Nights of Cabiria **Sydney Lumet:** 12 Angry Men	**Alfred Hitchcock:** Vertigo **Jacques Tati:** Mon Oncle **Orson Welles:** Touch of Evil	**Jean-Luc Godard:** À Bout de Souffle **Alfred Hitchcock:** North by Northwest **François Truffaut:** Les Quatre Cents Coups
Nanna Ditzel: wicker hanging chair for Bonacina **Gerd Müller:** Kitchen Machine for Braun **Eero Saarinen:** Tulip chairs and table for Knoll	**Charles + Ray Eames:** Aluminum Group seating **Arne Jacobsen:** Swan chair + sofa for Fritz Hansen **Eric Marshall:** Ultra Radio	**Harley Earl:** Cadillac **Alec Issigonis:** Mini **WM Russell:** K2 Kettle
Jack Kerouac: On the Road **Boris Pasternak:** Dr Zhivago **Patrick White:** Voss	**Samuel Beckett:** Endgame + Malone Dies **Lawrence Durrell:** The Alexandrian Quartet **Jack Kerouac:** The Dharma Bums	**Laurie Lee:** Cider with Rosie **Norman Mailer:** Advertisements for Myself **Alan Sillitoe:** The Loneliness of the Long-Distance . . .
Nat King Cole: Love is the Thing **Alan Jay Lerner + Frederick Loewe:** My Fair Lady **Elvis Presley:** Loving You	**Cannonball Adderley:** Somethin' Else **R Rogers + O Hammerstein:** South Pacific **Frank Sinatra:** Only the Lonely + Come Fly With Me	**The Dave Brubeck Quartet:** Time Out **Miles Davis:** Kind of Blue **The Kingston Trio:** At Large
Europe: ATypI forms **UK:** Macmillan's Never Had It So Good speech **USSR:** launch Sputnik I	**Brazil:** win the football World Cup **Sweden:** Dr Ake Senning: first heart pacemaker **US:** Explorer I satellite into orbit	**UK:** influential US design exhibition at US embassy **UK:** M1, first British motorway opens **US:** The Sound of Music opens on Broadway
George de Mistral: Velcro **US:** Drunkometer first tested on drivers	**Berthold Foundry:** Diatype photosetting available **Burroughs Corp:** designs E13 computer alphabet **Ole Kirk + Godtfred Christiansen:** Lego toy bricks	**Christopher Cockerell:** Hovercraft **Letraset:** transfer lettering company formed, London **Kilby + Robert Noyce:** microchip
Europe: Economic Community (EEC) established **UK:** Anthony Eden resigns **UK:** Harold Macmillan becomes prime minister	**China:** Mao Tse-tung launches Great Leap Forward **Europe:** French settlers revolt in Algeria **US:** NASA founded	**Fidel Castro:** becomes dictator of Cuba **Charles de Gaulle:** becomes president of France **Dalai Lama:** flees Tibet
Humphrey Bogart: dies **Christian Dior:** dies **Senator Joseph McCarthy:** dies	**Alfred Noyes:** dies **Tyrone Power:** dies **Ralph Vaughan Williams:** dies	**Billie Holiday:** dies **Buddy Holly:** dies **Cecile B de Mille:** dies

60	61	62
››› **Fortunato Depero:** dies **Vilmos Huszar:** dies	**Augustus John:** dies **Eero Saarinen:** dies **James Thurber:** dies	**Will Bradley:** dies **Yves Klein:** dies **Franz Kline:** dies
››› **J Müller-Brockmann:** Zurich City Police poster **J Müller-Brockmann:** Der Film poster **Hans Neuburg:** Italienische Maler exhibition poster	**J Müller-Brockmann:** Deutschlands Weg exhibition **Dieter Rot:** Bok4A experimental book **Emil Ruder:** TM typographic covers	**Richard P Lohse:** Kunstgewerbemuseum poster **Bruno Monguzzi:** IBM discpac booklet cover **Wolf D Zimmermann:** Fischer book cover
››› **Saul Bass:** Psycho film titles + Exodus graphics **Leo Lionni:** Fortune New York cover **George Lois:** begins Esquire statement covers	**Lou Dorfsman:** Exhilarate CBS TV print advert **Rudolph de Harak:** McGraw Hill paperback covers **Leo Lionni:** resigns from Fortune magazine	**Maurice Binder:** Dr No film titles **Herb Lubalin:** Eros + Saturday Evening Post mags **Bradbury Thompson:** final Westvaco Inspirations
››› **Robert Brownjohn + Bob Gill:** arrive in London **Tom Eckersley:** Swedish seminar poster **Romek Marber:** Penguin Crime Series covers	**Dennis Bailey:** Architecture Today poster **Robin Fior:** Call to Action! Committee of 100 poster **Colin Forbes:** signage system for Heathrow Airport	**Fletcher/Forbes/Gill:** form **Ken Garland:** forms Ken Garland & Associates **Raymond Hawkey:** The Ipcress File book cover
››› **Germano Facetti:** art director, Penguin Books **Abram Games:** Over My Shoulder **J Müller-Brockmann:** The Graphic Artist + his . . .	**Aaron Burns:** Typography book **Johannes Itten:** The Art of Colour **Ladislav Sutnar:** Visual Design in Action	**Walter Allner:** art director, Fortune magazine **Marshall McLuhan:** The Gutenberg Galaxy **G Moore:** art editor, Sunday Times colour section
››› **Lester Beall:** International Paper Company **Chermayeff & Geismar:** Chase Manhattan Bank **Raymond Loewy:** International Harvester	**Peter Caplan:** Peter Dixon Ltd **Wim Crouwel:** Omniscreen silkscreen printers **Norbert Dutton:** The Plessey Co Ltd	**Otl Aicher, T Gonda, F Querengässer +:** Lufthansa **David Collins:** Cyprus Airways **Kenneth Lamble:** Dunlop Footwear Co Ltd
››› **José Mendoza y Almeida:** Pascal **SL Hartz:** Molé Foliaté **Hoffmann + Miedinger:** NHG renamed Helvetica	**Albert Bolton + Albert Hollenstein:** Eras **Freeman Craw:** Ad Lib **Günter Gerhard Lange:** type director, Berthold AG	**Roger Excoffon:** Antique Olive (began) **Berthold type foundry:** Standard **Aldo Novarese:** Eurostile
››› **Reid Miles:** Jimmy Smith: Midnight Special **Reid Miles:** Lou Donaldson: Sunny Side Up **Woody Woodward:** Various: This is the Blues	**Reid Miles:** Dexter Gordon: One Flight Up **Marvin Schwartz:** Puccini: Madame Butterfly **Jim Silke:** Judy Garland: at Carnegie Hall	**Karl Gerstner:** Bech Electronik Centre **Robert Jones:** Lena Horne: Lena . . . Lovely + Alive **Reid Miles:** Freddie Hubbard: Hub-Tones
››› **Andre Francois:** Pirelli poster **George Giusti:** Holiday magazine cover, Rome issue **Ben Shahn:** Stop H-Bomb Tests poster	**Edward Bawden:** Faber & Faber book jackets **Ivan Chermayeff:** Blind Mice + Other Numbers **Bob Gill:** A to Z children's book	**S Chwast + M Glaser:** Filmsense poster **Roman Cieslewicz:** Cyrk poster **Paul Rand:** Little 1 children's book
››› **Eve Arnold:** Marilyn Monroe **René Burri:** São Paulo **Alberto Korda:** Che Guevara	**Eve Arnold:** Jacqueline Kennedy . . . **David Bailey:** Jean Shrimpton, Tower Bridge **Mario Giacomelli:** I Have No Hands to Caress . . .	**Cecil Beaton:** Edith Sitwell **Lee Friedlander:** Galax, Virginia **Lee Friedlander:** Newark, New Jersey
››› **Dennis Bailey:** tutor, Cental School, London **RO Blechman:** tutor, School of Visual Arts, NY **FHK Henrion:** tutor, RCA, London	**Anthony Froshaug:** tutor, RCA, London **Karl Gerstner:** visual communication tutor, Ulm	**Paul Gredinger:** visual communication tutor, Ulm **Carlo Vivarelli:** visual communication tutor, Ulm
››› **Edward Killingsworth:** Triad (CSH #23) **Eric Lyons:** Span Development Group **Viljo Revell:** Cemetery Chapel	**Philip Johnson:** New Harmony Shrine **Ponti, Nervi + Associates:** Pirelli Building **Eero Saarinen:** TWA Terminal	**John Graham:** Space Needle **Eero Saarinen:** Dulles Airport **Sir Basil Spence:** St Michael's Cathedral
››› **Jean (Hans) Arp:** Siamosis **Anthony Caro:** Midday **Julio Le Parc:** Continual Light (mobile)	**Barbara Hepworth:** Single Form **Jasper Johns:** Zero Through Nine **Yves Klein:** FC–11 Anthropometry – Fire	**Jim Dine:** Wiring the Unfinished Bathroom **Victor Pasmore:** Relief Construction in . . . **Andy Warhol:** Soup Can
››› **Federico Fellini:** La Dolce Vita **Alfred Hitchcock:** Psycho **Billy Wilder:** The Apartment	**Luis Buñuel:** Viridiana **François Truffaut:** Jules et Jim **Robert Wise:** West Side Story	**John Frankenheimer:** The Manchurian Candidate **David Lean:** Lawrence of Arabia **Andrei Tarkovsky:** Ivan's Childhood
››› **Kenneth Grange:** Kenwood Chef **Verner Panton:** Panton plastic stacking chair **Dieter Rams:** director of design, Braun AG	**NASA:** Apollo spacecraft **Tobia Scarpa:** Bastiano sofa + chair for Gavina **Reinhold Weiss:** Braun desk fan	**Castiglioni brothers:** Arco floor lamp **Charles + Ray Eames:** Tandem 2600 airport seating **H Gugelot + GA Müller:** Braun Sixtant shaver
››› **DH Lawrence:** Lady Chatterley's Lover (uncensored) **Harold Pinter:** The Caretaker **Sylvia Plath:** The Colossus + Other Poems	**Ian Fleming:** Thunderball **Joseph Heller:** Catch-22 **Muriel Spark:** The Prime of Miss Jean Brodie	**Anthony Burgess:** A Clockwork Orange **Carl Jung:** Memories, Dreams, Reflections **Henry Miller:** Tropic of Capricorn
››› **Luciano Berio:** Circles **Olivier Messiaen:** Time-colouring **Elvis Presley:** GI Blues	**Leonard Bernstein:** West Side Story **Henry Mancini:** Breakfast at Tiffany's **Elvis Presley:** Blue Hawaii	**The Beatles:** Love Me Do **Nat King Cole:** Ramblin' Rose **The Oscar Peterson Trio:** Night Train
››› **Fluxus:** art movement begins **Rome:** Olympics **UK:** Lady Chatterley's Lover cleared of obscenity . . .	**Letraset:** introduce instant dry transfer lettering **Tanzania:** Dr Louis Leakey discovers Homo habilis **USSR:** Yuri Gagarin: first man in space	**UK:** first issue of Private Eye **US:** first Pop Art exhibition at Sidney Janis Gallery **US:** Telstar communication satellite launch
››› **Theodore H Maiman:** lasers **US:** Echo 1 communications satellite launches **US:** Tiros 1 first meteorological satellite launches	**JW Dawson:** Computer in Building Design article **IBM:** Selectric phototypesetting machine **UK:** contraceptive pill available	**Ermal Clayton Fraze:** tab-opening drink can **Polaroid:** introduce colour instant film **UK:** first push-button controlled Panda crossing
››› **South Africa:** Sharpeville massacres **US:** John F Kennedy elected president **USSR:** Leonid Brezhnev becomes head of state	**Europe:** Berlin Wall erected **US:** founds Peace Corps **US:** American-backed Bay of Pigs attack in Cuba fails	**Algeria:** claims independence from France **Cuba:** Missile Crisis **US:** sends troops to Vietnam
››› **Albert Camus:** dies **Clark Gable:** dies **Boris Pasternak:** dies	**George Formby:** dies **Ernest Hemingway:** dies **Carl Jung:** dies	**Charles Laughton:** dies **Marilyn Monroe:** dies **Vita Sackville-West:** dies

63	64	65
Georges Braque: dies **Jean Cocteau:** dies **Tristan Tzara:** dies	**Thomas M Cleland:** dies **Giorgio Morandi:** dies **Gerrit Rietveld:** dies	**Carlo Carra:** dies **Le Corbusier:** dies **Max Ernst:** dies
W Crouwel, F Kramer + B Wissing: form Total **K Gerstner, P Gredinger + M Kutter:** form GGK **Karl Gerstner:** Designing Programmes book	**Yusaku Kamekura:** Tokyo Olympic posters **Josef Müller-Brockmann:** Tonhalle festival poster **Rosmarie Tissi:** E Lutz advertisements	**Jacques Blanchard:** Secours d'Hiver Op Art poster **Josef Müller-Brockmann:** Gruppe 21 ads **Rosmarie Tissi:** Univac invitation
Robert Brownjohn: From Russia with Love film titles **Pablo Ferro:** Dr Strangelove film titles **Giovanni Pintori:** Olivetti newspaper ad	**Alexey Brodovitch:** Art in America cover **Chermayeff & Geismar:** Mobil identity programme **Lou Dorfsman:** becomes director of design, CBS	**Louis Danziger:** The First Generation exhibition **Erik Nitsche:** A History of Astronomy book **Cipe Pineles:** appointed consultant, Lincoln Centre
D Birdsall (BDMW): 17 Graphic Designers London **Tom Eckersley:** Keep Britain Tidy poster **Ian Hamilton Finlay:** XM concrete poem	**Robert Brownjohn:** Goldfinger film titles **Anthony Froshaug:** Typographic Norms manual **J Kinneir + M Calvert:** British motorway signage	**Birdsall, Forsyth, Curtis + Hackett:** form Omnific **Matthew Carter:** becomes staff designer, Linotype **Bob Gill:** leaves Fletcher/Forbes/Gill
Alan Aldridge: art editor of fiction, Penguin Books **R de Harak:** Twisted Tales from Shakespeare cover **Tom Wolsey:** art director, Queen magazine	**Ken Garland:** First Things First manifesto **Marshall McLuhan:** Understanding Media **H Spencer:** The Reponsibilities of . . . essay	**Gui Bonsiepe:** Visual / Verbal Rhetoric essay **Armin Hofmann:** Graphic Design Manual . . . **Harry Peccinotti:** art editor, Nova magazine, London
AM Cassandre: Yves Saint Laurent **Fletcher/Forbes/Gill:** D&AD **M Minale + B Tattersfield:** Hawker Sidley	**Gerald Barney + Milner Gray (DRU):** British Rail **Armin Hofmann:** Swiss National Exhibition Centre **Yusaku Kamekura:** Tokyo Olympics	**Paul Rand:** ABC **Francesco Saroglia:** International Wool Secretariat **Hans Schleger:** John Lewis Partnership
Fred Lambert: Compacta **Ricard Giralt Miracle:** Gaudi **Hermann Zapf:** Hunt Roman	**Chris Brand:** Apollo **Adrian Frutiger:** Albertina **Georg Trump:** Jaguar	**Arthur Baker:** Baker Signet **Matthew Carter:** Auriga **Louis Minott:** Davida Bold
Don Hunstein: Bob Dylan: The Freewheelin' . . . **Reid Miles:** H Hancock: Inventions + Dimensions **Reid Miles:** Lee Morgan: The Sidewinder	**Milton Glaser:** The Sound of Harlem **Reid Miles:** Eric Dolphy: Out to Lunch **Unknown:** Joan Baez / 5	**Barry Feinstein:** The Byrds: Mr Tambourine Man **Robert Freeman:** The Beatles: Help **Reid Miles:** Herbie Hancock: Maiden Voyage
John Burningham: Borka, The Adventures . . . book **Maurice Sendak:** Where the Wild Things Are book **Ben Shahn:** Love + Joy about Letters book	**John Furnival:** The Fall of the Tower of Babel **Jan Lenica:** Wozzeck poster **Robert Massin:** La Cantatrice Chauve book	**RO Blechman:** CBS TV ad **Robert Massin:** Eugène Ionesco's Délire à Deux book **Henryk Tomaszewski:** Cyrk poster
Eve Arnold: Liz Taylor + Richard Burton **Elliot Erwitt:** The Funeral of President . . . **Lewis Morley:** Christine Keeler	**Cecil Beaton:** Audrey Hepburn **Horst Faas:** A Father's Tragic Burden **Shomei Tomatsu:** Ruinous Gardens	**Bernd + Hilla Becher:** Cooling Tower **Marc Riboud:** A Street In Old Beijing **Malick Sidibé:** Twist
Otl Aicher: rector, Institute of Design, Ulm **J Müller-Brockmann:** tutor, Institute of Design, Ulm	**Paul Davis:** tutor, school of Visual Arts, New York **Tomàs Maldonado:** rector, Institute of Design, Ulm	**Wim Crouwel:** tutor, Delft Technical University **Emil Ruder:** director, Basel School of Design **Dietmar Winkler:** joins MIT design services dept
W Gropius + P Belluschi: Pan Am Building **Carlo Scarpa:** Castelvecchio Museum **Alejandro de la Sota:** apartment block	**Eric Bedford +:** Post Office Tower **Alison + Peter Smithson:** Economist Building **Kenzo Tange:** Tokyo Olympic Stadium	**Snowdon, Price + Newby:** Northern Aviary **Team 4:** Reliance Controls Factory **JL Wormersley:** Park Hill + Hyde Park Estate
Josef Albers: Homage to the Square – Curious **Victor Pasmore:** Abstract in White, Ochre . . . **Antoni Tàpies:** Ocre	**Ad Reinhardt:** Black Painting No 34 **Bridget Riley:** Shuttle I **Andy Warhol:** Saturday Disaster	**Patrick Caulfield:** Still Life with Jug + Bottle **Joseph Kosuth:** One + Three Chairs **Roy Lichtenstein:** Girl with Hair Ribbon
Federico Fellini: 8½ **Joseph Losey:** The Servant **Tony Richardson:** Tom Jones	**Jacques Demy:** Les Parapluies de Cherbourg **Stanley Kubrick:** Dr Strangelove . . . **Richard Lester:** A Hard Day's Night	**Fred Coe:** A Thousand Clowns **David Lean:** Dr Zhivago **Sidney Lumet:** The Spy Who Came in from the Cold
Robin Day: Mark II polypropylene stacking chair **H Gugelot + R Hocker:** Kodak carousel projector **Eliot Noyes:** IBM typewriter 72	**George Nelson:** Action Office **Eliot Noyes:** IBM Computer System 360 **M Zanuso + R Sapper:** TS 502 radio	**Castiglioni Brothers:** RR120 Stereo Hi Fi **Cesare (Joe) Columbo:** 4867 chair **Charles + Ray Eames:** IBM Pavilion, New York
Betty Friedan: The Feminine Mystique **Mary McCarthy:** The Group **John Robinson:** Honest to God	**Saul Bellow:** Herzog **William Burroughs:** The Naked Lunch **Len Deighton:** Funeral in Berlin	**Seamus Heaney:** Eleven Poems **Norman Mailer:** An American Dream **Harold Pinter:** The Homecoming
The Beatles: Please Please Me + With the Beatles **Bob Dylan:** The Freewheelin' Bob Dylan **Andy Williams:** Days of Wine and Roses	**John Barry:** Goldfinger **Peter, Paul + Mary:** Peter, Paul + Mary **Elvis Presley:** Roustabout	**The Beatles:** Help + Rubber Soul **Bob Dylan:** Highway 61 Revisited **R Rodgers + O Hammerstein:** The Sound of Music
UK: Printing + the Mind of Man exhibition, Earls Court **US:** Apollo space programme launch **US:** Martin Luther King Jr: I Have a Dream speech	**Tokyo:** Olympics **UK:** Conran opens Habitat **US:** Op Art first termed in Time magazine	**Maria Callas:** Puccini's Tosca: final performance **MOMA:** The Responsive Eye: Opt Art exhibition **Japan:** Bullet Train opens
DEC: introduce the first minicomputer **Philips:** introduce compact cassette player **Polaroid:** Land Camera Automatic 100	**Douglas C Engelbart:** computer mouse **IBM:** Operating System 360 **J Kemeny + T Kurtz:** BASIC computer language	**Dr Rudolf Hell:** Digiset phototypesetting machine **IBM:** develop the means to digitally store type **PDP-8 Mini:** first integrated circuit computer
UK: Alec Douglas-Home becomes prime minister **US:** John F Kennedy assassinated **US:** Lyndon B Johnson becomes president	**South Africa:** N Mandela sentenced to life in prison **US:** Civil Rights Act passed **USSR:** Khrushchev deposed by Brezhnev + Kosygin	**India:** invades Pakistan **US + Europe:** anti-war protests **US:** Malcolm X assassinated
Aldous Huxley: dies **CS Lewis:** dies **Edith Piaf:** dies	**Ian Fleming:** dies **Harpo Marx:** dies **Cole Porter:** dies	**Winston Churchill:** dies **Nat King Cole:** dies **TS Eliot:** dies

66	67	68
Jean Hans Arp: dies **Andre Breton:** dies **Alberto Giacometti:** dies	**Johannes Itten:** dies **René Magritte:** dies **Stanley Morison:** dies	**AM Cassandre:** dies **Marcel Duchamp:** dies **Sir Herbert Read:** dies
Inge Druckrey: Orta Soft Drinks poster **Siegfried Odermatt:** Union Safe Co trademark **Massimo Vignelli (Unimark):** Knoll identity	**Wim Crouwel:** New Alphabet + brochure **Hans Neuberg:** Paul Schuitema exhibition poster **Massimo Vignelli:** Knoll poster	**Anton Stankowski:** Berlin Design Programme **R Tissi + S Odermatt:** establish studio, Zurich **Lance Wyman:** Mexico City Olympic graphics
Rick Griffin: Jook Savage Art Show poster **George Lois:** Nauga trade character for Naugahyde **Massimo Vignelli (Unimark):** NY Subway map	**Paul Davis:** Che Guevara cover for Evergreen Review **Charles + Ray Eames:** Powers of Ten film **Rudolph de Harak:** McGraw Hill covers	**S Chwast + M Glaser:** Lincoln Centre poster **Pablo Ferro:** The Thomas Crown Affair film titles **Massimo Vignelli:** NY Subway signage
Tom Eckersley: Cooks poster **Hans Schleger:** designer, Edinburgh Festival **Michael Wolff + Wally Olins:** form Wolff Olins	**Ken Garland:** Here Are Some Things We Must Do **Fred Lambert:** A Comprehensive selection . . . **Herbert Spencer:** Traces of Man book + cover	**Derek Birdsall:** art director, Nova magazine **Ken Garland:** attends Hornsey College of Art sit-ins **Richard Hollis:** MoRADE poster
Bob Cobbing: Worm concrete poem **Bruno Munari:** Arte Come Mestiere **Hans Schmoller:** Nikolaus Pevsner: Berkshire	**Marshall McLuhan:** The Medium is the Massage **Emil Ruder:** Typography: A Manual of Design **Emmett Williams:** An Anthology of Concrete Poetry	**Herb Lubalin:** Avant Garde magazine **James Sutton + Alan Bartram:** Atlas of Typeforms **Hermann Zapf:** Manuale Typographicum
Gerstner, Gredinger + Kutter AG (GGK): BOAC **H Schleger + R Fry:** Allen Lane the Penguin Press **Lance Wyman:** Mexico Olympics	**R Armstrong + M Gray (DRU):** Capper-Neil Ltd **Herb Lubalin + Tom Carnase:** Mother + Child **Karen Munck:** Smiths Food Group Ltd	**Rupert Armstrong + Milner Gray (DRU):** ICI **David Gentleman:** British Steel **Armin Vogt:** Fiat
Matthew Carter: Cascade Script **Dick Dooijes:** Lectura **Jan Tschichold:** Sabon	**Wim Crouwel:** New Alphabet **Adrian Frutiger:** Serifa **Richard Isbell:** Americana	**Adrian Frutiger + ECMA:** OCR-B **Milton Glaser:** Baby Teeth **Hermann Zapf:** Firenze
Ed Thrasher: Frank Sinatra: Strangers in The Night **Klaus Voorman:** Beatles: Revolver **Guy Webster:** The Byrds: Turn! Turn! Turn!	**Peter Blake +:** The Beatles: Sgt Pepper's Lonely . . . **P Brown:** The Small Faces: Ogdens' Nut Gone Flake **Andy Warhol:** The Velvet Underground + Nico	**Milton Glaser:** The Band: Music from Big Pink **R Hamilton + G House:** Beatles: The White Album **John Lennon +Yoko Ono:** Unfinished Music No 1
A Katzman + W Bowart: East Village Other mag **Victor Moscoso:** Neon Rose posters **Tadanori Yokoo:** Koshimaki Osen poster	**Robert Crumb:** Cheap Thrills record cover **Milton Glaser:** Bach + Dylan posters **Tomi Ungerer:** Kiss for Peace anti-Vietnam poster	**Robert Crumb:** Zap Comix **Grapus:** form **S Thorgerson + A Powell:** form Hipgnosis
Bruce Nauman: Self-Portrait as Fountain **Lütfi Özkök:** Portrait of Samuel Beckett **Art Sinsabaugh:** Chicago Landscape #117	**Diane Arbus:** Boy with Straw Hat Waiting to . . . **Philip Jones Griffith:** Civilian Victim, Vietnam **Ed Ruscha:** State Board of Equalizations . . .	**Eddie Adams:** Execution of a Vietcong Prisoner **Lee Friedlander:** New Orleans **Will McBride:** Overpopulation
Tomàs Maldonado: leaves Institute of Design, Ulm **Herbert Ohl:** rector, Institute of Design, Ulm **Geoff White:** tutor, Ravensbourne College	**Muriel Cooper:** first art director, MIT press **Hans Hollein:** chair of Architecture, Düsseldorf Acad **G Kepes:** founds Advanced Visual Studies Cntr, MIT	**Hochschule für Gestaltung:** in Ulm closes **Armin Hofmann:** director, Basel School of Design **Wolfgang Weingart:** begins teaching at Basel
Gillespie, Kidd + Coia: St Peter's College **Richard Seifert:** Centre Point **Max Urbahn +:** Vehicle Assembly Building	**Frederick Gibberd:** Liverpool Catholic Cathedral **Bertrand Goldberg:** Marina City **LCC Architects Dept:** Hayward Gallery	**GLC Architects Dept:** Elgin Estate **Denys Lasdun:** Student Housing (UEA) **Schipporeit–Heinrich:** Lake Point Tower
Carl Andre: Lever **Dan Flavin:** Monument for V Tatlin **Willem de Kooning:** The Visit	**Patrick Heron:** Manganese in Deep Violet **Victor Vasarely:** Arny **Andy Warhol:** Index Book	**Dan Flavin:** Untitled (to the innovator . . .) **Eva Hesse:** Contingent **Donald Judd:** Untitled
Michelangelo Antonioni: Blow Up **Lewis Gilbert:** Alfie **Andrei Tarkovsky:** Andrei Rublev	**James Clavell:** To Sir With Love **Norman Jewison:** In the Heat of the Night **Mike Nichols:** The Graduate	**Lindsay Anderson:** If . . . **Stanley Kubrick:** 2001: A Space Odyssey **Frank Perry:** The Swimmer
Cedric Hartman: 1U VW / Pharmacy floor lamp **Ingo Maurer:** Bulb lamp **Marco Zanuso + Richard Sapper:** Grillo telephone	**Arne Jacobson:** Cylinda Line tea service **Verner Panton:** Panton plastic stacking chair for Vitra **Sir Archibald Russell +:** Concorde	**Henry Dreyfus:** Trimline telephone **Gatti, Paolini + Teodoro:** Sacco bean bags **Richard Neagle:** Nike chair
JG Ballard: The Crystal World **Truman Capote:** In Cold Blood **Thomas Pynchon:** The Crying of Lot 49	**Gabriel Garcia Marquez:** 100 Years of Solitude **Joe Orton:** Loot **Tom Stoppard:** Rosencrantz + Guildenstern are Dead	**Allan Ginsberg:** Airplane Dreams **Dennis Potter:** The Nigel Barton Plays **Gore Vidal:** Myra Breckinridge
The Beach Boys: Pet Sounds **The Beatles:** Revolver **Bob Dylan:** Blonde on Blonde	**The Beatles:** Sgt Pepper's Lonely Hearts Club . . . **Jimi Hendrix:** Are You Experienced? **The Velvet Underground:** The Velvet Underground	**The Beatles:** The White Album **Simon + Garfunkel:** The Graduate **Sly + the Family Stone:** Stand!
UK: introduce the postcode **UK:** England win football World Cup **UK:** Wales: Aberfan coal slide tragedy	**Christian Barnard:** performs first heart transplant **US:** San Francisco: Summer of Love hippy demos **US:** first Super Bowl	**Mexico:** Olympics **Paris:** student uprising + protests **UK:** de Stijl exhibition, Camden Arts Centre
M De Bakey: performs plastic heart valve implant **Hawker Harrier:** first vertical take-off aircraft **UK:** Barclaycard credit card introduced	**UK:** BBC transmit first colour TV **US:** Polaroid introduces 10-second film **Linotron:** phototypesetting machine	**UK:** epidural technique tests **UK:** introduce decimal coins **UK:** first heart transplant
China: Mao Tse-Tung proclaims Cultural Revolution **US:** Black Panther Party established **US:** Mass Draft protests	**China:** detonates hydrogen bomb **Israel:** seizes land in Six Day War **USSR:** Stalin's daughter defects to the west	**US:** Robert F Kennedy assassinated **US:** Martin Luther King Jr assassinated **US:** Richard Nixon becomes US president
Walt Disney: dies **Buster Keaton:** dies **Evelyn Waugh:** dies	**John Coltrane:** dies **Che Guevara:** dies **Siegfried Sassoon:** dies	**Enid Blyton:** dies **Tony Hancock:** dies **John Steinbeck:** dies

»» **Lester Beall:** dies
Walter Gropius: dies
Ludwig Mies van der Rohe: dies

»» **Wim Crouwel:** Visual Communications in NL poster
Ivan Picelj: Tendencies 4 exhibition poster
Ruedi Rüegg: Musiker-Handschriften poster

»» **Seymour Chwast:** The South issue Push Pin Graphic
Heinz Edelmann: graphics for Yellow Submarine
George Lois: Esquire covers: Warhol in Soup Can

»» **Ken Garland:** Galt Toys: Galy Tots brochure
Pearce Marchbank +: The Wall Sheet Journal
George Mayhew: The Revenger's Tragedy poster

»» **FHK Henrion:** Design Coordination + Corporate ...
Rob Roy Kelly: American Wood Type
Herbert Spencer: Pioneers of Modern Typography

»» **Saul Bass:** AT&T (Bell)
FHK Henrion: Westminster Press
Raymond Loewy: New Man

»» **Colin Brignall + Letraset:** Aachen + Premier
Günter Gerhard Lange: Concorde
Hans E Meier: Syntax

»» **B Cato + E Landy:** Van Morrison: Moondance
Henry Fox: Johnny Cash: At San Quentin
George Hardie: Led Zeppelin: Led Zeppelin

»» **S Chwast + M Glaser:** Audience magazine
Roman Cieslewicz: Lenin poster
Art Spiegelman: cartoonist, Cavalier, Dude + Gent

»» **Neil Armstrong:** Buzz Aldrin on the Moon
Henri Cartier-Bresson: Paris, Boulevard Diderot
Marc Riboud: Angkor Wat

»» **Muriel Cooper:** designs the Bauhaus opus at MIT
Ruedi Rüegg: visiting tutor, Ohio State University
Herbert Spencer: RCA co-publish The Visible Word

»» **Marcel Breuer + Herbert Beckhard:** Geller House II
Arne Jacobsen: Royal Danish Embassy
François Spoerry: Port Grimaud

»» **Christo:** Wrapped Coast
Chuck Close: Richard Serra
Sol LeWitt: Three Cubes with One Half – Off

»» **Dennis Hopper:** Easy Rider
Ken Russell: Women in Love
John Schlesinger: Midnight Cowboy

»» **L Castiglioni + G Frattini:** Boalum lamp
Giancarlo Piretti: Plia folding chair
Ettore Sottsass: portable Valentine typewriter

»» **Ted Hughes:** Oedipus
Philip Roth: Portnoy's Complaint
Kurt Vonnegut: Slaughterhouse Five

»» **Van Morrison:** Moondance
Rolling Stones: Let it Bleed
Led Zeppelin: Led Zeppelin + Led Zeppelin II

»» **UK:** Concorde maiden flight
US: Apollo 11 + Neil Armstrong first moon landing
US: Woodstock music festival

»» **UK:** first human eggs fertilised in test-tube
US: Arpanet: precursor to the internet created

»» **Yasser Arafat:** becomes leader of the PLO
Charles De Gaulle: resigns as French president
UK: abolishes Death Penalty

»» **Ho Chi Minh:** dies
Dwight D Eisenhower: dies
Judy Garland: dies

Key: symbols, abbreviations + acronyms

. . .
the three point ellipses marks the omission of
information that is too long to fit within the measure

+
the plus symbol is used as a replacement for and or &,
except when the & is part of an actual name

+:
the plus colon marks the omission of either a name
or names that are too long to fit within the measure

R
initials are used to replace first names when a pair or
group of people are too long to fit within the measure

[a]
anything contained within square brackets indicates
an alternative spelling

ABC: American Broadcasting Company
AGI: Alliance Graphique Internationale
ATypI: Association Typographique Internationale
AT&T: American Telephone and Telegraph Company
BOAC: British Overseas Airways Corporation
CBS: Columbia Broadcasting System
CCA: Container Corporation of America
CIBA: (Company for) Chemical Industry Basel
CSH #: Case Study House Program
ECMA: European Computer Manufacturers Association
FoB: Festival of Britain
GDC: General Dynamics Corporation
GM: General Motors
IBM: International Business Machines
ICA: Institute of Contemporary Arts, London
ICI: Imperial Chemical Industries
LCP: London College of Printing
MIT: Massachusetts Institute of Technology
MOMA: Museum of Modern Art, New York
RCA: Royal College of Art, London
UEA: University of East Anglia

Note
When a date is given on which an individual
worked with an organisation or at an educational
establishment this should not be taken as the
first or only connection between them, or that such
an appointment was of short or long duration.

In the publishing section entries are books unless
specified otherwise. Items are included for design
and/or authorship.

In the image-making section non-specified entries
have been used for a variety of purposes.

The primary research for this work was from
books + journals in libraries + collections; in pursuing
their own research, it is hoped that the reader
will extend their curiosity beyond standard internet
searches + return to study the printed page.

**Margaret Calvert's studio
1979 to the present**

When Margaret Calvert set
up her own practice she
moved some of the objects
from her previous studio
to her home. The objects,
gathered over 40 years
of working life, continue
to be added to still.

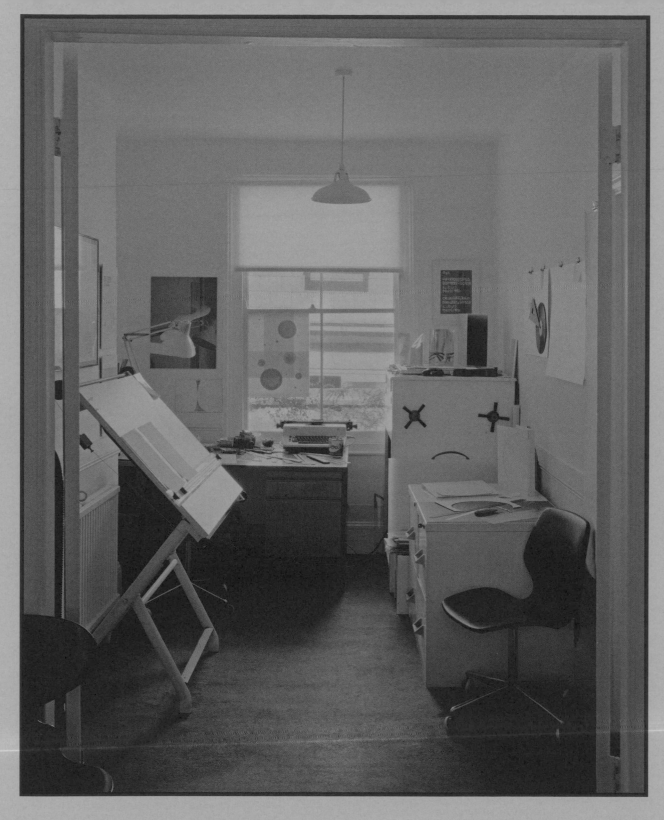

The dimensions
written, edited and compiled by
Lucienne Roberts
Ray Roberts
Kelvyn Laurence Smith
Rebecca Wright

Contributor biographies
written by
Rebecca Wright

The timeline
edited and compiled by
Kelvyn Laurence Smith
Rebecca Wright
designed by
Kelvyn Laurence Smith

Index
Indexing Specialists (UK)

Ray Roberts
Roberts graduated from the
Central School of Arts and Crafts
in 1947. After working under
Oliver Simon at the Curwen
Press, he set up his own design
practice in 1961. He has taught
at many British colleges and
universities including the
Central School of Art and
Design, Middlesex University
and the University of Reading.
In keeping with many of his
generation Roberts remains
as broadly engaged with
his subject today as over his
50 years of working life.

**Kelvyn Laurence Smith
Rebecca Wright**

Mr Smith runs a well-oiled
letterpress workshop in London.
He is of strong temperament
and is chiefly concerned
with all things typographic;
good practice and quality
workmanship.

Ms Wright is something of
a visual anthropologist. She is
a narrator of personal histories
and a teller of tales through
words, pictures and design.
She makes bespoke books
and printed ephemera.

Mr Smith and Ms Wright are
both senior lecturers in visual
communication and design
at highly regarded educational
establishments.

Together they publish limited
editions of their ongoing
enquiries into visual language;
Smith's Rules + Wright's Variations.

picture research
Sophia Gibb

photography
All reasonable attempts have
been made to trace, clear
and credit the copyright holders
of the images reproduced.
However, if any credits have
been inadvertently omitted,
the publisher will endeavour to
incorporate amendments in
future editions.

additional photography
Ian Bavington Jones
Andrew Penketh

cover
Andrew Penketh
based on an image by
Kelvyn Laurence Smith,
Rebecca Wright
and Lucienne Roberts

4, 5, 190, 191
Andrew Penketh

10, 11
Kelvyn Laurence Smith,
Rebecca Wright

18, 19
American poster
courtesy American
Antiquarian Society, Worcester,
Massachusetts, USA
Gustav Klimt
courtesy Albertina,
Vienna, Austria
Beggarstaff brothers
courtesy of the Board of
Trustees of the Victoria and
Albert Museum, London
El Lissitzky
private collection/
© DACS 2005

20, 21
Kurt Schwitters
private collection/
© DACS 2005
Herbert Bayer
© DACS 2005
Piet Zwart
private collection/
© DACS 2005
AM Cassandre
Collection Bibliothèque
Nationale, Cabinet
des Estampes, Paris, France
© Mouron. Cassandre/
all rights reserved/
license number 2005-27-05-03

22, 23
Abram Games
courtesy estate of
Abram Games
Herbert Matter
Kunstgewerbemuseum,
Zurich, Switzerland
Paul Rand
courtesy Marion Rand
Josef Müller-Brockmann
© DACS 2005

24, 25
War ruin
Betti Bora/Alinari
Archives-Florence, Italy
Festival of Britain
unattributed photograph for
Barnaby's Studios Ltd/
Mary Evans Picture Library

26, 27
Cadmore Lane Junior School
RIBA Library
Photographs Collection
Harlow
AP Archive/RIBA Library
Photographs Collection

56
Terminal Five posters
David Reinfurt (ORG)

61
Stedelijk Museum CS
Gert-Jan van Rooij (SMCS)

81
Connect
Harriet Crowder

113
Ground Zero
Peter Mauss/Esto

A book like this is impossible
to produce without the support
of others. I would like to thank
firstly all the interviewees who
gave their time so generously
and patiently; their wisdom
will serve to enlighten me for
the rest of my life.

Thank you: Wim Crouwel,
Milton Glaser, Ken Garland,
Rosmarie Tissi, Colin Forbes,
Geoff White, Karl Gerstner,
Margaret Calvert and
Ivan Chermayeff. Thanks are
also due to Experimental
Jetset, Brookie Maxwell,
Peter Smith, Sabina Oberholzer,
Michael Gericke, Rupert Bassett,
Helmut Schmidt Rhen,
Kerr Noble and Dirk Fütterer.

Thank you to Brian Morris
and all at AVA Publishing,
particularly my editor
Natalia Price-Cabrera whose
support has been hugely
appreciated. Thanks are
also due to Deirdre Murphy,
Susanne Dechant, Andrew
Penketh, Nick Deschamps,
Sophia Gibb and to my patient
friends Annette Pitura and
Diane Magee.

I want to thank above all
Putzi and Ray Roberts, my
parents, for opening my eyes.
Without them I wouldn't have
entered the world that this
book seeks to explore. I also
wouldn't know about Winnie-
the-Pooh, Vaughan Williams and
Singin' in the Rain... the things
that make life worth living.

I would also like to thank
Damian Wayling, the best
and most loving of friends,
John McGill technical wiz and
hugely supportive colleague,
the wonderful Mr Smith
and Ms Wright sparkle and
all, Bob Wilkinson for his
understanding and Dave Shaw
for taking me shopping just
at the right time.